Y0-CCN-821

WITHDRAWN
MAR 4 1993

Selected Sources: Extensive references were consulted during the map research, for the purposes of this map however, only a list of the most important sources is provided.

Dorion, Henri. *La Frontière Québec-Terre-Neuve*. Les Presses de L'Université Laval, 1963.

Ganong, W.F. "A Monograph on the Evolution of the Boundaries of New Brunswick." *Proceedings and Transactions of the Royal Society of Canada*, Second Series, Vol. VII, Section II. (1901) 139-449.

Ireland, Willard E. "The Evolution of the Boundaries of British Columbia." *British Columbia Historical Quarterly 3*. (October 1939) 263-282.

King, W.F. *Report upon the Title of Canada to the Islands North of the Mainland of Canada*. Ottawa: Government Printing Bureau, 1905.

Nicholson, N.L. *The Boundaries of the Canadian Confederation*. Toronto: Macmillan of Canada, 1979.

Ontario. *Statutes, Documents and Papers bearing on the Discussion respecting the Northern and Western Boundaries of the Province of Ontario etc.* Toronto: Hunter, Rose and Co., 1878.

White, J. "Boundary Disputes and Treaties." *Canada and its Provinces*, Vol. VIII, Part III. Toronto: The Publishers Association, 1913.

CANADA
125

CONSTITUTIONS

1763 — 1982

CANADA
125

ITS CONSTITUTIONS
1763 — 1982

EVOLUTION OF A DEMOCRACY

DIRECTED BY : J. FERNAND TANGUAY

INTRODUCTION BY SENATOR GÉRALD A. BEAUDOIN, O.C., Q.C.

Méridien

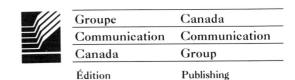

Groupe   Canada
Communication   Communication
Canada   Group
Édition   Publishing

All rights reserved. No part of this publication may be reproduced or transmitted in any form by means, electronic or mechanical, including photocopying and recording, or by any information storage or retrieval system, without the prior written permission of Éditions du Méridien, division of Société d'information et d'affaires publiques (SIAP) Inc., 1980 west Sherbrooke, room 710, Montreal (Quebec) H3H 1E8.

Typesetting and mounting: Daniel Huot

© Éditions du Méridien — 1992
ISBN 2-89415-091-1

© Canada Communication Group
ISBN 0-660-14667-3
CAT— # P60-4/5 — 1992 E

Legal deposit 3rd trimester 1992
— Bibliothèque nationale du Québec
— National Library of Canada

Printed in Canada

ST. JAMES · ASSINIBOIA

To all parliamentarians who dedicated their life
to the evolution of democracy in Canada.

ST. JAMES-ASSINIBOIA

TABLE OF CONTENTS

OUR CANADA

One hundred and twenty five years under the same constitution without a revolution or major uprising is a record of which all Canadians can be proud. Whether one is born on this territory or has come from abroad by virtue of the power given by this constitution, all have a reason to celebrate.

This overall evaluation of the Canada Act (1867) is impressive. We find five generations of Canadians, neo-Canadians of all origins, races and creeds and over half a million aboriginals living in a climate of peace, liberty and prosperity; a situation which is not common place in our world. Only a very mature and dynamic people could achieve such a balanced way of life.

This anniversary provides a golden opportunity to look back and take note of the evolution of democracy in our country from the very beginning. The constant respect for democratic principles and the Rule of Law has allowed Canada not only to develop internally in a peaceful manner but also to radiate throughout the international community.

During the past three decades I had the great privilege of serving my country in the Foreign Service in various countries and to travel extensively on all five continents. I lived with my family in prosperous industrialized countries and under communist regimes in Eastern Europe, as well as spending some time in the third world. I came to realize, that Canada is a country with no enemies, past or present and that we Canadians are the envy of many other peoples: sometimes for our natural resources which are apparently unlimited, sometimes because of our easy access to wide open spaces, sometimes. for our sense of tolerance and our educational system which is next to none, and sometimes for our cultural diversity.

There is a direct link between the constitution and the influence of Canada in the world. Indeed how could a country with acute social, economic or political problems, or with domestic discord speak with authority at the United Nations or other international fora? The influence of a country in the world is clearly related to the political stability, economic prosperity and the cultural and spiritual development of its people.

In this regard Canada has allowed the great majority of Canadians the opportunity to develop a happy family life, prosperous professionnal activities and a stimulating cultural and spiritual life. Along with a clean environment, this harmonious way of life is undoubtedly the most precious heritage we can leave to future generations. All of these values are reflected in the Constitution which enshrined the best of the British and French traditions, adapted of course to the continent and territory we occupy. This unique constitution has allowed us to govern ourselves in a balanced way, thus avoiding the excesses of some of the absurd ideologies of the 20th century which resulted in massive purges, Holocaust, genocides and a serious deterioration of the spiritual and emotional fiber of millions of human beings in various parts of the world. Our constitution has served as a shield against impulses of fundamentalism or anarchy.

Canadian history is not written with blood; our political system based on the separation of the legislative, executive and judiciary powers has allowed us to maintain this equilibrium and provided a climate in which Canadians can flourish. For example, the independence of the judiciaty which is taken for granted by Canadians, is still violated in many countries.

As a result of the stability provided by our constitution and under the leadership of men and women who have had the ability to think globally, Canada has been able to play a prominent international role. Canada's views and positions are highly respected by the world community. As one of the founding peoples of the U.N. almost half a century ago, Canadians have acquired vast experience in multilateral diplomacy. Furthermore Canada has always implemented the decisions of the Security Council for instance through an Act of the Canadian parliament (R.S.C. 275), the United Nations Act which authorizes full implementation of sanctions decreeded under article 41 of the Charter. In addition, Canada has faithfully ratified major international conventions and given serious consideration to Declarations and Resolutions of the General Assembly.

Even in times of economic hardship, Canada has always fulfilled its financial commitments and has made its full share of voluntary contributions to causes such as humanitarian assistance for famine, ecological or human disasters, sustainable development in the third world, or the improvement of the fate of the 20 million refugees in various parts of the world. Canada led the way at the recent Summit in Rio de Janeiro dedicated to Planet Earth by supporting fully the proposals put forward by the U.N. under the leadership of a Canadian, Maurice Strong. Strong is a member of a distinguished group of Canadian men and women who have dedicated part of their lives to the improvement of living conditions for mankind through the ideals promoted by the U.N. and its specialized agencies. Several of these Canadians have been recognized by the international community for their outstanding contributions. To mention but two examples, soon after the founding of the U.N. a distinguished Canadian jurist, John P. Humphrey submitted the first draft of a document which in 1948 was to become the Universal Declaration of Human Rights. A few years later, Lester B. Pearson, then Secretary of State for External Affairs, was awarded the Nobel Peace Prize for his important contribution to solving the Suez crisis.

The influence of Canadians at the U.N. and in its specialized agencies is impossible to measure but we can be proud of the role played by our distinguished compatriots in such organisations as the International Labour Organisation, the World Health Organisation, UNICEF and UNESCO to name a few, or at major international conferences on key issues such as Disarmement, the Law of the Sea, and the International Control of Drugs and Narcotics. We can also be proud of the unique role played by members of the Canadians Forces in practically every U.N. Peace Keeping Operation in the world. The Conference which led to the foundation of the Food and Agriculture Organization (FAO) was held in Quebec City and Montreal became the permanent seat of the International Civil Aviation Organization which is now under the leadership of D[r] Assad Kotaite.

This ability to think globally was stimulated by the adoption of the Statute of Westminster in 1931 which created the Commonwealth; through the acquired powers Canada was able to start exercising its influence outside its borders. It was not a surprise when a Canadian, Arnold Smith, a career foreign service officer, was chosen as the first Secretary General of the Commonwealth. In keeping with its sense of balance Canada played a highly visible role when *La Francophonie Internationale* was founded in the 70s. Its main agency, l'*Agence de Coopération culturelle et technique* which has its headquarters in Paris is, at present, headed by the former publisher of *Le Devoir*, Jean-Louis Roy.

Anniversaries such as the one we are celebrating recall so many accomplishments of which every Canadian can be proud. It is our good fortune that our pride of the past does not prevent us from thinking ahead and striving to improve our lot by making major adjustments and the fine tuning necessary in this age of high technology and rapid communications. During the first fifty years of Confederation if one wanted to witness an event in some other part of the country, one had to spend numerous hours on the train; later in the 30s one could fly there during the same day; since the 50s one can simply turn on the television. The impact of such rapid technological development is felt throughout the lives of every Canadian.

Another interesting development of the last two decades is the emergence in many countries of a group of specialists on Canada referred to as *Canadianists*; there are 5000 of them in some thirty countries. They study, lecture, publish for scholarly reviews in various disciplines of the social sciences and humanities. There are associations in each of these 30 countries which are grouped under an international council which has its headquarters in Ottawa but whose president is a distinguished professor of Literature at the University of Trier in Germany: Prof. Hans-Josef Niederehe. This very successful programme was initiated and encouraged by the Department of External Affairs under the leadership of Allen E. Gotlieb, now President of the Canada Council; that department is still funding this programme in the framework of its Academic Relations Division, headed by Brian Long.

It is hard to imagine a country like ours which is so throughly studied on all continents is still being discovered by its own citizens. The various constitutions which have governed this country over time are but one aspect a lot of Canadians need to discover. It is in this vein that les Éditions du Méridien in cooperation with the Canada Communication Group-Publishing is presenting this album, containing all the major texts of our current constitution and the previous ones to assist us in appreciating the rapid evolution towards democracy (1791) and towards full sovereignty (1931). This album does not pretend to replace text books in constitutional law which contain additional technical material, but rather intends to offer

Canadians on this important occasion an overview of the legislative acts which brought Canada together, the Canada we know today — *our Canada*.

We wish to express our deep gratitude to Senator Gérald A. Beaudoin, O.C., Q.C., who readily accepted to provide us with a remarquably concise and comprehensive overview of constitutional developments in Canada.

We also wish to thank Marcel Pelletier, Q.C., professor of parliamentary law at the University of Ottawa for his outstanding contribution to the preparation of this album at all stages.

Our sincere appreciation to Pierrette Pelletier whose cooperation in transcribing the complex legal texts was invaluable.

The encouragement and assistance received at an early stage from the British High Commissionner Sir Brian Fall, now Ambassador in Moscow, was highly appreciated.

HAPPY ANNIVERSARY!

On this First Day of July 1992

J. Fernand Tanguay
Chairman
Les Éditions du Méridien

CHRONOLOGY

1492 – Discovery of America by Christopher Columbus, an Italian navigator at the service of Spain.

1497 – First voyage by John Cabot (Giovanni Caboto) in the North Atlantic searching for the country of the Great Khan (Asia). He was sponsored by King Henry VII of England.

1500 –
1501 A Portuguese, Gaspar Corte-Real sailed to Labrador and the northern part of Newfoundland, believing he had reached Asia. He was lost at sea on his return to Portugal.

1524 – Giovanni da Verrazzano, a Florentine navigator was sent by King Francis I of France in search of the western passage. He explored the Atlantic coast from Florida to Newfoundland.

1524 –
1525 Esteban Gomez made the same attempt on behalf of Spain, but unsuccessfully.

1534 – Francis I asked Jacques Cartier, a navigator from St. Malo, to undertake the exploration of a route to the Orient through North America. On July 24, he erected a cross at Gaspé bearing the arms of France, thus officially taking possession of the land.

1535 – Second voyage of Cartier. He discovered the estuary of the great Hochelaga (St. Lawrence) River which he explored further, reached Stadacona (Quebec) and Hochelaga (Montreal) and spent the winter in Sainte-Croix (St. Charles). He departed for France where he arrived in July 1536 with ten Indians, including the Huron Chief, Donnacona, and a crew decimated by scurvy, but the bearer of revealing stories and meticulous descriptions.

1541 – Attempted settlement by Jean-François de la Rocque de Roberval who was appointed Viceroy of Canada, Newfoundland and Labrador by Francis I, on 15 January.

1557 – Jacques Cartier died on 1 September, at Limoilou, near St. Malo.

1576 –
1577
1578   Martin Frobisher, a British navigator, led three explorations in North Atlantic and discovered the bay which now bears his name.

1578 –   Humphrey Gilbert attempted to found a colony in Newfoundland but could not achieve his goal. He nevertheless took possession of the island for Elizabeth I.

1585 –
1586   John Davis, hoping to find the passage to the East, entered the strait
1587   to which he gave his name.

1598 –   Troilus de Mesgoues, Marquis de la Roche, appointed by King Henri IV Lieutenant-General of New France, Newfoundland and Labrador, built a colony in Sable Island which was abandoned five years later.

1603 –   Samuel de Champlain sailed from France in March to explore the St. Lawrence River with Pierre du Gua de Monts, the new Lieutenant-General of New France, who obtained a monopoly of the fur trade for ten years.

1604 –   Du Gua de Monts established a settlement in Acadia, first at St. Croix Island and then, moved it to Port-Royal in 1605. The trading monopoly granted to de Monts was withdrawn in 1607, and all the colonists returned to France.

1608 –   Champlain founded Quebec, July 3, when he began to build the "**Abitation**" at the foot of the cliff, the present Place Royale. He spent the winter at Quebec.

1609 –   Champlain set out to explore the Richelieu River and discovered a large lake to which he gave his name.

1610 –   English navigators sailed further to the North and entered Hudson Strait, and the Frobisher, Baffin and Hudson Bays.

1613 –   Champlain returned to St. Malo in August and published an account of his journey and a map of New France.

1615 –   Champlain reached Huronia and discovered Lake Attigouantan (Huron). Wounded in a fight with the Iroquois, he wintered in Huronia and returned to Quebec on July 11.

1617 –   Louis Hébert, the first farmer in the country, landed with his wife, Marie Rollet and their three children.

1623 – The feudal system began in New France on February 4, when Louis Hébert was granted the fief of Sault-au-Matelot, at Quebec.

1625 – The first Jesuits arrived at Quebec, April 26.

1627 – Armand-Jean de Plessis, Cardinal Richelieu, Prime Minister under Louis XIII, formed the **Company of New France**, also called the **One Hundred Associates**, on April 29. This private, but important company was given full seigniorial ownership in New France, in addition to a perpetual fur trade monopoly. It was also granted a 15 year duty free trade monopoly on land and on sea (except for cod and whale fishing rights). The government of the colony was delegated to a Governor nominated by the Company and appointed by the King. The Company was to develop trade in the new colony, establish garrisons, bring in clergymen, but principally settle 4000 French colonists in 15 years and support them for three years.

1628 – Four ships, sent to New France by the One Hundred Associates with 400 people and the supplies necessary for their settlement, were intercepted and seized by the Kirke brothers, English navigators. The expedition, organized by London merchants, was authorized by King Charles I.

1629 – Unable to resist any longer, Champlain surrendered on July 19, leaving Quebec to the Kirke brothers. He was taken to England and then to France, where he arrived in December, urging the return of the colony to France.

– Sir William Alexander seized Port-Royal, in Acadia, with the authorization of Charles I of England.

1629 – The English occupied Quebec until 1632.

1632 – Quebec and Port-Royal were returned to France by the Treaty of Saint-Germain-en-Laye, signed by England and France on March 29.

1633 – Champlain returned to Quebec on May 22 and proceeded to rebuild the "**Abitation**" from its ruins and build the church of Notre-Dame-de-la-Recouvrance.

1635 – Death of Champlain at Quebec, December 25.

1636 –   Charles Huault de Montmagny arrived at Quebec as the first titular Governor of New France and Champlain's successor, holding military, civil and judicial powers. Trade and the financial administration of the colony came under the authority of the secretary of the One Hundred Associates.

1641 –   The Iroquois formally declared war against the French.

1642 –   Paul de Chomedey de Maisonneuve founded Ville-Marie (Montreal) on May 18. He served as Governor of the new town until 1665.

1643 –   Louis XIII died on May 14 and was succeeded by Louis XIV who was then only four years old.

1647 –   By an edict called "**Arrest du 27 mars 1647 portant Règlemens pour les habitants de la nouvelle france**", Louis XIV set up the Council of Quebec composed of the Governor of Quebec, the Governor of Ville-Marie and the superior of the Jesuits. This decree, better known as the Regulation of 1647, may be considered as the first political constitution of New France, as the Council had authority in all matters of finance, fur trade regulations and general policy of the country. The Council appointed naval officers and also clerks and functionaries.

1651 –   A trial court with jurisdiction in civil and criminal matters, called "Sénéchaussée" (Seneschalsy), was created at Quebec and Trois-Rivières. Ville-Marie already had its seigniorial tribunal. Decisions of the Sénéchaussée and the Ville-Marie tribunal could be appealed to the Governor as the final resort.

1659 –   François de Montmorency, Monseigneur de Laval, arrived in the colony on June 16, as Vicar-apostolic in New France. He became Bishop of Quebec in 1674.

1663 –   The Company of One Hundred Associates conveyed all its assets and interests in New France to Louis XIV on February 24. The King appointed a new Governor and an Intendant responsible for police, justice and finance.

–   On September 18, the **Sovereign Council of Quebec** was established by a royal edict which provided for civil government in the new royal province. The Council, which had jurisdiction over political, commercial and financial matters, consisted of the Governor, the Bishop, an Attorney General, five councillors (seven, after 1674) and one secretary. The Intendant sat at the Council as of 1665. This regime was to endure until the Conquest in 1760.

1664 – A Royal edict introduced into New France the civil laws and usages of France ("us et coutumes de Paris") as codified in 1510.

1665 – Intendant Jean Talon arrived at Quebec and endeavoured to strengthen royal authority in the colony, encourage the settlement of colonists and increase and diversify the settlers' production. Another Intendant, Louis Robert, appointed in 1663, never came to New France.

1670 – King Charles II of England granted a charter to the **Hudson's Bay Company** to develop the fur trade in the north western part of the country, between Labrador and the Rocky Mountains. The area was called Rupert's Land. The Company kept competing with traders established along the St. Lawrence River.

1672 – Louis de Buade, Comte de Palluau et de Frontenac, godson of Louis XIII, was appointed Governor of New France, on April 6. He served for ten years, and again from 1689 until his death in 1698.

   – Talon left Quebec forever to return to France. Louis XIV, who was then engaged in a European conflict, did not appoint a successor until 1675. As a result, the rise of the colony's economy slowed down and diminished. The fur trade became once more the main economic activity.

1713 – The Treaty of Utrecht ended the War of the Spanish Succession and forced the King of France to give up to England Acadia in its entirety, Newfoundland and the Hudson's Bay with its hydrographic basin. France retained the islands of St. Pierre and Miquelon, Ile Royale (Cape Breton Island) and Ile Saint-Jean (Prince Edward Island).

   – Pierre Gaultier de la Verendrye, his sons and his associates began their expeditions to find the northwest sea. They reached the present Manitoba and Saskatchewan and established many new trading posts.

1749 – Halifax was founded on July 9 and replaced Annapolis Royal as the capital of Nova-Scotia, where over 2,500 people settled.

1754 – Anthony Henday, an employee of the Hudson's Bay Company was the first European to journey as far across the prairies as the present area of Alberta. This expedition sought to encourage the Indians to trade with the Company.

1755 –   François-Pierre de Rigaud, Marquis de Vaudreuil, appointed in January, was the last Governor of New France, serving from July 10, 1755 to September 8, 1760.

    –   Capitulation of Forts Beausejour and Gaspareau in Nova Scotia. The Acadians who refused to take the oath of allegiance to England were deported to the American colonies.

1758 –   England authorized the establishment of a Legislature for Nova-Scotia consisting of a Legislative Assembly, an Executive Council and a Legislative Council. It was the first Legislature with a popularly elected House to be instituted in one of the British North American colonies which were to form the Canadian Confederation of 1867. The colony already had its own judicial system with a Chief Justice.

1759 –   Capitulation of Quebec on September 18 after a siege of three months by Maj.-Gen. James Wolfe and a battle in formation on the Plains of Abraham. The French troops defending Quebec were led by Louis Joseph, Marquis de Montcalm, Commander-in-Chief. Both Commanders were killed in the battle. The town was surrendered to General George Townshend and Admiral Charles Saunders by Commander Jean-Baptiste de Ramezay.

1760 –   Threatened by the troops of General Jeffrey Amherst, the Commander-in-Chief of the British Forces, Montreal capitulated on September 8. Governor General de Vaudreuil surrendered Montreal to General Amherst, and consequently the whole colony. Thus, North America, from the Gulf of Mexico to the Hudson's Bay, came under British rule.

    –   A proclamation of September 22 by Governor General Amherst outlined the main aspects of the new administration which divided Canada into three military districts. James Murray remained in office as military Governor of Quebec, Thomas Gage was appointed to Montreal and Ralph Burton to Trois-Rivières.

    –   Murray issued a proclamation on October 31 to establish military courts in Quebec.

1763 –   England, France, Spain and Portugal ended the Seven Year's War with the signature of the Treaty of Paris, on February 10. France was the great loser, keeping only the islands of St. Pierre and Miquelon and New-Orleans in North America. The Treaty authorized freedom of religion according to the rites of the Church of Rome, in as much as permitted by British law, and it also allowed the inhabitants to emigrate within eighteen months following the exchange of ratifications of the Treaty.

–   On October 7, George III signed a **Proclamation** setting up a civilian government for the conquered territories. It established four distinct governments, of which only one was in Canada. Even the name "Canada" disappeared and was replaced by that of "Province of Quebec". Canada's territory was considerably reduced and a vast region was created in the west with a view to pacifying the Indians. The French civil law (**Coutume de Paris**) was replaced by British law, contrary to the terms of the capitulations, and new courts of law were established in which English was the only official language.

–   James Murray was appointed civil Governor of the new Province of Quebec on November 21 and received detailed instructions signed by the King on December 7. He was ordered to appoint a Council and call a general assembly of the citizens. No such assembly was ever called, because the members of both the Council and the assembly were required to subscribe the Test Oath which was unacceptable to the Catholics who were thus excluded from any public office.

1764 –   Civil government was officially established on August 10 when James Murray took office.

–   Montague Wilmot succeeded Charles Lawrence as Lieutenant-Governor of Nova-Scotia, assuming office in May.

1766 –   Murray was recalled by the government of England, further to the discontent of the English minority in the colony. Guy Carleton, a career officer, was charged with the administration of the country as Lieutenant-Governor. He then served as Governor from 1768 to 1778.

1769 –   St. John Island was detached from Nova Scotia and recognized as a distinct province with a separate government. The first Governor, Walter Patterson, was appointed on July 14. The name of the province will only be changed to Prince Edward Island in 1799.

1773 –   The first Assembly of St. John Island was convened in July.

1774 –   Adoption of the **Quebec Act** by the British Parliament. First introduced in early May, the Bill received Royal Assent from George III on June 22 and came into force May 1, 1775. It was the first time that the Imperial Parliament intervened in the establishment of a colonial government. The Act restored the boundaries of the colony to those preceding the Royal Proclamation of 1763; it established French civil law and the British criminal law system, with trial by jury; it granted religious freedom to Roman Catholics, authorized the clergy to collect the tithe, and substituted a new form of oath for the Test Oath. An enlarged Legislative Council appointed by the Crown was established instead of an assembly as promised in the **Royal Proclamation of 1763**.

1775 – First session of the Legislative Council at Quebec, from August 17 to September 7.

1784 – New Brunswick was detached from Nova Scotia on August 16 and became a new colony with a nominated council and an elected assembly.

– Cape Breton Island was separated from Nova Scotia as a distinct colony with its own council, on August 26.

– St. John Island (P.E.I.) was reunited to Nova Scotia on September 11, but retained a separate local government.

1786 – The first Assembly of New Brunswick, elected in 1785, met for the first time on January 9 at St. John.

– St. John Island (P.E.I.) was again separated from Nova Scotia to become a province.

1788 – On July 24, Governor Carleton issued a proclamation dividing the area to be known later as Upper Canada into four judicial districts, namely Lunenburg, Mecklenburg, Nassau and Hesse. A judge and a sheriff were designated for each district.

1791 – On June 10, the British Parliament adopted the **Constitutional Act** which established the first representative government in Canada. The Act made provision for the division of Quebec into two provinces: Upper and Lower Canada, granting to each separate parliamentary institutions. In each, the Lieutenant Governor acted with the advice and consent of the Legislative Council, the members of which were appointed by the King for life, and an elected Assembly. Lower Canada would continue with the French civil law, whereas Upper Canada would be under the English common law. English criminal law continued to apply to both.

– By an Order-in-Council dated August 24, the province of Quebec was divided into Upper Canada with a capital at Newark (Niagara-on-the-Lake) and Lower Canada with a capital at Quebec City.

– In the absence of Governor-in-Chief Carleton, now Lord Dorchester, the Lieutenant Governor of Lower Canada, Allured Clarke, issued a proclamation dated November 18, declaring that the Act would come into effect on December 26.

1792 – Lower-Canada was divided into fifty electoral districts on May 7, and Upper Canada followed suit in July with sixteen districts.

– A general election was held on June 15 in Lower Canada and a Legislative Council of fifteen members was appointed.

– John Graves Simcoe took office as Lieutenant Governor of Upper Canada on July 8, and on the 29th William Osgoode, the Chief Justice, was appointed Speaker of the Legislative Council.

– The first session of the Legislature of Upper Canada was convened on September 17. Colonel John Macdonell was elected presiding officer of the Legislative Assembly.

– The Legislature of Lower Canada opened its first session on December 17 at the Bishop's Palace in Quebec City. Chief Justice William Smith was appointed by the Crown to take the Chair of the Legislative Council. Jean-Antoine Panet, a lawyer, was elected Speaker of the Legislative Assembly. One of the first items of business of the Assembly was to order that all motions, bills and other proceedings be put in both languages.

1796 – On February 1, York (Toronto) became the new capital of Upper Canada.

– The fifth and last session of the first Parliament of Upper Canada closed on June 3, and a general election was called.

– Proclamation dissolving the Parliament of Lower Canada, May 31, and ordering the return of the writs on July 20.

1799 – St. John Island officially became Prince Edward Island on June 3.

1803 – On August 11, a statute of the Imperial Parliament granted jurisdiction to the criminal courts of Upper and Lower Canada over criminal offences committed in Indian lands or other areas of British North America without a judicial organization.

1820 – George III died in August and was succeeded by George IV.

– Cape Breton Island was reannexed to Nova Scotia on October 16.

1833 –   Meeting at St. John's, January 1, of the first representative Assembly of Newfoundland.

1834 –   March 1, adoption by the Assembly of Lower Canada of the "Ninety-two Resolutions" expressing grievances against the administration and relating mainly to the control of revenue by the legislature, responsible government and an elected council.

1837 –   A rebellion broke out in Lower Canada, November 6, causing many disturbances and casualties among the "Patriotes" and their English Canadian rivals. A similar uprising began in Upper Canada, December 5. The chief instigators in both cases, Louis-Joseph Papineau and William Lyon Mackenzie, fled to the United States.

1838 –   The Constitution of 1791 was suspended in Lower Canada by virtue of an Act adopted on February 10. The Governor was empowered to appoint a special council to make laws, within restrictions. The British Colonial Office retained ultimate power.

   –   On March 30, John George Lambton, Earl of Durham, was appointed Governor-in-Chief of British North America (except Newfoundland), and High Commissioner to investigate on the affairs of British North America and inquire into the political situation and the form of government to be granted to the colony. Durham served from May 29 to November 1. In his report, laid before the British Parliament, February 11, 1839, he recommended a legislative union between Upper and Lower Canada, a colonial government responsible to the elected Assembly and the systematic anglicization of French Canadians.

1840 –   The **Union Act** was adopted by the British Parliament and assented to on July 23, to become effective February 10, 1841. The Act united the provinces of Upper and Lower Canada which became respectively Canada West and Canada East. It further provided for an elected Assembly of 84 members and a Legislative Council appointed for life or good behaviour. The Crown appointed a Governor General as the royal representative in the Province of Canada, as well as an Executive Council. English was made the only official language.

1841 –   Charles Edward Poulett Thomson, Baron Sydenham, was sworn in, February 10, as the first Governor General of Canada. He died in office, September 19.

   –   Kingston was designated the new capital of Canada.

–   General elections having been held in March and April, the first session of the first Parliament of United Canada opened on June 14, at Kingston, and lasted until September 18.

1844 –   The capital of Canada was moved from Kingston to Montreal on May 10.

1848 –   Robert Baldwin of Canada West and Louis-Hyppolite Lafontaine of Canada East formed a Reform cabinet supported by the majority of the members elected in the preceding elections. Sworn in on March 11, the new ministry marked the beginning of responsible government in Canada.

1849 –   A Bill designed to compensate for property damage in Lower Canada during the Rebellion of 1837 caused a revolt which culminated in the burning of the Parliament building on April 25, the day the Bill was assented to by Governor General Elgin. As a compromise, the seat of government was removed from Montreal and the Assembly met alternatively in Toronto and Quebec City.

1851 –   The Legislative Council of Vancouver Island opened its first session on August 30.

1857 –   Ottawa was chosen by Queen Victoria, December 31, to be the new capital of Canada. It became official on September 24, 1859.

1858 –   The British Parliament adopted an Act, August 2, to grant British Columbia the status of Crown colony with her own government. The colony did not include Vancouver Island.

1864 –   The Charlottetown Conference on Maritime Union was convened on September 1, and was attended by representatives of Nova Scotia, New Brunswick, and Prince Edward Island, who were later joined by delegates of the Province of Canada. A proposal for a British North American confederation was presented by John A. Macdonald and Georges-Etienne Cartier.

–   A second Conference was held at Quebec City, from October 10 to 28, and concluded with the adoption of "Seventy-two Resolutions" to be submitted to the approval of the Imperial government.

1865 –   On February 20, the Legislative Council of the province of Canada adopted an Address urging the Imperial Parliament to pass legislation, based on the Quebec Resolutions, to achieve the Union of British North America. The Legislative Assembly adopted the same Address on March 11.

–   Proclamation by Queen Victoria, October 20, making Ottawa the permanent seat of the government of Canada.

1866 – The political union of mainland British Columbia and Vancouver Island was accomplished by an enactment of the British Parliament on August 6.

–   Representatives of the provinces of Canada, New-Brunswick and Nova Scotia met for a conference in London, beginning December 4, to consider new terms of a union of the British North American colonies. They adopted further resolutions which were transmitted by John A. Macdonald to the Secretary of State for the colonies, December 26, together with the last of seven draft bills based on the London Resolutions.

1867 – The **British North America Act**, introduced in the House of Lords on February 7 and adopted by Parliament on March 8, was assented to by Queen Victoria on March 29 and came into effect on July 1. It united the Provinces of Canada, New Brunswick and Nova Scotia into the "Dominion of Canada", a combination of federalism and the British parliamentary system.

–   Sir Charles Stanley, Viscount Monck, was commissioned first Governor General of Canada on June 1.

–   John A. Macdonald won the first federal election, September 18, and formed a Conservative government. The first session of the first Parliament opened on November 6, and the Ontario and Quebec legislatures held their first sittings on December 27.

1869 – The Hudson's Bay Company surrendered Rupert's Land to the Canadian government, effective December 1. This caused discontent amongst the people of the Red River District who rebelled under Louis Riel.

1870 – The Canadian Parliament adopted the **Manitoba Act** on May 12; it came into effect on July 15, making Manitoba the fifth province of Canada. The Northwest Territories became part of the Dominion of Canada under the terms of an Order of Her Majesty in Council dated June 23.

1871 – On March 10, the first Legislative Council of Manitoba sat for the first time.

—   British Colombia became the sixth province of Canada, July 20, pursuant to an Order of May 16 made by Queen Victoria. The Legislature met for the first time since Confederation on February 15, 1872.

1873 —   By Order-in-Council made June 26 at the Court at Windsor, Prince Edward Island was admitted into the Canadian Confederation, effective July 1.

1875 —   The Northwest Territories became a political entity, separate from Manitoba on April 8, with a Lieutenant Governor and a council appointed by the Governor General and exercising legislative and executive powers.

—   Creation of the Supreme Court of Canada by an Act of the Canadian Parliament adopted on April 5. William Buell Richards was appointed Chief Justice. The Court sat for the first time, January 17, 1876, in the Railway Committee Room of the House of Commons.

1883 —   Opening of the first session of the Northwest Territories Legislative Council at Regina on August 20.

1898 —   An Act of the Canadian Parliament, assented to June 13, constituted the Yukon as a separate territory with a Commissioner and a Legislative Council partly elected and partly appointed by the Governor General.

1901 —   Queen Victoria died on January 22. Edward VII was proclaimed King the next day.

1905 —   The provinces of Alberta and Saskatchewan were created by two federal Acts which received Royal Assent on July 20 to be effective September 1. Edmonton and Regina became the respective capitals.

1910 —   Death of King Edward VII on May 6, and accession of his son, George V.

1918 —   The **Canada Elections Act**, adopted on May 24, enfranchised all women for federal elections. Agnes Campbell McPhail was the first woman elected to the House of Commons on December 6, 1921.

1921 —   The Arms of Canada were proclaimed by King George V as the country's national symbol on November 21.

1923 –   Canada obtained from the King the necessary powers authorizing Ernest Lapointe, the Minister of Marine and Fisheries, to negotiate and sign independently for Canada, March 2, the "Halibut Treaty" with the United States, without the participation of an Imperial delegate.

1929 –   The Judicial Committee of the Imperial Privy Council reversed a decision of the Supreme Court of Canada and ruled, October 18, that women were eligible to sit in the Senate. Cairine Reay Wilson became the first woman senator on February 15, 1930.

1931 –   On December 11, the **Statute of Westminster** received Royal Assent, establishing legislative equality between Imperial and Dominion Parliaments. This Statute gave effect to the reports of the 1926 and 1930 Imperial Conferences, setting up a Commonwealth of sovereign nations freely united by a common allegiance to the Crown. The Imperial Parliament would no longer legislate for a Dominion (unless it was so requested) and Dominion laws would have extra-territorial effect.

1936 –   Abdication of King Edward VIII on December 10. George VI succeeded him.

1939 –   Canada declared war on Germany, September 10, seven days after Britain and France.

1940 –   The Canadian Constitution was amended to give Parliament exclusive jurisdiction over unemployment insurance. This British statute was assented to on July 10.

1947 –   On September 8, King George VI issued Letters Patent constituting the office of Governor General of Canada and authorizing the Governor General to exercise all powers and authorities lawfully belonging to the King in respect of Canada.

1949 –   Newfoundland became the tenth Province of Canada by virtue of an Act of the Westminster Parliament adopted on March 23. The first session of the Legislature opened at St. John's, July 13.

–   All appeals from the Supreme Court of Canada to the British Privy Council in civil matters were abolished on December 10. Appeals in criminal cases had already been abolished in 1933.

–   At Canada's request, the federal Parliament was granted a general power to amend the Canadian Constitution, except in matters pertaining to the legislative powers of the provincial legislatures, the use of the English and French languages, the maximum duration of the mandate of a House of Commons and the requirement for an annual session.

1952 – Vincent Massey became the first Canadian-born Governor General on January 24.

– Death of King George VI on February 6, and accession to the Throne of Queen Elizabeth II. She was crowned on June 2, 1953.

1957 – On June 21, Ellen Louks Fairclough was the first woman to be appointed to the Canadian Cabinet.

– For the first time in Canada, the reigning monarch, Queen Elizabeth II, opened Parliament on October 14.

1960 – The **Canadian Bill of Rights** was enacted on August 10 as an ordinary statute of the federal Parliament and did not apply to provincial legislation.

– The retirement age of Superior Court judges was fixed at 75 years, pursuant to a statute of the United Kingdom Parliament passed on December 20, at the request of Canada.

1965 – A new national Flag of Canada was proclaimed for February 15. The Proclamation, dated January 28, was the first one signed in Canada by a reigning Sovereign. The Royal Union Flag (Union Jack) continued to be used as a symbol of Canada's allegiance to the Crown and membership in the Commonwealth.

– A federal statute amending the Constitution required Senators appointed after June 1 to retire at the age of 75.

1967 – Canada's centennial year was marked by celebrations attended by the Queen and many Heads of States. The Order of Canada came into being on July 1, and Expo' 67 opened in Montreal on April 27.

1968 – The Quebec Legislature abolished the Legislative Council, effective December 31. The name of the Legislative Assembly was changed to the **National Assembly**.

1969 – The **Official Languages Act** was assented to, July 9, and came into force on September 7. English and French were declared the official languages of the Federal administration which had to provide bilingual services to the public.

1972 –   Muriel McQueen Fergusson was the first woman appointed Speaker of the Senate on December 15.

1974 –   The first woman to be appointed Lieutenant Governor in a Canadian province was Pauline McGibbon of Ontario on January 17.

–   Ralph Steinhauer, the first Indian to hold the position of Lieutenant Governor (in Alberta), was appointed on July 2. He was a former chief of the Saddle Lake Indian Band.

1975 –   Federal legislation was passed, March 13 and June 19 respectively, to add one seat for the Northwest Territories in the House of Commons, and one seat each in the Senate for the Yukon and the Northwest Territories.

–   On March 24, Royal Assent was given to a Private Member's Bill, sponsored by Sean O'Sullivan, making the beaver (Castor canadensis) one of the official symbols of Canada. The beaver had already been used as an emblem by certain Indian tribes; it was on the coat of arms of the Hudson's Bay Company, and also on those of Sir William Alexander (the founder of Nova Scotia), Count Frontenac, Governor of New France, and Sir Guy Carleton, Governor General of Canada.

1977 –   The first sitting of the House of Commons to be televised was on October 18.

1980 –   Jeanne Sauvé was the first woman to become Speaker of the House of Commons on April 14.

–   A referendum held in the Province of Quebec, May 20, denied the Parti Québécois Government, by a 60 to 40 per cent margin, the mandate to negotiate national sovereignty and economic association with Canada.

–   *O Canada* was officially declared the national anthem by an Act of Parliament adopted on June 27 at the initiative of Francis Fox, Secretary of State.

–   On October 6, the federal government announced its intention to patriate the Constitution unilaterally, in view of the failure of the First Ministers to reach an agreement at the September conference. The matter was referred to the Supreme Court of Canada which ruled, on September 28, 1981, that the proposal was strictly legal, but it offended the constitutional convention requiring a substantial degree of provincial consent.

1981 – At the initiative of Prime Minister Pierre Elliott Trudeau the House of Commons on December 2, and the Senate on December 8, adopted a resolution for a Joint Address to the Queen asking the British Parliament to pass legislation to patriate the **British North America Act, 1867**, adding to it a Charter of Rights and Freedoms and an amending formula.

1982 – On March 4, Bertha Wilson, a Justice of the Ontario Court of Appeal, was the first woman appointed to the Supreme Court of Canada.

– At the request of the Canadian Parliament, the British House of Commons passed the **Canada Act 1982** on March 8. The Act, which contained the **Constitution Act, 1982**, was adopted by the House of Lords on March 25 and was given Royal Assent by Queen Elizabeth II on March 29, precisely 115 years after Queen Victoria had assented to the **British North America Act, 1867**. The new Constitution Act ended British legislative jurisdiction over the Canadian Constitution and entrenched a Charter of Rights and Freedoms and an amending formula. **The Constitution Act, 1982** came into effect on April 17, with the signing of a Proclamation by Queen Elizabeth II, in Ottawa. It was only the second time in our history that a reigning monarch had signed a proclamation in Canada.

1983 – A first ministers' conference on aboriginal constitutional matters took place, March 15 and 16, and resulted in the successful use of the new amending formula. Representatives of the aboriginal peoples of Canada and of the governments of the Yukon and the Northwest Territories participated in the discussions. The **Constitution Amendment Proclamation, 1983**, respecting the identification and definition of the rights of aboriginal peoples, was signed by Governor General Jeanne Sauvé on June 21, 1984, thus completing the formal amending process.

1984 – The first woman Governor General of Canada, Jeanne Sauvé, assumed office on May 14.

1985 – Having been the first black member elected to the House of Commons and made a federal cabinet minister, Lincoln Alexander was appointed Lieutenant Governor of Ontario, September 20, the first black person to hold the vice-regal position in Canada.

1987 – Further proposals to amend the Constitution of Canada were unanimously accepted in principle by the first ministers at Meech Lake on April 30. The "Meech Lake Accord", a legal text reflecting the proposals, resulted in unanimous agreement at the Langevin Block meeting of June 2 and 3. The Accord required the ratification of both Houses of Parliament and all Provincial Legislatures within a three-year maximum ratification period following the adoption of the resolution initiating the process. The Quebec National Assembly adopted such a resolution on June 23, 1987, thereby initiating the process. Meanwhile, changes in government occurred in three provinces, and by June 23, 1990, legislative authorization was granted in New Brunswick, but not in Manitoba; it was rescinded in Newfoundland.

1988 – On June 4, Governor General Jeanne Sauvé authorized the creation of the Canadian Heraldic Authority, having received on that day new Letters Patent signed by the Queen, on the advice of Her Canadian Privy Council, and empowering the Governor General to grant armorial bearings in the country. Canada is the only Commonwealth country lawfully authorized to exercise the armorial prerogative.

1990 – A **Commission on Quebec's future constitutional arrangements** was created by an Act of the National Assembly on September 4. This "Expanded Parliamentary Committee", made up of 18 members of the National Assembly, three members of the House of Commons, and of non-parliamentarians, was co-chaired by Michel Bélanger and Jean Campeau, two representatives of the business community. It was mandated to study and analyze the political and constitutional status of Quebec. It reported to the National Assembly on March 27, 1991.

– On November 1, Prime Minster Brian Mulroney announced the creation of the **Citizens' Forum on Canada's Future**, headed by Keith Spicer, to seek opinions and solutions from the people of Canada and to report its findings by July 1, 1991.

– A resolution establishing a Special Joint Committee of Parliament was passed by the House of Commons on December 17 and by the Senate on January 30, 1991, with the mandate to study the process for amending the Constitution of Canada. The co-chairmen, Senator Gérald Beaudoin and Jim Edwards, M.P., reported their findings to Parliament on June 20, 1991.

1991 – A **Special Joint Committee on a Renewed Canada** (also referred to as the Beaudoin-Dobbie Committee) was established by an Order of the House of Commons of June 19 and a similar Order adopted by the Senate two days later. The Committee was instructed to inquire into and make recommendations to Parliament on a set of constitutional proposals for the renewal of Canada which the federal government made public on September 24. The Committee held its first meeting the next day and, during a five month period, sought broad public participation and discussion on Canada's constitutional future.

– On August 26, the Government of Canada established the Royal Commission of Inquiry on Aboriginal Peoples with the broad mandate to examine the evolution of relations between Aboriginal peoples, the Canadian government and Canadian society as a whole, as well as social, economic and justice issues, and Aboriginal self-government.

1992 – On the occasion of Canada's 125th anniversary, numerous special events and activities are taking place throughout the country, including 125 days of celebrations in the nation's Capital from May 6 to September 7, and an unprecedented Canada Day on July 1 on Parliament Hill.

Her Majesty Queen Elizabeth II, Queen of Canada. — Rideau Hall.

His Excellency the Right Honourable Ramon John Hnatyshyn, P.C., C.C., C.M.M., C.D., Q.C., Governor General of Canada. — Karsh/Rideau Hall.

It is with great pleasure that I extend my warmest greetings to the readers of this album commemorating Canada's 125th birthday.

Canada has recently been defined by the United Nations as the best country in the world in which to live. The dynamic energy of Canadians has resulted in a quality of life that is recognized and admired internationally for its richness and diversity. As we celebrate the 125th year of our coming together as a country, we cherish the opportunity not only to look back on what we have accomplished, but to look forward to what we have yet to achieve as we lay the foundations for the next 125 years and beyond.

The sense of pride in our country that has allowed us to live in peace, freedom and security is as strong today as it was in 1867. It is that pride, as well as our shared hopes and dreams for the future, which will ensure that Canada remains united and prosperous.

I congratulate the staff at Meridien on their efforts, and I know that you will all enjoy leafing through the pages of this fine publication.

Brian Mulroney

OTTAWA
1992

The Right Honourable Brian Mulroney, Prime Minister of Canada

Jacques Cartier. Théophile Hamel (1817-1870) Oil. — National Archives of Canada (C-11226).

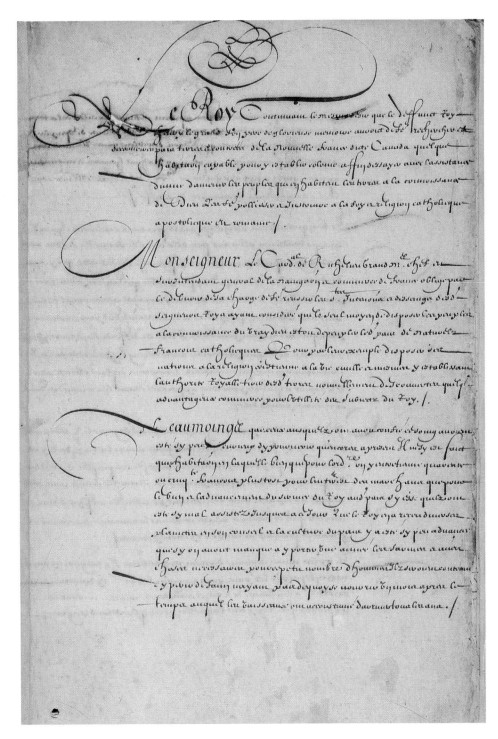

Constitution of the Company of New France, also called the One Hundred Associates, Paris, April 29, 1627. — National Archives of Canada, Manuscript Division (C-137541).

Great Seal Deputed for the "Province of Quebec", 1763. On the obverse of the seal, King George III points with his sceptre to his new colony on a map of North America. The reverse of the seal bears the royal arms. The seal was used on a proclamation of July 23, 1793. — National Archives of Canada, Manuscript Division (Obverse, C-131487 and reverse, C-131486).

New Brunswick Legislature Meeting in Mallard House, St. John, N.B., 1786. C.W. Simpson (1878-1942) Oil on canvas. — National Archives of Canada (C-13936).

No 60.

Downing Street,
31 December 1857.

Sir,

By my Despatch of the 17th April last I informed you that Her Majesty had been graciously pleased to comply with the prayer of the Address presented to Her by the Legislative Council and Assembly of Canada, namely, that She would

exercise The Royal Prerogative by the selection of some place for the permanent Seat of Government in Canada.

This question has now been considered by Her Majesty and by Her Government, with that attention which its great importance demanded.

The statements and arguments contained in the various Memorials laid before them in consequence of your invitation to the Mayors of the several Cities chiefly interested, have been fully weighed.

I am commanded by the Queen to inform you that in the judgment of Her Majesty, the city of Ottawa combines greater advantages than any other place in Canada for the permanent Seat of the future Government of the Province: and is selected by Her Majesty accordingly.

I have the honor to be
Sir,
Your most obedient
humble servant
Whitehall

Governor
The Right Honble
Sir E. Head Bart
&c &c
Canada.

Dispatch of 31 December 1857 from Henry Labouchere, Secretary of State for the Colonies informing Sir Edmund Head, Governor in Chief, that Queen Victoria had selected Ottawa for the permanent seat of the future Government of the Province of Canada. — National Archives of Canada, Manuscript Division (C-20384, C-20385 and C-20386).

Convention at Charlottetown, Prince Edward Island, of Delegates from the Legislatures of Canada, New Brunswick, Nova Scotia and Prince Edward Island to take into consideration the union of the British North American Colonies, September 1, 1864. — G.P. Roberts/National Archives of Canada (C-733).

"Our Future Queen", 1837. Portrait of Queen Victoria. Sir G.W. Hayter (1792-1871) Engraving.
— National Archives of Canada (C-95246).

First sitting of the Legislative Council of the United Colony of British Columbia, January 24, 1867, in the Legislative Council Hall formerly the main Barracks of the Royal Engineers at New Westminster. C.W. Simpson (1878-1942) Oil. — National Archives of Canada (C-13960).

Northwest Territories Council Meeting, Fort Garry, 1870. C.W. Simpson (1878-1942) Oil.
— National Archives of Canada (C-13940).

Conference of the Marquis of Lorne, Governor General of Canada, and Chief Crowfoot with Blackfeet Indians, 1881. Sydney Prior Hall (1842-1917) Pastel. — National Archives of Canada (C-121918)

The Hon. John Norquay, Premier of Manitoba, 1881. A descendant of a metis woman and a Hudson's Bay Company officer, Norquay was elected by acclamation to Manitoba's first Legislative Assembly, December 27, 1870, and retained his seat until his death. He was Premier of Manitoba from November 1878 to December 1887. Sydney Prior Hall (1842-1917) Pencil. — National Archives of Canada (C-12882).

George R.I.

George by the Grace of God, of the United Kingdom of Great Britain and Ireland and of the British Dominions beyond the Seas King, Defender of the Faith, Emperor of India. &c. &c. &c.

To all and singular to whom these Presents shall come, Greeting:

Whereas for the better treating of and arranging certain matters which are now in discussion, or which may come into discussion between Us and Our Good Friends the United States of America, relating to the regulation of the Pacific Halibut Fishery We have judged it expedient to invest a fit person with Full Power to conduct the said discussion on Our Part. Know Ye therefore that We, reposing especial trust and confidence in the wisdom loyalty diligence and circumspection of Our Trusty and Well-beloved the Honourable Ernest Lapointe, one of Our Counsel learned in the Law, Member of the Parliament of Canada, Member of Our Privy Council for Canada, Minister of Marine and Fisheries of Our Dominion of Canada, have named, made, constituted and appointed, as We do by these Presents name, make, constitute, and appoint him Our undoubted Commissioner Procurator and Plenipotentiary: Giving to him all manner of power and authority to treat adjust and conclude with such Minister or Ministers as may be vested with similar power and authority on the part of Our Good Friends the United States of America, any Treaty, Convention, or Agreement that may tend to the attainment of the above-mentioned end, and to sign for Us, and in Our Name, everything so agreed upon and concluded, and to do and transact all such other matters as may appertain thereto in as ample manner and form, and with equal force and efficacy as We Ourselves could do if personally present: Engaging and Promising upon Our Royal Word that whatever things shall be so transacted and concluded by Our said Commissioner Procurator and Plenipotentiary shall, subject if necessary to Our Ratification be agreed to, acknowledged and accepted by Us in the fullest manner and that We will never suffer either in the whole or in part any person whatsoever to infringe the same, or act contrary thereto, as far as it lies in Our power. In witness whereof We have caused the Great Seal of Our United Kingdom of Great Britain and Ireland to be affixed to these Presents which We have signed with Our Royal Hand.

Given at Our Court of Saint James the First ——— day of February ——— in the year of Our Lord one thousand nine hundred and Twenty-three and in the Thirteenth ——— year of Our Reign.

Commission signed by King George V granting Ernest Lapointe, Minister of Marine and Fisheries, full powers to conclude a Treaty with the United States on halibut fishing in the Pacific Ocean, February 1, 1923. — National Archives of Canada, Manuscript Division (MG 27, III B 10).

THE CANADIAN BILL OF RIGHTS

An Act for the Recognition and Protection of Human Rights and Fundamental Freedoms.
Statutes of Canada 1960, 8-9 Elizabeth II, Chapter 44, assented to 10th August 1960.

THE Parliament of Canada, affirming that the Canadian Nation is founded upon principles that acknowledge the supremacy of God, the dignity and worth of the human person and the position of the family in a society of free men and free institutions;

Affirming also that men and institutions remain free only when freedom is founded upon respect for moral and spiritual values and the rule of law;

And being desirous of enshrining these principles and the human rights and fundamental freedoms derived from them, in a Bill of Rights which shall reflect the respect of Parliament for its constitutional authority and which shall ensure the protection of these rights and freedoms in Canada:

THEREFORE Her Majesty, by and with the advice and consent of the Senate and House of Commons of Canada, enacts as follows:

PART I
BILL OF RIGHTS

1. It is hereby recognized and declared that in Canada there have existed and shall continue to exist without discrimination by reason of race, national origin, colour, religion or sex, the following human rights and fundamental freedoms, namely,

a) the right of the individual to life, liberty, security of the person and enjoyment of property, and the right not to be deprived thereof except by due process of law;

b) the right of the individual to equality before the law and the protection of the law;

c) freedom of religion;

d) freedom of speech;

e) freedom of assembly and association; and

f) freedom of the press.

2. Every law of Canada shall, unless it is expressly declared by an Act of the Parliament of Canada that it shall operate notwithstanding the *Canadian Bill of Rights*, be so construed and applied as not to abrogate, abridge or infringe or to authorize the abrogation, abridgment or infringement of any of the rights or freedoms herein recognized and declared, and in particular, no law of Canada shall be construed or applied so as to

a) authorize or effect the arbitrary detention, imprisonment or exile of any person;

b) impose or authorize the imposition of cruel and unusual treatment or punishment;

c) deprive a person who has been arrested or detained

   (i) of the right to be informed promptly of the reason for his arrest or detention,

   (ii) of the right to retain and instruct counsel without delay, or

   (iii) of the remedy by way of *habeas corpus* for the determination of the validity of his detention and for his release if the detention is not lawful;

d) authorize a court, tribunal, commission, board or other authority to compel a person to give evidence if he is denied counsel, protection against self crimination or other constitutional safeguards;

e) deprive a person of the right to a fair hearing in accordance with the principles of fundamental justice for the determination of his rights and obligations;

f) deprive a person charged with a criminal offence of the right to be presumed innocent until proved guilty according to law in a fair and public hearing by an independent and impartial tribunal, or of the right to reasonable bail without just cause; or

g) deprive a person of the right to the assistance of an interpreter in any proceedings in which he is involved or in which he is a party or a witness, before a court, commission, board or other tribunal, if he does not understand or speak the language in which such proceedings are conducted.

3. The Minister of Justice shall, in accordance with such regulations as may be prescribed by the Governor in Council, examine every proposed regulation submitted in draft form to the Clerk of the Privy Council pursuant to the *Regulations Act* and every Bill introduced in or presented to the House of Commons, in order to ascertain whether any of the provisions thereof are inconsistent with the purposes and provisions of this Part and he shall report any such inconsistency to the House of Commons at the first convenient opportunity.

4. The provisions of this Part shall be known as the *Canadian Bill of Rights*.

"I am a Canadian, a free Canadian, free to speak without fear, free to worship God in my own way, free to stand for what I think right, free to oppose what I believe wrong, free to choose those who shall govern my country. This heritage of freedom I pledge to uphold for myself and all mankind.

The Right Honourable John G. Diefenbaker, Prime Minister of Canada,
House of Commons Debates, July 1, 1960.

PARLIAMENT BUILDINGS · OTTAWA

Roger Duhamel, F.R.S.C., Queen's Printer, Ottawa, Canada.

Déclaration Canadienne des Droits

Loi ayant pour objet la reconnaissance et la protection des droits de l'homme et des libertés fondamentales. Statuts du Canada 1960, 8-9 Élisabeth II, Chapitre 44. Sanctionnée le 10 août 1960.

Le Parlement du Canada proclame que la nation canadienne repose sur des principes qui reconnaissent la suprématie de Dieu, la dignité et la valeur de la personne humaine ainsi que le rôle de la famille dans une société d'hommes libres et d'institutions libres;

Il proclame en outre que les hommes et les institutions ne demeurent libres que dans la mesure où la liberté s'inspire du respect des valeurs morales et spirituelles et du règne du droit;

Et afin d'expliciter ces principes ainsi que les droits de l'homme e les libertés fondamentales qui en découlent, dans une Déclaration de droits qui respecte la compétence législative du Parlement du Canada et qui assure à sa population la protection de ces droits et de ces libertés,

En conséquence, Sa Majesté, sur l'avis et du consentement du Sénat et de la Chambre des communes du Canada, décrète:

PARTIE I

DÉCLARATION DES DROITS

1. Il est par les présentes reconnu et déclaré que les droits de l'homme et les libertés fondamentales ci-après énoncés ont existé et continueront à exister pour tout individu au Canada quels que soient sa race, son origine nationale, sa couleur, sa religion ou son sexe:

a) le droit de l'individu à la vie, à la liberté, à la sécurité de la personne ainsi qu'à la jouissance de ses biens, et

le droit de ne s'en voir privé que par l'application régulière de la loi;
b) le droit de l'individu à l'égalité devant la loi et la protection de la loi;
c) la liberté de religion;
d) la liberté de parole;
e) la liberté de réunion et d'association, et
f) la liberté de la presse.

2. Toute loi du Canada, à moins qu'une loi du Parlement du Canada ne déclare expressément qu'elle s'appliquera nonobstant la *Déclaration canadienne des droits,* doit s'interpréter et s'appliquer de manière à ne pas supprimer, restreindre ou enfreindre l'un quelconque des droits ou des libertés reconnus et déclarés aux présentes, ni à en autoriser la suppression, la diminution ou la transgression, et en particulier, nulle loi du Canada ne doit s'interpréter ni s'appliquer comme

a) autorisant ou prononçant la détention, l'emprisonnement ou l'exil arbitraires de qui que ce soit;
b) infligeant des peines ou traitements cruels et inusités, ou comme en autorisant l'imposition;
c) privant une personne arrêtée ou détenue
 (i) du droit d'être promptement informée des motifs de son arrestation ou de sa détention,
 (ii) du droit de retenir et constituer un avocat sans délai, ou
 (iii) du recours par voie d'*habeas corpus* pour qu'il soit jugé de la validité de sa détention et que sa libération soit ordonnée si la détention n'est pas légale;
d) autorisant une cour, un tribunal, une commission, un office, un conseil ou une autre autorité à contraindre une personne à témoigner si on lui refuse le secours d'un avocat, la protection contre son propre témoi-

gnage ou l'exercice de toute garantie d'ordre constitutionnel;
e) privant une personne du droit à une audition impartiale de sa cause, selon les principes de justice fondamentale, pour la définition de ses droits et obligations;
f) privant une personne accusée d'un acte criminel du droit à la présomption d'innocence jusqu'à ce que la preuve de sa culpabilité ait été établie en conformité de la loi, après une audition impartiale et publique de sa cause par un tribunal indépendant et non préjugé, ou la privant sans juste cause du droit à un cautionnement raisonnable; ou
g) privant une personne du droit à l'assistance d'un interprète dans des procédures où elle est mise en cause ou est partie, ou témoin, devant une cour, une commission, un office, un conseil ou autre tribunal, si elle ne comprend ou ne parle pas la langue dans laquelle se déroulent ces procédures.

3. Le ministre de la Justice doit, en conformité de règlements prescrits par le gouverneur en conseil, examiner toute proposition de règlement soumise, sous forme devant-projet, au greffier du Conseil privé, selon la *Loi sur les règlements,* comme tout projet ou proposition de loi soumis au présenté à la Chambre des communes, en vue de constater si l'une quelconque de ses dispositions est incompatible avec les fins et dispositions de la présente Partie, et il doit signaler toute semblable incompatibilité à la Chambre des communes dès qu'il en a l'occasion.

4. Les dispositions de la présente Partie, doivent être connues sous la désignation: *Déclaration canadienne des droits.*

Je suis Canadien, un Canadien libre, libre de m'exprimer sans crainte, libre de servir Dieu comme je l'entends, libre d'appuyer les idées qui me semblent justes, libre de m'opposer à ce qui me semble injuste, libre de choisir les dirigeants de mon pays. Ce patrimoine de liberté, je m'engage à le sauvegarder pour moi-même et pour toute l'humanité.

[signature]

Le très honorable John G. Diefenbaker, premier ministre du Canada, Débats de la Chambre des Communes, le 1ᵉʳ juillet 1960.

LE PARLEMENT-OTTAWA

Roger Duhamel, M.S.R.C. Imprimeur de la Reine, Ottawa, Canada.

ELIZABETH THE SECOND,

BY THE GRACE OF GOD OF THE UNITED KINGDOM, CANADA AND HER OTHER REALMS AND TERRITORIES QUEEN, HEAD OF THE COMMONWEALTH, DEFENDER OF THE FAITH.

TO ALL TO WHOM THESE PRESENTS SHALL COME OR WHOM THE SAME MAY IN ANYWISE CONCERN,

GREETING:

A PROCLAMATION

Attorney General of Canada

WHEREAS the Senate of Canada, by resolution dated the 17th day of December, in the year of Our Lord one thousand nine hundred and sixty-four, has recommended that there be designated, as the National Flag of Canada, the flag hereinafter described;

AND WHEREAS the House of Commons of Canada, on the 15th day of December, in the year of Our Lord one thousand nine hundred and sixty-four, did concur in the recommendation, made on the twenty-ninth day of October, in the year of Our Lord one thousand nine hundred and sixty-four, by a Special Committee thereof, that the flag, hereinafter described, be designated as the National Flag of Canada:

NOW KNOW YE that by and with the advice of Our Privy Council for Canada, We do by this Our Royal Proclamation appoint and declare as the National Flag of Canada, upon, from and after the fifteenth day of February, in the year of Our Lord one thousand nine hundred and sixty-five, a red flag of the proportions two by length and one by width, containing in its centre a white square the width of the flag, bearing a single red maple leaf, or, in heraldic terms, described as gules on a Canadian pale argent a maple leaf of the first:

OF ALL WHICH Our Loving Subjects and all others whom these Presents may concern are hereby required to take notice and to govern themselves accordingly:

IN TESTIMONY WHEREOF We have caused these Our Letters to be made Patent and the Great Seal of Canada to be hereunto affixed. Given the 28th day of January, in the Year of Our Lord One Thousand Nine Hundred and Sixty-five and in the thirteenth Year of Our Reign.

By Her Majesty's Command

Prime Minister of Canada

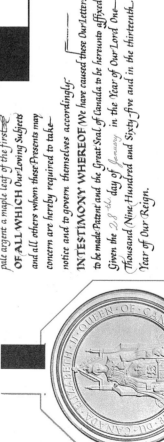

GOD SAVE THE QUEEN

ELISABETH DEUX, PAR LA

GRÂCE DE DIEU, REINE DU ROYAUME-UNI, DU CANADA ET DE SES AUTRES ROYAUMES ET TERRITOIRES, CHEF DU COMMONWEALTH ET DÉFENSEUR DE LA FOI.

A TOUS CEUX À QUI LES PRÉSENTES PARVIENDRONT OU QU'ICELLES POURRONT DE QUELQUE MANIÈRE CONCERNER,

SALUT:

PROCLAMATION

Procureur général du Canada

CONSIDÉRANT que le Sénat du Canada, par une résolution datée du 17e jour de décembre, en l'an de grâce mil neuf cent soixante-quatre, a recommandé que soit désigné, comme Drapeau national du Canada, le drapeau ci-après décrit;

ET CONSIDÉRANT que la Chambre des communes du Canada, le 15e jour de décembre, en l'an de grâce mil neuf cent soixante-quatre, a approuvé la recommandation formulée le vingt-neuvième jour d'octobre, en l'an de grâce mil neuf cent soixante-quatre, par un Comité spécial d'icelle et portant que le drapeau ci-après décrit soit désigné comme Drapeau national du Canada:

SACHEZ DONC MAINTENANT que, de et par l'avis de Notre Conseil privé pour le Canada, Nous désignons et déclarons comme Drapeau national du Canada, à compter du quinzième jour de février, en l'an de grâce mil neuf cent soixante-cinq, un drapeau rouge dont les proportions sont de deux de longueur sur un de largeur, à carré blanc au centre, haut de la largeur accollée à la hampe et portant une seule feuille d'érable rouge ou, en termes d'héraldique, de gueules, au pal canadien d'argent, chargé d'une feuille d'érable du premier:

DE CE QUI PRÉCÈDE, Nos féaux sujets et tous ceux que les présentes peuvent concerner sont par les présents requis de prendre connaissance et d'agir en conséquence.

EN FOI DE QUOI Nous avons fait émettre Nos présentes Lettres Patentes et à icelles fait apposer le Grand Sceau du Canada. Donné ce 28e jour de janvier en l'an de grâce mil neuf cent soixante-cinq, le treizième de Notre Règne.

Par ordre de Sa Majesté

Le premier ministre du Canada,

DIEU SAUVE LA REINE

TO ALL TO WHOM

THESE PRESENTS SHALL COME OR WHOM THE SAME MAY IN ANYWAY CONCERN, GREETING:

BY Robert Douglas Watt, Chief Herald of Canada:

WHEREAS THE HONOURABLE RAMON JOHN HNATYSHYN former President of the Queen's Privy Council for Canada, Companion of the Order of Canada, Commander of the Order of Military Merit, one of Her Majesty's Counsel learned in the Law, Bachelor of Arts and Bachelor of Laws of the University of Saskatchewan, whom Her Majesty has appointed to be Governor General of Canada to succeed Her Excellency the Right Honourable Jeanne Sauvé, has represented unto the Chief Herald of Canada his wish to be granted armorial bearings by lawful authority; AND WHEREAS a Warrant has been received from Leopold Henri Amyot, Herald Chancellor of the Canadian Heraldic Authority dated the 10th day of October 1989, authorizing the Chief Herald of Canada to grant to THE HONOURABLE RAMON JOHN HNATYSHYN such armorial bearings as are fitting and appropriate: NOW KNOW YOU that pursuant to the authority vested in Her Excellency the Right Honourable Jeanne Sauvé, a Member of the Queen's Privy Council for Canada, Chancellor and Principal Companion of the Order of Canada, Chancellor and Commander of the Order of Military Merit upon whom has been conferred the Canadian Forces Decoration, Governor General and Commander-in-Chief of Canada, to exercise the armorial prerogative of Her Majesty Queen Elizabeth II as Queen of Canada by Letters Patent dated the 4th day of June 1988, and the terms of my Commission of office, I, the Chief Herald of Canada do by these Presents grant and assign to THE HONOURABLE RAMON JOHN HNATYSHYN the armorial bearings as are set out in my Commission the following Arms: Per fess Bleu Céleste and Or in chief a lion passant guardant or royally crowned proper holding in its dexter paw a maple leaf Gules fimbriated Or in base a lion passant guardant Bleu Céleste holding in its dexter paw a heart Gules; And for a Crest: Above a helmet mantled Bleu Céleste doubled Or on a wreath Or and Bleu Céleste a demi-lion Gules charged on each shoulder with a maple leaf Argent holding in its dexter fore paw Scales of Justice Or; And for a Motto: MODERATIO IN OMNIBUS; to be borne and used for ever hereafter by THE HONOURABLE RAMON JOHN HNATYSHYN and by his descendants with due and proper differences upon Seals, Shields, Banners, Flags or otherwise according to the Law of Arms of Canada; AND I DO FURTHER grant and assign the following supporters: Dexter a white-tailed deer per fess Bleu Céleste and Or attired and gorged with a collar all Or pendant therefrom a bezant charged with a representation of the badge of the House of Commons of Canada proper, sinister a bull per fess Bleu Céleste and Or gorged with a collar Vert fimbriated Argent pendant therefrom a prairie lily flower proper charged with the Tryzub of the Ukraine Bleu Céleste the whole set upon a compartment party per pale of trees of the boreal forest Vert and a wheat field Or rising above barry wavy Azure and Argent to be borne and used by THE HONOURABLE RAMON JOHN HNATYSHYN during his life-time according to the Law of Arms of Canada; As are more plainly here depicted and entered in Volume I, page 70 of the Public Register of Arms, Flags and badges of Canada; GIVEN under my hand and the seal of the Canadian Heraldic Authority at Rideau Hall in the City of Ottawa this sixteenth day of January in the year of Our Lord one thousand nine hundred and ninety, in the sixth year of Her Excellency's service in office and in the thirty-eighth year of Her Majesty's reign.

IN TESTIMONY WHEREOF the Herald Chancellor, Leopold Henri Amyot, and the Deputy Herald Chancellor, Lieutenant-General François Richard, have witnessed this action with their signatures.

TOUS CEUX

QUI VERRONT LES PRÉSENTES OU QUE LES PRÉSENTES CONCERNENT, SALUT:

DE la part de Robert Douglas Watt, Héraut d'armes du Canada:

CONSIDÉRANT que L'HONORABLE RAMON JOHN HNATYSHYN, ancien Président du Conseil privé de la Reine pour le Canada, Compagnon de l'Ordre du Canada, Commandeur de l'Ordre du Mérite militaire, l'un des conseillers juridiques de Sa Majesté, Bachelier ès arts et Bachelier en droit de l'Université de Saskatchewan que a été nommé Gouverneur général par Sa Majesté pour succéder à Son Excellence la très honorable Jeanne Sauvé, a avisé le Héraut d'armes du Canada qu'il désirait porter des armoiries officielles; ET CONSIDÉRANT que Leopold Henri Amyot, Chancelier d'armes de l'Autorité héraldique du Canada, a émis un Mandat daté du 10e jour d'octobre 1989 autorisant le Héraut d'armes du Canada à concéder à L'HONORABLE RAMON JOHN HNATYSHYN des armoiries convenables et appropriées; SACHEZ QUE conformément à l'autorité dont est investie Son Excellence la très honorable Jeanne Sauvé, membre du Conseil privé de la Reine pour le Canada, Chancelier et Compagnon principal de l'Ordre du Canada, Chancelier et Commandeur de l'Ordre du Mérite militaire à qui a été décernée la Décoration des Forces canadiennes, Gouverneur général et Commandant en Chef du Canada, d'exercer la prérogative en matière d'armoiries que lui a concédée Sa Majesté la Reine Elizabeth II à titre de Reine du Canada par lettres patentes datées du 4e jour de juin 1988, et conformément aux dispositions de notre commission d'officier; Nous, le Héraut d'armes du Canada par les présentes, concédons et assignons à L'HONORABLE RAMON JOHN HNATYSHYN les armoiries suivantes: Coupé de bleu céleste sur or en chef un léopard d'or ceint de la couronne royale au naturel et tenant de sa patte dextre une feuille d'érable de gueules bordée d'or et en pointe un léopard de bleu céleste tenant de sa patte dextre un cœur de gueules; l'écu timbré d'un heaume avec des lambrequins de bleu céleste doublés d'or et une torque d'or et de bleu céleste; Et pour cimier: Un lion issant de gueules chargé sur chaque épaule d'une feuille d'érable d'argent et tenant de sa patte dextre la balance de la justice d'or; Et pour devise: MODERATIO IN OMNIBUS pour être portées et utilisées à perpétuité par L'HONORABLE RAMON JOHN HNATYSHYN et ses descendants avec les brisures convenables et appropriées sur des sceaux, des écus, des bannières, des drapeaux ou autrement en conformité du droit héraldique du Canada; ET EN OUTRE concédons et assignons les supports suivants: À dextre un caribou coupé de bleu céleste sur or l'ramé et portant un collier d'or d'où pend un besant aussi d'or chargé d'une représentation de l'insigne de la Chambre des communes du Canada au naturel, à senestre un taureau coupé de bleu céleste sur or portant un collier de sinople bordé d'argent d'où pend un lis de la prairie au naturel chargé d'un tridend de l'Ukraine de bleu céleste le tout soutenu d'un mont parti d'arbres de la forêt boréale de sinople et d'un champ de blé d'or soutenu de burelé-ondé pour être portés et utilisés par L'HONORABLE RAMON JOHN HNATYSHYN de son vivant en conformité du droit héraldique du Canada; AINSI qu'ils sont figurés sur les présentes et consignés dans le volume I page 70 du Registre public des armoiries, drapeaux et insignes du Canada; DONNÉ sous notre seing et le sceau de l'Autorité héraldique du Canada à la résidence du Gouverneur général, dans la ville d'Ottawa, le seizième jour de janvier en l'an grâce mil neuf cent quatre-vingt-dix, la sixième année que Son Excellence exerce ses fonctions et le trente-huitième du règne de Sa Majesté.

EN FOI DE QUOI le Chancelier d'armes, Leopold Henri Amyot, et le Vice-chancelier d'armes, Lieutenant-général François Richard, se portent témoins en apposant leur signature.

Chancelier d'armes

Chef Héraut of Canada / Héraut d'armes du Canada

Deputy Herald Chancellor

Herald Chancellor

Vice-chancelier d'armes

Great Seal of Canada in use since 1952. Queen Elizabeth II. Designed by the Canadian artist Eric Aldwinckle. Engraved by Thomas Shingles of the Canadian Royal Mint. — National Archives of Canada (C-33866).

The **Royal Proclamation of October 7, 1763**, by King George III (First page). — National Archives of Canada, Manuscript Division (MG 40, E1)/Crown copyright, reproduced with the permission of the Controller of HMSO.

The Quebec Act, 1774 (First page). — National Archives of Canada, Manuscript Division (MG 40, E1)/Crown copyright, reproduced with the permission of the Controller of HMSO.

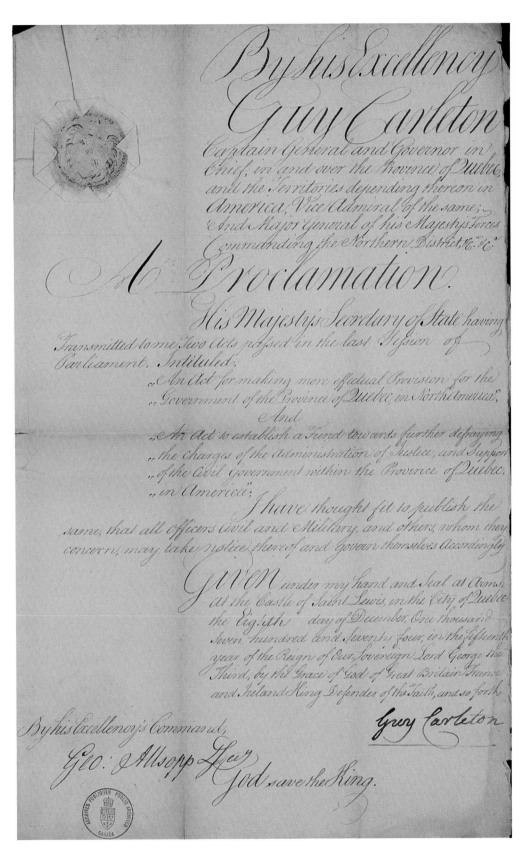

Proclamation of December 8, 1774, by Governor Guy Carleton announcing that he had received and published two Acts of Parliament, including the Quebec Act. — National Archives of Canada, Manuscript Division (RG4, B3, vol. 1).

The **Constitutional Act, 1791** (First page) — National Archives of Canada, Manuscript Division (MG 40, E1)/Crown copyright, reproduced with the permission of the Controller of HMSO.

The **Union Act, 1840** (First page). — National Archives of Canada, Manuscript Division (MG40, E1)/Crown copyright, reproduced with the permission of the Controller of HMSO.

ANNO TRICESIMO

VICTORIÆ REGINÆ.

✸✸✸

C A P. III.

An Act for the Union of *Canada, Nova Scotia,* and *New Brunswick,* and the Government thereof; and for Purposes connected therewith. *29th March 186*

WHEREAS the Provinces of *Canada, Nova Scotia,* and *New Brunswick* have expressed their Desire to be federally united into One Dominion under the Crown of the United Kingdom of *Great Britain* and *Ireland,* with a Constitution similar in Principle to that of the United Kingdom:

And whereas such a Union would conduce to the Welfare of the Provinces and promote the Interests of the *British* Empire:

And whereas on the Establishment of the Union by Authority of Parliament it is expedient, not only that the Constitution of the Legislative Authority in the Dominion be provided for, but also that the Nature of the Executive Government therein be declared:

And whereas it is expedient that Provision be made for the eventual Admission into the Union of other Parts of *British North America:*

Be it therefore enacted and declared by the Queen's most Excellent Majesty, by and with the Advice and Consent of the Lords Spiritual

C   and

"**British North America Act, 1867**", now **The Constitution Act, 1867** (First page). — National Archives of Canada, Manuscript Division (MG40, E1)/Crown copyright, reproduced with the permission of the Controller of HMSO.

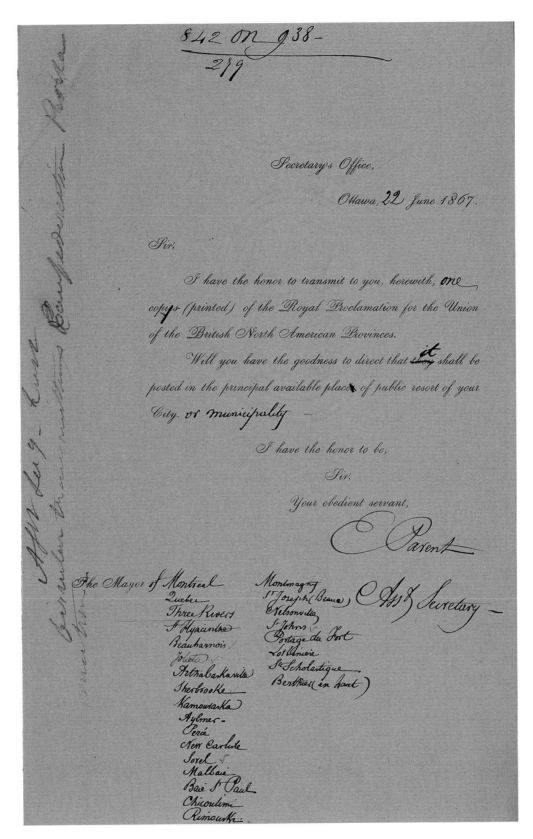

842 on 938 —
279

Secretary's Office,

Ottawa, 22 June 1867.

Sir,

I have the honor to transmit to you, herewith, one copies (printed) of the Royal Proclamation for the Union of the British North American Provinces.

Will you have the goodness to direct that it shall be posted in the principal available place of public resort of your City or municipality —

I have the honor to be,

Sir,

Your obedient servant,

Parent

Ass. Secretary —

The Mayor of Montreal
Quebec
Three Rivers
St Hyacinthe
Beauharnois
Joliete
Arthabaskaville
Sherbrooke
Kamouraska
Aylmer
Percé
New Carlisle
Sorel
Malbaie
Baie St Paul
Chicoutimi
Rimouski

Montmagny
St Joseph (Beauce)
Nelsonville
St Johns
Portage du Fort
Lot Aimée
Ste Scholastique
Berthier (en haut)

Letter from the Assistant Provincial Secretary, E. Parent, directing the mayors to publicize the Proclamation of May 22, 1867. — National Archives of Canada, Manuscript Division (C-138956).

Par la REINE.

UNE PROCLAMATION

Pour unir les Provinces du Canada, de la Nouvelle Ecosse et du Nouveau Brunswick, en une seule et même Puissance sous le nom de Canada.

CONSIDERANT que par un acte du Parlement passé le vingt-neuvième jour de Mars, mil huit cent soixante-et-sept, dans la trentième année de Notre Règne, intitulé : " Acte concernant l'Union " et le Gouvernement du Canada, de la Nouvelle " Ecosse et du Nouveau Brunswick, ainsi que les " objets qui s'y rattachent," après l'énumération de diverses autres dispositions, il est décrété "qu'il sera " loisible à la Reine, de l'avis du Très Honorable " Conseil Privé de Sa Majesté, de déclarer par pro-" clamation, qu'à compter du jour y désigné,—mais " pas plus tard que six mois après la passation du " présent Acte,—les provinces du Canada, de la " Nouvelle Ecosse et du Nouveau Brunswick ne for-" meront qu'une seule et même Puissance sous le " nom de Canada ; et que dès ce jour, ces trois pro-" vinces ne formeront, en conséquence qu'une seule " et même puissance sous ce nom ;" et qu'il est de plus décrété que " les premières personnes appelées " au Sénat seront celles que la Reine, par mandat, " sous le seing manuel de Sa Majesté, jugera à propos " de désigner, et que leurs noms seront insérés dans " la Proclamation de la Reine décrétant l'Union ;" à ces causes, Nous avons de l'avis de Notre Conseil Privé, jugé à propos d'émettre Notre Proclamation Royale, et nous déclarons et ordonnons, qu'à compter du premier jour de Juillet, mil huit cent soixante-et-sept, les Provinces du Canada, de la Nouvelle Ecosse et du Nouveau Brunswick, ne formeront qu'une seule et même Puissance sous le nom de Canada.

Et nous déclarons et ordonnons, en outre, que les personnes dont les noms sont insérés et énumérés dans la présente Proclamation sont celles que, par mandat revêtu de Notre Seing manuel, Nous avons jugé à propos d'appeler les premières au Sénat du Canada.

Pour la Province d'Ontario.

John Hamilton.
Roderick Matheson.
John Ross.
Samuel Mills.
Benjamin Seymour.
Walter Hamilton Dickson.
James Shaw.
Adam Johnston Fergusson Blair.
Alexander Campbell.
David Christie.
James Cox Aikins.
David Reesor.
Elijah Leonard.
William MacMaster.
Asa Allworth Burnham.
John Simpson.
James Skead.
David Lewis Macpherson.
George Crawford.
Donald Macdonald,
Oliver Blake.
Billa Flint.
Walter McCrea.
George William Allan.

Pour la Province de Québec.

James Leslie.
Asa Belknap Foster.
Joseph Noël Bossé.
Louis A. Olivier.
Jacques Olivier Bureau.
Charles Malhiot.
Louis Renaud.

Luc Letellier de St. Just.
Ulric Joseph Tessier.
John Hamilton.
Charles Cormier.
Antoine Juchereau Duchesnay.
David Edward Price.
Elzear H. J. Duchesnay.
Léandre Dumouchel.
Louis Lacoste.
Joseph F. Armand.
Charles Wilson.
William Henry Chaffers.
Jean Baptiste Guévremont.
James Ferrier.
Sir Narcisse Fortunat Belleau, Chevalier.
Thomas Ryan.
John Sewell Sanborn.

Pour la Province de la Nouvelle Ecosse.

Edward Kenny.
Jonathan McCully.
Thomas D. Archibald.
Robert B. Dickey.
John H. Anderson.
John Holmes.
John W. Ritchie.
Benjamin Wier.
John Locke.
Caleb R. Bill.
John Bourinot.
William Miller.

Pour la Province du Nouveau Brunswick.

Amos Edwin Botsford.
Edward Barron Chandler.
John Robertson.
Robert Leonard Hazen.
William Hunter Odell.
David Wark.
William Henry Steeves.
William Todd.
John Ferguson.
Robert Duncan Wilmot.
Abner Reid McClelan.
Peter Mitchell.

Donné à notre cour, au *château de Windsor*, ce vingt-deuxième jour de *Mai*, mil huit cent soixante et sept, dans la trentième année de notre règne.

DIEU sauve la REINE.

Nominations.

SECRETARIAT PROVINCIAL, (Est.)
Ottawa, 22 Juin, 1867.

Il a plu à SON EXCELLENCE L'ADMINISTRATEUR DU GOUVERNEMENT nommer George Landry, de Carleton, Ecuyer, Evaluateur pour la municipalité de Carleton, Comté de Bonaventure, en remplacement de Pierre Landry.

Ordre Généraux de Milice.

QUARTIERS GÉNÉRAUX.

Ottawa, 14 Juin, 1867.
ORDRES GÉNÉRAUX.

MILICE VOLONTAIRE.

No. 1.

1. Des arrangements ont été faits pour l'échange des Carabines maintenant en la possession des Volontaires, pour des Carabines Enfield Snider se chargeant par la culasse.

2. L'échange sera faite dans le plus court délai possible, et dans ce but des dépôts de ces carabines et de munitions propres à ces armes seront établis à Québec, Montréal, Prescott, Kingston, Toronto et London, d'où les Officiers d'Etat-Major de district pourront en retirer pour fournir aux corps dans leurs divers districts.

French translation of the Proclamation by Queen Victoria, May 22, 1867, announcing the coming into force of the Act of 1867 and the appointment of the first members of the Senate. Published in the Canada Gazette. — National Archives of Canada, Manuscript Division (C-138957).

CHAPTER 4.

An Act to give effect to certain resolutions passed
by Imperial Conferences held in the years 1926
and 1930.   [11th December 1931.]

A.D. 1931.

WHEREAS the delegates of His Majesty's Governments in the United Kingdom, the Dominion of
Canada, the Commonwealth of Australia, the Dominion
of New Zealand, the Union of South Africa, the Irish
Free State and Newfoundland, at Imperial Conferences
holden at Westminster in the years of our Lord
nineteen hundred and twenty-six and nineteen hundred
and thirty did concur in making the declarations
and resolutions set forth in the Reports of the said
Conferences :

And whereas it is meet and proper to set out by
way of preamble to this Act that, inasmuch as the
Crown is the symbol of the free association of the
members of the British Commonwealth of Nations, and
as they are united by a common allegiance to the Crown,
it would be in accord with the established constitutional
position of all the members of the Commonwealth in
relation to one another that any alteration in the law
touching the Succession to the Throne or the Royal Style
and Titles shall hereafter require the assent as well of
the Parliaments of all the Dominions as of the Parliament
of the United Kingdom :

And whereas it is in accord with the established
constitutional position that no law hereafter made by

The **Statute of Westminster, 1931** (First page). — National Archives of Canada, Manuscript Division (C-136592)/Crown copyright, reproduced with the permission of the Controller of HMSO.

INTRODUCTION*

On the occasion of the 125th anniversary of the Canadian federation, the publishing house Les Éditions du Méridien, under the editorial direction of Mr. Fernand Tanguay, is publishing the legal documents that constitute the Constitution of Canada, the fundamental law of the country.

Notwithstanding the crises we have experienced, particularly in recent years, the Canadian Constitution of 1867 continues to endure. It is one of the oldest in the world. It was the first federal constitution in the British Empire, and Canada was the first federation to combine a parliamentary regime with the system of responsible government.

The Constitution is the supreme law. All other laws derive their validity from the Constitution.

Our Constitution is federal and parliamentary. Canada is both a constitutional monarchy and a democratic state, one of the most democratic in existence. In 1982, Canada enshrined a *Charter of Rights and Freedoms* in its Constitution.

A Supreme Court, established in 1875 and becoming truly supreme in 1949, exercises ultimate control over the constitutionality of federal and provincial legislation. This judicial review is strictly exercised. The Court is composed of nine judges, three of whom are trained in the civil law system.

I. BACKGROUND

For thousands of years, Canada was inhabited by aboriginal peoples who had their own ways and customs. Then the Europeans arrived. The navigator Jacques Cartier, sailing from St-Malo in 1534, claimed possession of Canada on behalf of the King of France. Cartier made several voyages, but no one stayed behind to populate the colony. It was not until 1608, when Samuel de Champlain established a settlement in what is now Quebec City, that New France was firmly established. Colonization spread from Quebec to other points in America. During this period, the English set foot in America, particularly in the territory that was to become the United States of America. Canada, or New France, lived under French rule until the decisive armed conflict of 1759, during the *Seven Years War*. The *Capitulation of Quebec* occurred on September 18, 1759 and the *Capitulation of Montreal* on September 8, 1760. Until the *Treaty of Paris* of February 10, 1763, the colony was administered by General Amherst. Under this treaty, France renounced all claim to Nova Scotia and Acadia, and ceded Canada and Cape Breton to the United Kingdom.

Beginning in 1759, Canada experienced a second regime, that of Britain. The *Royal Proclamation* of October 7, 1763 may be considered our first constitution

---

* The author has borrowed to some degree from the opening pages of his treatise on the Canadian Constitution, *La Constitution du Canada*, published in 1990 by Wilson & Lafleur. He wishes to thank Mr. Pierre Thibault for his collaboration.

following the Conquest. It abolished the French civil law, granted the first civilian government and created a judicial system. Canada became a British colony, gradually acquiring its internal autonomy, a responsible government and, in 1867, a federal constitution. But it was not until 1931 that the country's formal political independence was genuinely enshrined in a constitutional document.[1] The country's independence was acquired between 1919 and 1931, as the Supreme Court of Canada stated in the *Offshore Mineral Rights Reference*.[2]

From 1763 to 1774 Canada lived under a system of absolute government. On the eve of America's declaration of independence, with the winds of revolt blustering south of the frontier, the *Quebec Act of 1774* came into force; adopted by the Parliament in Westminster, it re-established the French civil law, allowed the exercise of the Roman Catholic religion and the tithe, and exempted Quebec residents from the application of the *Test Act*. In 1774, for the first time, the expression *property and civil rights* appeared in our Constitution; it is still there today. The *Quebec Act* may be considered our second constitution. After American independence, recognized by the *Treaty of Paris of 1783*, many American Loyalists emigrated to Canada. They settled in Ontario, Quebec and the Maritime provinces.

In 1791, in the *Constitutional Act*, the British Parliament divided the colony into two provinces, Upper Canada and Lower Canada (Ontario and Quebec), and introduced the representative and parliamentary system. Ontario adopted the common law as its legal framework. The elected representatives of the people in both Quebec and Ontario subsequently fought to obtain a genuinely responsible government, that is, a government that had to retain the confidence of the members of Parliament in order to remain in office. These struggles led to the Rebellion of 1837-38 in both Upper and Lower Canada, which was repressed by force of arms.

The third constitution, that of 1791, was then suspended. Lord Durham was appointed Governor General and came to conduct an on-the-spot investigation that lasted five months.

His report, published in January 1839, recommended *inter alia* the union of the two Canadas into a single province. On July 23, 1840, the British Parliament enacted the *Act of Union*, our fourth constitution, which united the two Canadas in the centre into a single political system. The use of French was explicitly ruled out as the language of legislation and the Parliament, and was restored only in 1848 thanks in part to the efforts of Louis-Hippolyte LaFontaine. LaFontaine in Quebec and Baldwin in Ontario were also the major artisans of the advent of responsible government, in 1847. In Nova Scotia, this form of government came into existence in 1846.

Because the two central provinces, which were now only one, were fundamentally quite different in terms of language, law, culture and religion, a certain *de facto* federalism developed between 1840 and 1867. Some laws applied only to one or the other province.

In 1857 Sir George-Étienne Cartier, the attorney general of Lower Canada, took the initiative in putting to a vote a law establishing a Commission to codify

---

[1] *Statute of Westminster, 1931*, 22 George V, c. 4 (U.K.).

[2] *Re: Offshore Mineral Rights of British Columbia*, [1967] S.C.R. 792.

the civil law of Lower Canada. This Commission tabled eight reports. The work was submitted to the legislature on January 31, 1865 and came into force on August 1, 1866.

As early as 1859-60 Canada felt the need to establish itself as a federation. The matter had already been under discussion for several years. And the fragility of the scattered British colonies to the north of the American republic was even more apparent in the wake of the violent civil war in the United States, which lasted four years, from 1861 to 1865.

Political, economic and military factors played a role in the federation of the British colonies. Canada feared the armies of the victorious North, especially since the mother country, the United Kingdom, had supported the South in the War of Secession. Furthermore, the governments in the Province of Canada were unstable; the Union regime was no longer functioning very well. And there was a desire to strengthen the economy of the country, some sectors of which were quite shaky. A free-trade treaty between Canada and the United States, which lasted ten years, came to an end in 1864, when the Americans lost interest in it. Railways needed to be built in the British colonies. In 1858 the Macdonald-Cartier ministry had set its sights on creating a federation.

The foundations of the Canadian federation were laid in three constitutional conferences. The first was held in Charlottetown in September 1864, the second in Quebec City from October 11 to 27, 1864, and the third in London from December 4 to 24, 1866. In Quebec and London, the Fathers of Confederation adopted Resolutions registering the political compromise they had reached. The 72 *Quebec Resolutions* and the 69 *London Resolutions* laid the groundwork for the *British North America Act* our fifth constitution adopted by the Parliament of Westminster on March 29, 1867, and which came into force on July 1, 1867. Thus a British statute serves as our Constitution.

Sir John A. Macdonald, the leader of the Ontario delegation, who was subsequently to become the first prime minister of the Canadian federation, wanted a legislative union. It was only under the insistent pressure of Sir George-Étienne Cartier, the leader of the Quebec delegation, and the delegates from Nova Scotia and New Brunswick, that Macdonald agreed to a federative form of government, improperly named "Confederation". The *Constitution Act, 1867* (as our fundamental law of 1867 has been known since the patriation of the Constitution on April 17, 1982) is therefore the product of a great political compromise. It does, however, contain some features of a unitary constitution: appointment of the lieutenant governors and judges of the superior provincial courts by the federal executive, the federal powers of reservation and disallowance of provincial statutes, and the federal declaratory power. The powers of reservation and disallowance are no longer used. The declaratory power still exists, although it has a limited scope, as the Supreme Court of Canada emphasized in 1981 in the *Patriation Reference*.[3]

Sir George-Étienne Cartier played a major role in these negotiations. He ensured that "property and civil rights" remained a matter of provincial jurisdiction, allowing Quebec to maintain intact its *Civil Code* and the other provinces to

---

[3] [1981] 1 S.C.R. 753.

retain the system of the common law. Education was made a matter of exclusive provincial jurisdiction. The French language was protected in Quebec and in federal government institutions. Several sections, although few in number, acknowledged Quebec's peculiar character; among these are sections 94 and 98.

Later events were to indicate that this fundamental law of 1867, notwithstanding some deficiencies that were subsequently remedied, was, when all is said and done, fairly well conceived for its time, and fulfilled the major needs of the moment.

The Constitution of 1867 was not the Constitution of an independent country. It was that of a federal colony enjoying extensive domestic autonomy. In 1867, Canadian external affairs continued to be largely the responsibility of the government in London.

The Constitution of 1867 did not include any constitutional charter of rights and freedoms like the U.S. *Bill of Rights*. However, the courts have recognized the constitutional existence in Canada of a number of rights and freedoms, based on the preamble of this constitution, which states that we have a Constitution similar in principle to that of the United Kingdom.

Until 1982 this Constitution was amended on several occasions by the Parliament of Westminster, to respond to our needs.

In 1919, Canada had put its own signature on the *Treaty of Versailles*, and, in 1923, the *Halibut Treaty*. In 1926 the *Balfour Declaration on the Dominions* was issued following the Imperial Conference of that year. This declaration dealt with the status of the Dominions:

> They are autonomous Communities within the British Empire, equal in status, in no way subordinate one to another in any aspect of their domestic or external affairs, though united by a common allegiance to the Crown, and freely associated as members of the British Commonwealth of Nations.[4]

Canada's political independence, which had been achieved between 1919 and 1931, as the Supreme Court was to declare in its 1967 judgment on offshore mineral rights,[5] was definitively recognized by the *Statute of Westminster, 1931*. The statute confirmed certain statements made by delegates to the Imperial Conferences of 1926 and 1930.

There remained, however, the controversial issue of the general amending formula and patriation. We were less than successful in developing a general amending formula. The Parliament of Westminster would have been more than happy to be rid of its exclusive power to amend the Canadian Constitution, which had become an embarrassment that it exercised only reluctantly. But it required more than ten constitutional conferences to reach an agreement on what the formula should contain.

Weary of these repeated failures, Mr. Pierre Elliott Trudeau, in October 1980, attempted patriation with the agreement of only two provinces. The issue finally went to the Supreme Court of Canada, which in September 1981 stated that, legally, the two houses of the federal Parliament could unilaterally apply to the Westminster

---

[4.] Imperial Conference of 1926, *Summary of Proceedings*, p. 12.

[5.] *Supra*, note 2.

Parliament to patriate the Constitution, but under constitutional conventions the federal government had to obtain a substantial degree of support from the provinces before doing so.[6] Mr. Trudeau then convened the famous constitutional conference of November 1981. On November 5, nine provinces and the federal government agreed on the principle of patriation and on the content of the *Constitution Act, 1982*.

Quebec withheld its agreement and subsequently referred the issue to its Court of Appeal and eventually the Supreme Court of Canada. Both courts concluded that Quebec did not enjoy a right of veto.[7]

Accordingly, patriation, which was achieved on April 17, 1982, was consistent with law and constitutional conventions. That is, Quebec is bound by the *Constitution Act, 1982* and the *Canada Act 1982*.

The *Canada Act 1982*, a statute of the British Parliament, therefore brought about patriation. Schedule A of the *Canada Act* constitutes the official French version: "*Loi de 1982 sur le Canada*" and the *Constitution Act, 1982* is Schedule B. The *Constitution Act, 1982* is of prime importance. It provides us with a constitutional charter of rights, provides a general formula for amending the Constitution, and expands the provincial legislative sphere through the addition of a section 92A dealing with natural resources, indirect taxation by the provinces and interprovincial trade in some areas.

The Parliament of Westminster therefore renounced all legislative authority over Canada in 1982. As the Supreme Court was to state in the *Patriation Reference*,[8] this final badge of subservience, the need to resort to the British Parliament to amend the 1867 Act, "did not carry any diminution of Canada's legal right in international law, and as a matter of Canadian constitutional law, to assert its independence in external relations, be they with Great Britain or other countries".[9]

The *Statute of Westminster, 1931* and the *Constitution Act, 1982* are the two most important constitutional provisions enacted since 1867. Since 1982, Canada has finally been the complete master of its Constitution.

II. DEFINITION OF THE CONSTITUTION

The Constitution has been defined as "the system of laws and conventions by which a state is governed".[10]

In the *Patriation Reference*, the Supreme Court defined it as "the global system of rules and principles which govern the exercise of constitutional authority in the whole and in every part of the Canadian state".[11]

In Canada we do not have a single document that includes the entire Constitution. The *Constitution Act, 1867* and all of its amendments constitute the major

---

6. *Re: Resolution to Amend the Constitution, supra*, note 3.
7. *Re: Objection to a Resolution to Amend the Constitution*, [1982] 2 S.C.R. 793.
8. *Supra*, note 3.
9. *Ibid.*, at 802-803.
10. E.A. Driedger, "Constitutional Amendment in Canada", (1962) 5 Can. Bar J. 52, at p. 53.
11. *Supra*, note 3, at 874.

part of our written Constitution. But the Constitution is also found in other documents and a part of it is unwritten.

III. SOURCES AND ELEMENTS OF THE CONSTITUTION

Section 52 of the *Constitution Act, 1982* states that the Constitution of Canada includes the *Canada Act 1982* (which brought about the patriation of the Constitution), the *Constitution Act, 1982* and the Acts and orders referred to in the Schedule to the *Constitution Act, 1982*. Since the 1982 patriation, the various *British North America Acts* are titled *Constitution Acts, 1867 to 1982*. They are part of the "Constitution of Canada".

The Canadian Constitution includes three elements: (a) legislative rules; (b) common law rules; and (c) constitutional conventions.[12]

The legislative rules and common law rules make up Canadian constitutional law. The third element, conventions, are certainly a part of the Constitution. They "form an integral part of the Constitution and of the constitutional system", the Court said: "constitutional conventions plus constitutional law equal the total Constitution of the country."[13]

The courts can rule on legislative rules and common law rules.

However, constitutional conventions are not judiciable. Thus, "the sanction for breach of a convention will be political rather than legal."[14]

In the 1981 *Patriation Reference*, the Supreme Court adopted the definition of a convention given by Chief Justice Freedman of Manitoba: "a convention occupies a position somewhere in between a usage or custom on the one hand and a constitutional law on the other."[15]

In the *Quebec Veto Reference*,[16] the Supreme Court emphasized the normative character that a convention must have. The *Patriation Reference* of 1981 and the *Quebec Veto Reference* of 1982 must be read together.

Canada's Constitution, it has been said, is partly unwritten: for example, the principle of responsible government, confidence votes, the position of prime minister and its method of selection, and the existence and role of the cabinet are not explicitly referred to or described in the *Constitution Act, 1867*. Yet these are fundamental features of the Canadian Constitution. Constitutional conventions, therefore, complement legislative rules and the common law. In the *Patriation Reference*,[17] the Court emphasized the very great importance of conventions in matters involving the royal assent, the resignation of a government, and the choice of a prime minister. These rules, which originated in the United Kingdom, were

---

12. *Ibid.*
13. *Ibid.*, at 883-84.
14. *Ibid.*, at 883.
15. *Ibid.*, at 883.
16. *Supra*, note 7.
17. *Supra*, note 3.

imported to Canada. There are many such conventions, as the British professor Geoffrey Marshall has demonstrated.[18]

In terms of the distribution of legislative powers, the Constitution is of course a written one. It could not be otherwise. But the interpretation of this distribution by the highest court is crucial, as important as the document itself. The court gives the words their full scope and meaning.

Finally, federal-provincial conferences play a key role in Canada. Even if these meetings, which result in decisions of major importance, do not amend the written Constitution, they help to navigate Canadian federalism through the numerous grey areas in the Constitution. There are always possibilities for centralization or decentralization outside of the written documents and court decisions. Many "administrative arrangements" between the central government and one or more provinces have originated as a result of federal-provincial conferences.

In a country with a federative form, the constitution is supreme. Even when the principle of parliamentary supremacy is in operation as it is in Canada this supremacy is exercised only in those legislative areas allocated by the Constitution to each of the two orders of government. Plenary powers are exercised only in the framework outlined by the fundamental law.

The parliamentary dimension of the Canadian Constitution is based on a number of sections in the 1867 Constitution but also on several (unwritten) conventions of the Constitution.

This Constitution, as Chief Justice Thibaudeau Rinfret stated, does not belong to either Parliament or the legislatures, but to the entire country.[19]

IV. SUPREMACY OF THE CONSTITUTION

Section 52 of the *Constitution Act, 1982* states that the Constitution is the supreme law of Canada and that any law that is inconsistent with the provisions of the Constitution is, to the extent of the inconsistency, of no force or effect.

The Constitution was already supreme when Canadian federalism came into being in 1867. The *Colonial Laws Validity Act, 1865* provided that colonial legislation was valid unless it was inconsistent with laws of the Parliament of Westminster applying to the colony, and only to the extent of the inconsistency.

The *British North America Act* of 1867 outlines the distribution of powers in sections 91 to 95, a distribution that, until 1982, only the Parliament of Westminster could amend.

Section 91 lists the federal powers, section 92 the provincial powers; section 93, a special section, allocates education to the provinces, and sections 92A.(3), 94A and 95 deal with concurrent powers.

---

[18] G. Marshall, *Constitutional Theory*, London, Oxford University Press, 1971; see also G. Marshall, *Constitutional Conventions, the Rules and Forms of Political Accountability*, Oxford, Clarendon Press, 1984, 247 pp.; and A. Heard, *Canadian Constitutional Conventions — The Marriage of Law and Politics*, Toronto, Oxford University Press, 1991, 189 pp.

[19] *A.G. for Nova Scotia* v. *A.G. of Canada*, [1950] 4 D.L.R. 369, at 371 and 372.

V. MAJOR FEATURES OF THE CANADIAN STATE

We can distinguish six major features in our system of government:
- – Canada is a constitutional monarchy;
- – Canada has a system of parliamentary democracy;
- – Canada is a federation;
- – The judiciary is strong and independent;
- – Rights and freedoms are constitutionally protected in Canada;
- – In Canada the principle of the rule of law exists.

A. Constitutional Monarchy

Canada acceded to political sovereignty gradually. In 1919, it signed the *Treaty of Versailles* after taking part in the first world conflict. In 1923 a Canadian minister, Ernest Lapointe, signed a treaty on behalf of Canada without the presence of British plenipotentiaries; in 1926 we appointed an ambassador to Washington. The *Balfour Declaration* of 1926 recognized our status of independence of and equality with the United Kingdom. In the *Reference on Offshore Mineral Rights*, the Supreme Court stated that Canada became a sovereign state during the period between 1919 and 1931.[20]

In Canada the Queen embodies the Executive, as section 9 of the *Constitution Act, 1867* expressly provides.

This monarchy, however, is constitutional:

Most of the powers of the Crown under the prerogative are exercised only upon the advice of the prime minister of the cabinet which means that they are effectively exercised by the latter, together with the innumerable statutory powers delegated to the Crown in council.[21]

The Queen also heads up the legislative power, since statutes are enacted by her upon the advice and consent of the Senate and the House of Commons. She is the fountain of justice. Justice is rendered in her name. She is the source of honours. Federally, she is represented by the governor general, who is appointed by the Queen on the advice of the prime minister of Canada, and provincially she is represented by a lieutenant governor who is appointed by the federal authority. Since 1952 we have had a Canadian governor general. The first was Mr. Vincent Massey, followed by Mr. Georges Vanier, Mr. Roland Michener, Mr. Jules Léger, Mr. Edward Schreyer, Ms. Jeanne Sauvé and Mr. Ramon Hnatyshyn. Francophones and anglophones have alternated consistently in this position since 1952. The Queen of the United Kingdom is at the same time the Queen of Canada. The same person is Queen of several different countries, several sovereign and equal kingdoms. Although, in theory, the Crown is indivisible, this is no longer the case in practice.[22]

---

[20] *Re: Offshore Mineral Rights*, *supra*, note 2, at 816. *Re: Resolution to Amend the Constitution*, *supra*, note 3, at 802.

[21] *Ibid.*, at 878. [The French version of this judgment states "[TRANSLATION] upon the advice of the prime minister *or* the cabinet...". — Tr.]

[22] Lord Denning, in *R.* v. *Secretary of State for Foreign and Commonwealth Affairs*, [1982] 2 All E.R. 118, states that the Crown by "usage and practice" has become divisible. In *A.G. of Alberta* v. *C.T.C.*, [1978] 1 S.C.R. 61, Chief Justice Laskin had earlier written (at p. 71): "There may

B. Parliamentary Democracy

We inherited our parliamentary system from Great Britain. At the federal level we have two chambers. The House of Commons has 295 members elected for a maximum of five years with a possible extension in case of emergency, and the Senate has 104 senators appointed by the central government. The provinces have no voice in the appointment of senators. The senators remain in office until the age of seventy-five. Each province has a legislative chamber. In Quebec, it is called the National Assembly. Bicameralism has existed in several provinces, but was eliminated over the years by amendments to the Constitution.

The provinces are not equally represented in the Senate. We have 24 senators for Ontario, 24 for Quebec, 24 for the Western provinces (6 for each province), 24 for the Atlantic provinces (10 for New Brunswick, 10 for Nova Scotia, 4 for Prince Edward Island), 6 for Newfoundland, 1 senator for the Yukon Territory and 1 for the Northwest Territories. In principle, the regions are equally represented in the Senate.[23]

Canadian parliamentary procedure is similar in principle to that of Britain. We have a "*Speaker*" or "*President*" to preside over the House of Commons. Once elected by his or her peers at the outset of a Parliament, he or she breaks with party politics. In the Senate, the Speaker is designated by the prime minister of Canada.

In Canada we have a responsible government, i.e., the executive must command the confidence of the House of Commons in order to remain in power. Should the ministers lose this confidence, "they must either resign or ask the Crown for a dissolution of the legislature," the Supreme Court stated in the *Patriation Reference*.[24] We have experienced several parliamentary crisis, in particular in 1926 and in 1968. We have also had several governments that have been defeated in the House and have had to resign: for example, in 1926, 1963, 1974 and 1979. From 1867 to 1921 we had a two-party system. Since 1921 we have had more than two parties in the House of Commons. However, only the Conservatives and Liberals have held the reins of power since 1867. Occasionally they have had to rely on a third party. We have had several minority governments: 1925, 1926, 1957, 1962, 1963, 1965, 1972 and 1979.

The Senate, in principle, has the same powers as the House of Commons, subject to three exceptions: money bills must originate in the lower house (although the Senate must also vote on them), the government is not responsible to the Senate, and, on matters of constitutional amendment, the Senate has had only a 180-day suspensive veto since 1982.

The federal Parliament may amend the representation in the House of Commons as provided in section 51 of the *Constitution Act, 1867*, but it may not set aside the principle of representation by population except by constitutional amendment.[25]

---

be something to be said for the view that, having regard to the nature of Canada's federal system, the notion of the indivisibility of the Crown should be abandoned."

[23.] For the characteristics required to be appointed a senator, see section 23 of the *Constitution Act, 1867*.

[24.] *Supra*, note 3, at 878.

[25.] See, in general, section 42(1)(*a*) *of the Constitution Act, 1982* and, in the case of Prince Edward Island, see section 41(b) of the *Constitution Act, 1982*.

In Canada, as in the United Kingdom, there is not a clear separation of the three powers of the State. Of course, in Great Britain the judiciary is clearly divided from the other two, as Lord Denning has said,[26] and has been since the *Act of Settlement*. In Canada, the judiciary is also separate. However, the executive and legislative are not really separated in Canada. The prime minister, who with his Cabinet constitutes the *de facto* executive power, also dominates the legislative power and sits in the House of Commons.

It is the American congressional system that best embodies the separation of powers, as we know. It was based on Montesquieu's idea of the separation of powers in Great Britain. This fortunate misunderstanding by Montesquieu concerning the division of the three powers in the United Kingdom inspired the authors of the American system of "checks and balances" and resulted in the establishment of a new political system that has been prodigiously successful.

In *Dye*[27] and *Hickman*,[28] the Supreme Court of Canada demonstrated that the executive branch of the state is responsible to the elected representatives of the people in the House of Commons, and illustrated the role of the judiciary as well as the relationship between the executive and legislative branches.

C. Federal System

(1) A True Federation

Federalism is the most fundamental aspect of the Canadian Constitution, and the one that is ordinarily discussed the most. In the *Patriation Reference*, two justices of the Supreme Court stated: "It can fairly be said, therefore, that the dominant principle of Canadian constitutional law is federalism."[29] The Constitution of 1867 is the first to recognize a genuinely federative character in our country.

The United States were the first in America to adopt the federative form. The Canadian parliamentarians in 1867 had studied the American constitution.[30] They modelled their concept of federalism on the American formula while shaping it to the needs of our own country.

Lord Carnarvon, in presenting the federative proposal to the House of Lords, emphasized its federal nature.[31]

---

26. "The Spirit of the British Constitution", (1951) 29 Can. Bar Rev. 1180.

27. *Auditor General of Canada* v. *Minister of Energy, Mines and Resources*, [1989] 2 S.C.R. 49 ("the Dye case").

28. *Hickman* v. *A.G. of Nova Scotia*, [1989] 2 S.C.R. 796.

29. *Supra*, note 3, at 821.

30. R. Ares, *Dossier sur le pacte confédératif de 1867*, Montreal, Éditions Bellarmin, 1967, at pp. 17 and 18. The author writes that the Fathers of Confederation and British statesmen frequently used the words "federal compact" "contract", or "treaty". The *Federalist*, for its part, crossed the boundary. In 1865 Macdonald had stated: "...we had the advantage of the experience of the United States. ...I am not one of those who look upon it as a failure. I think and believe that it is one of the most skillful works which human intelligence ever created.... To say that is has some defects is but to say that it is not the work of Omniscience, but of human intellects." (*Parliamentary Debates on the subject of the Confederation of the British North American Provinces*, Quebec 1865, p. 32.) It is also worth reading a work by Jean-Charles Bonenfant, *La naissance de la Confédération*, Montreal, éd. Léméac, 1965, 155 pp., and, by the same author, *Les institutions politiques canadiennes*, Québec, P.U.L., 1954, 204 pp., pp. 11-19.

31. W.F. O'Connor, *Report to the Speaker of the Senate*, 1939, Appendix 4, "Note re Conference at Charlottetown, Quebec and London (1864-1867); Note re Quebec Conference (1864)", Lord Carnarvon, p. 87.

The American historian Mason Wade, in his monumental work on the French Canadians, is prepared to state that Cartier was the major architect of the "federative" character of the Constitution of 1867.[32]

This federative character of our Constitution is above all apparent in the actual constitutional documents of 1867.

The word "federally" appears in the first paragraph of the preamble to the *Constitution Act, 1867*. Part V of the Act is devoted to "Provincial Constitutions". Part VI deals with the distribution of legislative powers. Subsection 7(3) of the *Statute of Westminster, 1931* expressly preserves the legislative distribution effected by the *Constitution Act, 1867* at the time when Canada became an independent country.

Section I of the *Quebec Resolutions of 1864* begins with the words: "A federal union". Section I of the *London Resolutions of 1866* is similar.

For eighty years the Judicial Committee of the Privy Council interpreted our Constitution, and strove to balance the distribution of powers. It went so far as to make this preservation of the balance of powers a basic rule of construction.

The British constitutional scholar K.C. Wheare has defined a federal state as one in which the central and regional governments are sovereign, each in its respective sphere, and in which the action of these governments is coordinated.[33]

The sovereign nature of the provincial legislatures within their sphere was clearly affirmed by the Judicial Committee of the Privy Council in a number of decisions.[34]

In the *Senate Reference*, the Supreme Court of Canada referred to the *Aeronautics Reference*, in which Lord Sankey spoke of the "compromise" and "contract" between the federating bodies, and fully endorsed this approach.[35] The Judicial Committee of the Privy Council used the words "treaty of union" in referring to Canada in an Australian case;[36] it referred to this case in the *Bonanza* judgment.[37] In the *Labour Conventions* case,[38] it used the expression "inter-provincial compact". It consistently did so.[39]

In *Edwards*,[40] the learned Law Lords wrote that the *Quebec Resolutions*, revised in London, were a compromise that constituted a monument to the political

[32] M. Wade, *The French Canadians, 1760-1945* (Toronto, 1956), p. 320.

[33] K.C. Wheare, *Federal Government*, 4th ed., New York, Oxford University Press, 1963, at p. 10.

[34] *Hodge v. The Queen*, [1883-84] 9 A.C. 117, at 132; *A.G. for Canada v. Cain*, [1906] A.C. 542, at 547; *In re The Initiative and Referendum Act*, [1919] A.C. 935, at 942 (Viscount Haldane); *British Coal Corporation v. The King*, [1935] A.C. 500, at 518; *The Liquidators of the Maritime Bank of Canada v. The Receiver-General of New Brunswick*, [1892] A.C. 437, at 442; *Edwards v. A.-G. for Canada*, [1930] A.C. 124, at 136; *In re The Regulation and Control of Aeronautics in Canada*, [1932] A.C. 54, at 70.

[35] *Re: Authority of Parliament in Relation to the Upper House*, [1980] 1 S.C.R. 54.

[36] *A.G. for The Commonwealth of Australia v. Colonial Sugar Refining Co.*, [1914] A.C. 237, at 253.

[37] *Bonanza Creek Gold Mining v. The King*, [1916] 1 A.C. 566, at 579.

[38] *A.G. for Canada v. A.G. for Ontario*, [1937] A.C. 326, at 351.

[39] L.-P. Pigeon, "Le problème des amendements à la Constitution", (1943) 3 Can. Bar Rev. 437.

[40] *Edwards v. A.G. for Canada*, *supra*, note 34, at 136.

ingenuity of the Canadian statesmen, and that these resolutions served as the basis for the *Constitution Act, 1867*. In the *Patriation Reference*,[41] the Supreme Court discussed the compact theory. However, it stated that this theory pertained to political science and not the legal domain as such.

In *Great West Saddlery*, Viscount Haldane commented that the *Constitution Act, 1867* established independent, overlapping powers, and that each government within its sphere is equal to the other.[42]

Finally, Lord Denning, in the *Mellenger* judgment, explains clearly that Canada is a federation, that legislative power is divided, and that each order of government is sovereign, independent and autonomous within its own sphere. The words he uses are highly descriptive.[43]

The action of these powers is coordinated. This is the second feature of the federal state. The great British jurist K.C. Wheare, in his précis *Federal Government*, analyzed the case of Canada. Because of certain unitary features in the Constitution, he concluded, that the Canadian Constitution is only quasi-federal. However, because of the actual dynamics of this Constitution, he added, "Its working is federal".[44]

It can be concluded that, beyond the shadow of a doubt, Canada is a federal state.

Although centralized on paper, and although comprising some features of a unitary state, Canada is a federation. The Judicial Committee of the Privy Council, through its interpretation of sections 91 and 92 of the *Constitution Act, 1867*, decentralized the distribution of powers.[45] In the *Patriation Reference*, the Supreme Court pointed out that: "Although there are what have been called unitary features in the *British North America Act*,... their modification of exclusive provincial authority does not detract from that authority to any substantial degree."[46]

(2) Canada is not a confederation

There is more than a difference of degree between a "federation" and a "confederation". They differ in both nature and substance.[47]

In its second report, entitled *Coming to Terms: The Words of the Debate*,[48] the Task Force on Canadian Unity highlighted the distinguishing features of confederations and federations, and unhesitatingly classified Canada as a federation.

---

41. *Supra*, note 3.

42. *Great West Saddlery Company Limited* v. *The King*, [1921] 2 A.C. 91, at 100.

43. *Mellenger* v. *New Brunswick Development Corporation*, [1971] 2 All E.R. 593, at 595-96.

44. K.C. Wheare, *Federal Government, supra*, note 33, at p. 20.

45. J. Beetz, "Les attitudes changeantes du Québec à l'endroit de la Constitution de 1867", in *L'avenir du fédéralisme canadien*, Montreal, P.U.M. 1965, pp. 113-18; R.M. Dawson, *The Government of Canada*, 5th ed., Toronto, University of Toronto Press 1970, at p. 81. See also the *Constitution Act, 1867* later in this work.

46. *Supra*, note 3, at 802.

47. Gérald-A. Beaudoin, *Essais sur la Constitution*, Ottawa, University of Ottawa Press, 1979, 422 pp., at pp. 65-74.

48. Task Force on Canadian Unity, *Coming to Terms: The Words of the Debate*, Supply and Services Canada, 1979, 111 p.

The report listed seven essential features of a federal political system: (a) two orders of government existing in their own right under the Constitution and each acting directly upon the same citizens; (b) a central government directly elected by the electorate of the whole federation and exercising authority directly by legislation and taxation upon the country as a whole; (c) regional units of government, each directly elected by and directly acting by legislation and taxation upon its own regional electorate; (d) a formal distribution of legislative and executive authority and of sources of revenue between the two orders of government; (e) a written constitution that cannot be amended unilaterally; (f) an umpire to rule upon disputes relating to respective governmental powers; and (g) processes and institutions to facilitate intergovernmental interaction.[49]

The report indicated the major characteristics of a confederation:

Generalizing from these examples, a confederation may be described as an association in which sovereign states are joined together by a pact or treaty of international law, or a constitution, in which they delegate specific limited authority, especially in matters of foreign affairs (defence and diplomacy), to a central agency. It may be called a "diet," "assembly," "council" or "congress" and its members are usually mandated delegates appointed by the member states. (A delegate has less independent authority than an elected representative as the delegate must carry out the instructions of the government that appoints him.)

Membership in the central organization is usually on the basis of equality for the constituent states; decisions usually require unanimity, at least in important matters, and are generally implemented by the member states themselves.

The central agency, having no direct authority over citizens and acting upon citizens only through the constituent state governments, is usually supported financially by "contributions" and militarily by "contingents" from the member states.

Usually there is also in the treaty or constitution creating the confederation a formal agreement on the part of the member states renouncing the right to go to war against each other, assuming the obligations of collective security with respect to each other, and agreeing to the arbitration of their conflicts.[50]

It is clear from the principles listed above that Canada is indeed a federation, and not a confederation.

(3) Particular nature of Canadian federalism

Canada is a type of federal state. It is a country in which federalism is alive and well. This federalism has evolved substantially and is continuing to evolve before our eyes.

Federalism is a form of government that now exists on all five continents. The definition of powers varies from one federation to another.

In 1867 Quebec and the Maritime provinces were unwilling to agree to anything other than a federation. Subsequently, the Maritime provinces came to envisage their survival in a more centralized form of government, with the federal authority vigorously pursuing a policy of federal grants to the provinces. Quebec

---

[49.] *Ibid.*, p. 24.

[50.] *Ibid.*, p. 25-26.

has consistently led the struggle for provincial autonomy. Since francophones are a majority in only this province, they favour a balanced federal state.

Quebec would be no more willing today than it was in 1867 to agree to a legislative union or unitary state. Since 1945, Quebec has undeniably been the province that is most vigilant in defending its conception of federalism.

In short, in 1867 there was a compromise that, when all is said and done, was quite acceptable for that period, given the diversity of languages, cultures and religions. There were, however, some serious deficiencies in terms of the lack of any general amending formula, the language of education, and the protection of the French language. It took more than a century to remedy these deficiencies, which have severely shaken Canadian federalism and sometimes come quite close to tolling its knell. Fortunately, Canada can and wishes to continue to live under this form of government.

While Canadian federalism has given rise to a great many disputes before the Judicial Committee of the Privy Council and the Supreme Court of Canada, this is because basically it is quite sound. Conflicts of jurisdiction between governments are in the very nature of things in any federation.

In our opinion, in contrast to what has happened in the United States, the *Canadian Charter of Rights and Freedoms* of 1982 will not relegate conflicts over the distribution of powers to the sidelines.

In Canada, federal-provincial constitutional conferences have assumed a scope and maintained a frequency that a foreigner would consider clearly excessive. This is in part attributable to the Canadian Senate, which has been unwilling or unable to assume the role that the founding fathers of 1867 hoped it would play. In a federation, the upper house should represent the needs and interests of the federated states. But the Canadian Senate, unlike the American, Australian, or other upper houses, is not an elected chamber but one whose members are appointed. Modelled on the British House of Lords, which operates in a unitary country, our Senate has been unable to play, within our federation on American soil, the role performed by the Lords in the United Kingdom. Innumerable proposals have been advanced for its reform, but so far no substantial reform has seen the light of day.

Canada is a country with a strong "constitutionalism". The Supreme Court, modelled on the U.S. Supreme Court, not only rules on fundamental rights but continues to exercise a profound influence on the course of Canadian federalism.

It is natural, in a federation, that there be tendencies at times toward centralization, and at other times toward decentralization. Several such trends can be observed in our own history. It is also normal that two schools of thought should exist, one favourable to centralization and the other to decentralization. A third school may even appear, promoting a more delicate balance of powers. Here, too, Canadian federalism is not lacking. Few federations in history have evidenced such a desire for self-interrogation and study of the distribution of powers, and its constant improvement.

Canadian federalism has changed a lot in the space of one century. The country has substantially increased in size: it has become a member of the Group of Seven (G-7). Canada is evolving toward a more pronounced bilingualization. Who would have thought so, at the turn of the century! Since the Quiet Revolution of the 1960s,

Quebecers' influence on the federal scene has been greater than at any other time in the country's history.

D. A Strong and Independent Judiciary

Canada is endowed with a strong and independent judiciary.

We have provincial and federal courts. At the apex is the Supreme Court of Canada.

The Supreme Court celebrated its centennial in 1975. The *Constitution Act, 1867* did not create the Canadian court of last resort; it confined itself to empowering the federal Parliament to establish through legislation a general court of appeal.

Erected in 1875, our highest court did not become truly supreme until 1949. Appeals to the Judicial Committee of the Privy Council in criminal matters were abolished in 1933, and in civil matters in 1949. Initially, the Court comprised six judges; the number was increased to seven in 1927 and to nine in 1949. At least three judges must be chosen from among the judges of the Court of Appeal or the Superior Court of Quebec, or from among Quebec lawyers. Among the purposes of the *Constitution Act, 1982* is the protection of the Supreme Court and particularly its composition.

The Court is a national one. Since its origin it has issued judgments in public and private law in areas of federal and provincial jurisdiction. Since 1975 most appeals have been heard only with leave.

An increasing proportion of the Court's work is devoted to public law. It issues judgments and opinions of very great significance. It has become the guardian of the Constitution.

It has issued a large number of judgments in the area of the distribution of powers between the federal government and the provinces that have exercised a powerful influence on the direction of Canadian federalism.

The advent of a constitutional Charter of rights in April 1982 substantially modified its role. No one can remain indifferent to its decisions and opinions in this area in particular. It has issued more than 200 judgments on the *Canadian Charter of Rights and Freedoms*, at least forty of which are landmark decisions.

In a country such as ours, in which control of the constitutional validity of the laws is strictly exercised, it is impossible to exaggerate the importance of this fundamental, bilingual, bi-juridical institution which is, perhaps, unique in the world.

E. Rights and Freedoms Constitutionally Entrenched Since 1982

In 1867 the Fathers of Confederation had a choice between following the American example of the *Bill of Rights* of 1789, or relying on the British way of protecting rights and freedoms. They chose the second course.

They stated in the preamble to the *Constitution Act, 1867* that we have a Constitution similar in principle to that of the United Kingdom. These words subsequently were used by the courts and the legal community to conclude that such major documents as the *Magna Carta*, the *Bill of Rights*, the *Act of Settlement* and the doctrine of *habeas corpus* are a part of our Constitution. In 1938 the

Supreme Court went so far as to add that some freedoms are implicitly guaranteed.[51]

The Fathers of Confederation took the trouble, however, to give special protection to particular freedoms, such as language rights (section 133), denominational schools (section 93), annual sittings of Parliament and periodic elections (sections 20 and 50), and independence of the judiciary (section 99).

This system bore some fruit. However, after the Second World War a movement developed to entrench a bill of rights in the actual written Constitution of the country. This movement grew stronger, and on April 17, 1982 Canada, as the United States had done, provided itself with an entrenched *Charter of Rights and Freedoms* in the Constitution.

This was a considerable event both legally and legislatively. The role of the courts, which in Canada ensure judicial review of the constitutional validity of statutes, was substantially increased.

F. Rule of Law in Canada

The opening words of the *Constitution Act, 1982* refer to the rule of law in Canada:

> Whereas Canada is founded upon principles that recognize the supremacy of God and the rule of law.

The preamble of the 1867 Constitution states that we have a Constitution similar in principle to that of the United Kingdom. We have therefore inherited in Canada the principle of the *rule of law*, which is one of the principles of the British constitution.

The rule of law, one of the most fundamental features of the Canadian Constitution, has been acknowledged in a number of judgments.

In *Re Manitoba Language Rights*,[52] the Supreme Court held that the obligations under section 23 of the *Manitoba Act, 1870* (the equivalent for Manitoba of section 133 of the *Constitution Act, 1867*, which is binding on Quebec) are mandatory, and that Manitoba statutes and regulations that were not enacted, printed and published in both English and French have no legal force and effect by reason of section 23 of the *Manitoba Act, 1870*. However, since the principle of the rule of law and the *de facto* doctrine are part of our system of government, the current statutes of the Manitoba Legislature that are of no force or effect should be deemed to have temporary force and effect for the minimum period of time necessary for their translation, re-enactment, printing and publication. Given that Manitoba could not "rectify *instantaneously* the constitutional defect",[53] this conclusion was necessary, the Court stated.

In *Mercure*,[54] the Supreme Court of Canada concluded that section 110 of the *North-West Territories Act* (which is likewise the equivalent of section 133 of the *Constitution Act, 1867*) is applicable to Saskatchewan under sections 14 and 16 of

---

51. *Re: Alberta Statutes*, [1938] S.C.R. 100.
52. [1985] 1 S.C.R. 721.
53. *Ibid.*, at 749.
54. [1988] 1 S.C.R. 234.

the *Saskatchewan Act, 1905*. However, Saskatchewan, under section 45 of the *Constitution Act, 1982*, may unilaterally, through a bilingual statute, extricate itself from this obligation, the Court said; the choice, however, must be made quickly. Meanwhile, because of the principle of the rule of law, the statutes enacted in English only were deemed valid during the minimum period of time necessary for their translation, re-enactment, printing and publication.[55]

Chief Justice Dickson had the following to say about the rule of law in *British Columbia Government Employees' Union*:

> There cannot be a rule of law without access [to the courts], otherwise the rule of law is replaced by a rule of men and women who decide who shall and who shall not have access to justice....
>
> [adopting the words of the B.C. Court of Appeal] ...the right to access to the courts is under the rule of law one of the foundational pillars protecting the rights and freedoms of our citizens.[56]

Let us say, finally, that in one judgment the Supreme Court stated that the principle of the rule of law applies to members of the military.[57]

VI. RENEWAL OF THE FEDERATION SINCE 1982

Only one province in Canada is in its majority French-speaking. No matter how far ahead we cast our vision, a similar situation is unlikely to occur in any other province, even if, in 1870 in Manitoba, more than one French-speaking leader so hoped. In New Brunswick, 34% of the population is French-speaking.

If we wish to keep Quebec within the Canadian federation a solution which, in our view, is by far the best for both Quebec and Canada, Canadian federalism will have to be refined. This is inevitable.

A pronounced "provincialism" would undermine the central Parliament and produce negative results. Moreover, a number of provinces do not want this. They argue that it would deprive them of their financial wherewithal. They are much too dependent for their survival on the financial assistance of the federal authorities.

Quebec would have a hard time adjusting to an overly centralized federal state.

Everything depends, then, on finding an acceptable degree of centralization or decentralization, suited to contemporary needs.

Provinces with sparse populations and low revenues do not need the additional powers that some Quebec governments demand occasionally, from time to time. This is the dilemma of Canadian federalism, its existential difficulty.

There is no reason to think that a new Canadian federalism could not adjust to a few asymmetries for Quebec in such areas as culture, marriage and divorce.

---

55. Saskatchewan soon made its decision. By a statute enacted in both languages it extricated itself for the future from the bilingualism obligation provided in section 110 of the *North-West Territories Act*. Alberta, which was in the same situation constitutionally, did likewise. Both provinces are willing to commit themselves to some measure of bilingualism, by stages.

56. *British Columbia Government Employees Union* v. *A.G. of British Columbia*, [1988] 2 S.C.R. 214, at 230.

57. [1943] S.C.R. 483.

Although legally bound by the patriation of April 17, 1982, Quebec wanted to "politically return" to and be reconciled within the Canadian family, subject to certain conditions. Mr. René Lévesque, the Quebec premier, took this path with a long list of his own terms in the spring of 1985, and in May 1986 Mr. Bourassa, the current premier, set forth five minimum conditions. In August 1986, in Edmonton, the federal government and the other provinces agreed to give priority to Quebec's "reintegration". On April 30, 1987, at Meech Lake, the eleven first ministers reached agreement in principle on the five points. Quebec heard from some experts in May, in its Commission on institutions. On June 3, 1987, in the Langevin Block in Ottawa, after more than 19 hours of deliberations, the eleven governments agreed on the legal wording of the "*Meech Lake Accord*", embellished by a few saveguard clauses and amendments.

It remained only for the Senate and the House of Commons, as well as the legislative assembly in each province, to adopt in both official languages the so-called amending resolution. Debates followed in the federal and provincial capitals.

At a conference of the eleven first ministers on June 9, 1990, the *Meech Lake Accord* came under very heavy fire. Unfortunately, the Accord lapsed through the failure of the Manitoba and Newfoundland legislatures to ratify it by June 22, 1990.

In the wake of the failure of the *Meech Lake Accord*, the federal government created the Spicer Commission, with a mandate to listen to Canadians in general, and the Beaudoin-Edwards parliamentary committee, with a mandate to propose amendments to the procedure for amending the Constitution of Canada.

The Beaudoin-Edwards Committee tabled its report on June 20, 1991 and proposed, *inter alia*, a new amending formula based on regional majorities (Atlantic Canada, Quebec, Ontario and the Western provinces) to replace the "7/50" formula and the unanimity requirement; a constitutional guarantee of the civilian component of the Supreme Court of Canada; participation of the aboriginal peoples and territories in future constitutional conferences, entrenchment in the Constitution of a provision authorizing the inter-parliamentary delegation of legislative powers and the enactment of a federal statute allowing the government of Canada to hold, at its discretion, a consultative referendum on a constitutional proposal.

The Committee on a Renewed Canada was established in September 1991 to examine proposals formulated by the Canadian government in its document *Shaping Canada's Future Together*. This committee (the Beaudoin-Dobbie committee, as it came to be called) tabled its report on February 28, 1992 and proposed a number of major constitutional changes, *including*: entrenchment in the Constitution of a Canada clause, recognition of Quebec's distinct society and the vitality and development of the official-language minorities, a constitutional guarantee, within certain parameters, of the inherent right of the aboriginal peoples to self-government, a new elected and more equitable Senate with a six-month suspensive veto over most bills, a new distribution of powers, a statement of economic union accompanied by a non-judiciable social charter, a provision on the Canadian common market, the enactment of federal legislation enabling the government of Canada to hold, at its discretion, a consultative referendum on a constitutional proposal, and the constitutional entrenchment of the civilian component of the Supreme Court of Canada.

More precisely, in the area of the distribution of powers, the Beaudoin-Dobbie Committee recommended that the federal spending power be limited, that the declaratory power be abrogated, that immigration agreements might be given constitutional authority, that Quebec's legislative jurisdiction over culture be confirmed and that it be given exclusive jurisdiction in matters of marriage and divorce. The Beaudoin-Dobbie Committee proposed that the federal government withdraw from the following areas of provincial jurisdiction: tourism, forests, mines, recreation, housing, municipal and urban affairs, energy, regional development, family policy, health, education and social services; that the provinces be given some legislative jurisdiction in matters of personal bankruptcy and inland fisheries; and that their jurisdiction in labour market training be confirmed. The Beaudoin-Dobbie Committee also recommended that a provision be entrenched in the Constitution that would allow, under certain conditions, the inter-parliamentary delegation of legislative powers, and a further provision that would protect federal-provincial agreements from unilateral amendment. Financial compensation would also be extended to all transfers of jurisdiction from the provinces to Parliament.

Finally, the Beaudoin-Dobbie Committee proposed a series of constitutional amending formulae, all of which give Quebec a right of veto.

While these lines were being written, the Beaudoin-Dobbie report was the subject of inter-ministerial discussions and negotiations under the chairmanship of the Right Honourable Joseph Clark.

Gérald-A. Beaudoin
8 juin 1992

THE ROYAL PROCLAMATION

October 7, 1763

BY THE KING, A PROCLAMATION
GEORGE R.

Whereas We have taken into Our Royal Consideration the extensive and valuable Acquisitions in America, secured to our Crown by the late Definitive Treaty of Peace, concluded at Paris, the 10th Day of February last; and being desirous that all Our loving Subjects, as well of our Kingdom as of our Colonies in America, may avail themselves with all convenient Speed, of the great Benefits and Advantages which must accrue therefrom to their Commerce, Manufactures, and Navigation, We have thought fit, with the Advice of our Privy Council, to issue this our Royal Proclamation, hereby to publish and declare to all our loving Subjects, that we have, with the Advice of our Said Privy Council, granted our Letters Patent, under our Great Seal of Great Britain, to erect, within the Countries and Islands ceded and confirmed to Us by the said Treaty, Four distinct and separate Governments, styled and called by the names of Quebec, East Florida, West Florida and Grenada, and limited and bounded as follows, viz.

First — The Government of Quebec bounded on the Labrador Coast by the River St. John, and from thence by a Line drawn from the Head of that River through the Lake St. John, to the South end of the Lake Nipissim; from whence the said Line, crossing the River St. Lawrence, and the Lake Champlain, in 45 Degrees of North Latitude, passes along he High Lands which divide the Rivers that empty themselves into the said River St. Lawrence from those which fall into the Sea; and also along the North Coast of the Baye des Chaleurs, and the Coast of the Gulph of St. Lawrence to Cape Rosieres, and from thence crossing the Mouth of the River St. Lawrence by the West End of the Island of Anticosti, terminates at the aforesaid River of St. John.

Secondly — The Government of East Florida, bounded to the Westward by the Gulph of Mexico and the Apalachicola River; to the Northward by a Line drawn from that part of the said River where the Chatahouchee and Flint Rivers meet, to the source of St. Mary's River, and by the course of the said River to the Atlantic Ocean; and to the Eastward and Southward by the Atlantic Ocean and the Gulph of Florida, including all Islands within Six Leagues of the Sea Coast.

Thirdly — The Government of West Florida, bounded to the Southward by the Gulph of Mexico, including all Islands within Six Leagues of the Coast, from the River Apalachicola to Lake Pontchartrain; to the Westward by the said Lake, the Lake Maurepas, and the River Mississippi; to the Northward by a Line drawn due East from that part of the River Mississippi which lies in 31 Degrees North Latitude, to the River Apalachicola or Chatahouchee; and to the Eastward by the said River.

Fourthly — The Government of Grenada, comprehending the Island of that name, together with the Grenadines, and the Islands of Dominico, St. Vincent's and Tobago. And to the end that the open and free Fishery of our Subjects may be extended to and carried on upon the Coast of Labrador, and the adjacent Islands, We have thought fit, with the advice of our said Privy Council to put all that Coast, from the River St. John's to Hudson's Streights, together with the Islands of Anticosti and Madelaine, and all other smaller Islands lying upon the said Coast, under the care and Inspection of our Governor of Newfoundland.

We have also, with the advice of our Privy Council, thought fit to annex the Islands of St. John's and Cape Breton, or Isle Royale, with the lesser Islands adjacent thereto, to our Government of Nova Scotia.

We have also, with the advice of our Privy Council aforesaid, annexed to our Province of Georgia all the Lands lying between the Rivers Alatamaha and St. Mary's.

And whereas it will greatly contribute to the speedy settling of our said new Governments, that our loving Subjects should be informed of our Paternal care, for the security of the Liberties and Properties of those who are and shall become Inhabitants thereof, We have thought fit to publish and declare, by this Our Proclamation, that We have, in the Letters Patent under our Great Seal of Great Britain, by which the said Governments are constituted, given express Power and Direction to our Governors of our Said Colonies respectively, that so soon as the state and circumstances of the said Colonies will admit thereof, they shall, with the Advice and Consent of the Members of our Council, summon and call General Assemblies within the said Governments respectively, in such Manner and Form as is used and directed in those Colonies and Provinces in America which are under our immediate Government; And We have also given Power to the said Governors, with the consent of our Said Councils, and the Representatives of the People so to be summoned as aforesaid, to make, constitute, and ordain Laws, Statutes, and Ordinances for the Public Peace, Welfare, and good Government of our said Colonies, and of the People and Inhabitants thereof, as near as may be agreeable to the Laws of England, and under such Regulations and Restrictions as are used in other Colonies; and in the mean Time, and until such Assemblies can be called as aforesaid, all Persons Inhabiting in or resorting to our Said Colonies may confide in our Royal Protection for the Enjoyment of the Benefit of the Laws of our Realm of England; for which Purpose We have given Power under our Great Seal to the Governors of our said Colonies respectively to erect and constitute, with the Advice of our said Councils respectively, Courts of Judicature and public Justice within our Said Colonies for hearing and determining all Causes, as well Criminal as Civil, according to Law and Equity, and as near as may be agreeable to the Laws of England, with Liberty to all Persons who may think themselves aggrieved by the Sentences of such Courts, in all Civil Cases, to appeal, under the usual Limitations and Restrictions, to Us in our Privy Council.

We have also thought fit, with the advice of our Privy Council as aforesaid, to give unto the Governors and Councils of our said Three new Colonies, upon the Continent full Power and Authority to settle and agree with the Inhabitants of our said new Colonies or with any other Persons who shall resort thereto, for such Lands, Tenements and Hereditaments, as are now or hereafter shall be in our Power to dispose of; and them to grant to any such Person or Persons upon such Terms, and under such moderate Quit-Rents, Services and Acknowledgments, as have been appointed and settled in our other Colonies, and under such other Conditions as shall appear to us to be necessary and expedient for the Advantage of the Grantees, and the Improvement and settlement of our said Colonies.

And Whereas, We are desirous, upon all occasions, to testify our Royal Sense and Approbation of the Conduct and bravery of the Officers and Soldiers of our Armies, and to reward the same, We do hereby command and impower our Governors of our said Three new

Colonies, and all other our Governors of our several Provinces on the Continent of North America, to grant without Fee or Reward, to such reduced Officers as have served in North America during the late War, and to such Private Soldiers as have been or shall be disbanded in America, and are actually residing there, and shall personally apply for the same, the following Quantities of Lands, subject, at the Expiration of Ten Years, to the same Quit-Rents as other Lands are subject to in the Province within which they are granted, as also subject to the same Conditions of Cultivation and Improvement; viz.

To every Person having the Rank of a Field Officer — 5,000 Acres.

To every Captain — 3,000 Acres.

To every Subaltern or Staff Officer, — 2,000 Acres.

To every Non-Commission Officer, — 200 Acres.

To every Private Man — 50 Acres.

We do likewise authorize and require the Governors and Commanders in Chief of all our said Colonies upon the Continent of North America to grant the like Quantities of Land, and upon the same conditions, to such reduced Officers of our Navy of like Rank as served on board our Ships of War in North America at the times of the Reduction of Louisbourg and Quebec in the late War, and who shall personally apply to our respective Governors for such Grants.

And whereas it is just and reasonable, and essential to our Interest, and the Security of our Colonies, that the several Nations or Tribes of Indians with whom We are connected, and who live under our Protection, should not be molested or disturbed in the Possession of such Parts of Our Dominions and Territories as, not having been ceded to or purchased by Us, are reserved to them, or any of them, as their Hunting Grounds. — We do therefore, with the Advice of our Privy Council, declare it to be our Royal Will and Pleasure, that no Governor or Commander in Chief in any of our Colonies of Quebec, East Florida, or West Florida, do presume, upon any Pretence whatever, to grant Warrants of Survey, or pass any Patents for Lands beyond the Bounds of their respective Governments, as described in their Commissions; as also that no Governor or Commander in Chief in any of our other Colonies or Plantations in America do presume for the present, and until our further Pleasure be known, to grant Warrants of Survey, or pass Patents for any Lands beyond the Heads or Sources of any of the Rivers which fall into the Atlantic Ocean from the West and North West, or upon any Lands whatever, which, not having been ceded to or purchased by Us as aforesaid, are reserved to the said Indians, or any of them.

And We do further declare it to be Our Royal Will and Pleasure, for the present as aforesaid, to reserve under our Sovereignty, Protection, and Dominion, for the use of the said Indians, all the Lands and Territories not included within the Limits of Our said Three new Governments, or within the Limits of the Territory granted to the Hudson's Bay Company, as also all the Lands and Territories lying to the Westward of the Sources of the Rivers which fall into the Sea from the West and North West as aforesaid.

And We do hereby strictly forbid, on Pain of our Displeasure, all our loving Subjects from making any Purchases or Settlements whatever, or taking Possession of any of the Lands above reserved, without our especial leave and Licence for that Purpose first obtained.

And, We do further strictly enjoin and require all Persons whatever who have either wilfully or inadvertently seated themselves upon any Lands within the Countries above described, or upon any other Lands which, not having been ceded to or purchased by Us, are still reserved to the said Indians as aforesaid, forthwith to remove themselves from such Settlements.

And whereas great Frauds and Abuses have been committed in purchasing Lands of the Indians, to the great Prejudice of our Interests, and to the great Dissatisfaction of the said Indians; In order, therefore, to prevent such Irregularities for the future, and to the end that the Indians may be convinced of our Justice and determined Resolution to remove all reasonable Cause of Discontent, We do, with the Advice of our Privy Council strictly enjoin and require, that no private Person do presume to make any purchase from the said Indians of any Lands reserved to the said Indians, within those parts of our Colonies where, We have thought proper to allow Settlement; but that, if at any Time any of the Said Indians should be inclined to dispose of the said Lands, the same shall be Purchased only for Us, in our Name, at some public Meeting or Assembly of the said Indians, to be held for that Purpose by the Governor or Commander in Chief of our Colony respectively within which they shall lie; and in case they shall lie within the limits of any Proprietary Government, they shall be purchased only for the Use and in the name of such Proprietaries, conformable to such Directions and Instructions as We or they shall think proper to give for that Purpose; And we do, by the Advice of our Privy Council, declare and enjoin, that the Trade with the said Indians shall be free and open to all our Subjects whatever, provided that every Person who may incline to Trade with the said Indians do take out a Licence for carrying on such Trade from the Governor or Commander in Chief of any of our Colonies respectively where such Person shall reside, and also give Security to observe such Regulations as We shall at any Time think fit, by ourselves or by our Commissaries to be appointed for this Purpose, to direct and appoint for the Benefit of the said Trade:

And we do hereby authorize, enjoin, and require the Governors and Commanders in Chief of all our Colonies respectively, as well those under Our immediate Government as those under the Government and Direction of Proprietaries, to grant such Licences without Fee or Reward, taking especial Care to insert therein a Condition, that such Licence shall be void, and the Security forfeited in case the Person to whom the same is granted shall refuse or neglect to observe such Regulations as We shall think proper to prescribe as aforesaid.

And we do further expressly enjoin and require all Officers whatever, as well Military as those Employed in the Management and Direction of Indian Affairs, within the Territories reserved as aforesaid for the use of the said Indians, to seize and apprehend all Persons whatever, who standing charged with Treason, Misprisions of Treason, Murders, or other Felonies or Misdemeanors, shall fly from Justice and take Refuge in the said Territory, and to send them under a proper guard to the Colony where the Crime was committed of which they stand accused, in order to take their Trial for the same.

Given at our Court at St. James's the 7th Day of October 1763, in the Third Year of our Reign.

GOD SAVE THE KING

THE QUEBEC ACT, 1774

14 George III, c. 83 (U.K.)

An Act for making more effectual Provision for the Government of the Province of Quebec in North America.

Preamble

"WHEREAS his Majesty, by his Royal Proclamation bearing Date the seventh Day of October, in the third Year of his Reign, thought fit to declare the Provisions which had been made in respect to certain Countries, Territories, and Islands in America, ceded to his Majesty by the definitive Treaty of Peace, concluded at Paris on the tenth day of February, one thousand seven hundred and sixty-three: And whereas, by the Arrangements made by the said Royal Proclamation, a very large Extent of Country, within which there were several Colonies and Settlements of the Subjects of France, who claimed to remain therein under the Faith of the said Treaty, was left, without any Provision being made for the Administration of Civil Government therein; and certain Parts of the Territory of Canada, where sedentary Fisheries had been established and carried on by the Subjects of France, Inhabitants of the said Province of Canada, under Grants and Concessions from the Government thereof, were annexed to the Government of Newfoundland, and thereby subjected to Regulations inconsistent with the Nature of such Fisheries:" May it therefore please your most Excellent Majesty that it may be enacted; and be it enacted by the King's most Excellent Majesty, by and with the Advice and Consent of the Lords Spiritual and Temporal, and Commons, in this present Parliament assembled, and by the Authority of the same, That all the Territories, Islands, and Countries in North America, belonging to the Crown of Great Britain, bounded on the South by a Line from the Bay of Chaleurs, along the High Lands which divide the Rivers that empty themselves into the River Saint Lawrence from those which fall into the Sea, to a Point in forty-five Degrees of Northern Latitude, on the Eastern Bank of the River Connecticut, keeping the same Latitude directly West, through the Lake Champlain, until, in the same Latitude, it meets the River Saint Lawrence; from thence up the Eastern Bank of the said River to the Lake Ontario; thence through the Lake Ontario, and the River commonly call Niagara; and thence along by the Eastern and South-eastern Bank of Lake Erie, following the said Bank, until the same shall be intersected by the Northern Boundary, granted by the Charter of the Province of Pennsylvania, in case the same shall be so intersected; and from thence along the said Northern and Western Boundaries of the said Province, until the said Western Boundary strike

The Territories, Islands, and Countries in North America, belonging to Great Britain

the Ohio: But in case the said Bank of the said Lake shall not be found to be so intersected, then following the said Bank until it shall arrive at that Point of the said Bank which shall be nearest to the Northwestern Angle of the said Province of Pennsylvania, and thence by a right Line, to the said Northwestern Angle of the said Province; and thence along the Western Boundary of the said Province, until it strike the River Ohio; and along the Bank of the said River, Westward, to the Banks of the Mississippi, and Northward to the Southern Boundary of the Territory granted to the Merchants Adventurers of England, trading to Hudson's Bay; and also all such Territories, Islands, and Countries, which have, since the tenth of February, one thousand seven hundred and sixty-three, been made Part of the Government of Newfoundland, be, and they are hereby, during his Majesty's Pleasure, annexed to, and made Part and Parcel of, the Province of Quebec, as created and established by the said Royal Proclamation of the seventh of October, one thousand seven hundred and sixty-three.

annexed to the Province of Quebec

Not to affect the Boundaries of any other colony;

II. Provided always, That nothing herein contained, relative to the Boundary of the Province of Quebec, shall in anywise affect the Boundaries of any other Colony.

nor to make void other Rights formerly granted

III. Provided always, and be it enacted, That nothing in this Act contained shall extend, or be construed to extend, to make void, or to vary or alter any Right, Title, or Possession, derived under any Grant, Conveyance, or otherwise howsoever, of or to any Lands within the said Province, or the Provinces thereto adjoining; but that the same shall remain and be in Force, and have Effect, as if this Act had never been made.

Former provisions made for the Province to be null and void after May 1, 1775

"IV. And whereas the Provisions, made by the said Proclamation, in respect to the Civil Government of the said Province of Quebec, and the Powers and Authorities given to the Governor and other Civil Officers of the said Province, by the Grants and Commissions issued in consequence thereof, have been found, upon Experience, to be inapplicable to the State and Circumstances of the said Province, the Inhabitants whereof amounted, at the Conquest, to above sixty-five thousand Persons professing the Religion of the Church of Rome, and enjoying an established Form of Constitution and System of Laws, by which their Persons and Property had been protected, governed, and ordered, for a long Series of Years, from the first Establishment of the said Province of Canada;" be it therefore further enacted by the Authority aforesaid, That the said Proclamation, so far as the same relates to the said Province of Quebec, and the Commission under the Authority whereof the Government of the said Province is at present administered, and all and every the Ordinance and Ordinances made by the Governor and Council of Quebec for the Time being, relative to the Civil Government and Administration of Justice in the said Province, and all Commissions to Judges and other Officers thereof, be, and the same are hereby revoked, annulled, and made void, from and after the first Day of May, one thousand seven hundred and seventy-five.

Inhabitants of Quebec may profess the Romish Religion, subject to the King's Supremacy, as by the Act 1 Eliz. and the Clergy enjoy their accustomed dues

"V. And, for the more perfect Security and Ease of the Minds of the Inhabitants of the said Province," it is hereby declared, That his Majesty's Subjects, professing the Religion of the Church of Rome of and in the said Province of Quebec, may have, hold, and enjoy, the free Exercise of the Religion of the Church of Rome, subject to the King's Supremacy, declared and established by an Act, made in the first Year of the Reign of Queen Elizabeth, over all the Dominions and Countries which then did, or thereafter should belong, to the Imperial Crown of this Realm; and that the Clergy of the said Church may hold, receive, and enjoy, their accustomed Dues and Rights, with respect to such Persons only as shall profess the said Religion.

Provisions may be made by his Majesty for the Support of the Protestant Clergy

VI. Provided nevertheless, That it shall be lawful for his Majesty, his Heirs or Successors, to make such Provision out of the rest of the said accustomed Dues and Rights, for the Encouragement of the Protestant Religion, and for the Maintenance and Support of a Protestant Clergy within the said Province, as he or they shall, from Time to Time, think necessary and expedient.

No Person professing the Romish Religion obliged to take the Oath of 1 Eliz. but to take, before the Governor, &c. the following Oath

VII. Provided always, and be it enacted, That no Person professing the Religion of the Church of Rome, and residing in the said Province, shall be obliged to take the Oath required by the said Statute passed in the first Year of the Reign of Queen Elizabeth, or any other Oaths substituted by any other Act in the Place thereof; but that every such Person who, by the said Statute, is required to take the Oath therein mentioned, shall be obliged, and is hereby required, to take and subscribe the following Oath before the Governor, or such other Person in such Court of Record as his Majesty shall appoint, who are hereby authorized to administer the same; *videlicet,*

The Oath

"I A.B. do sincerely promise and swear, That I will be faithful, and bear true Allegiance to his Majesty King George, and him will defend to the utmost of my Power, against all traitorous Conspiracies, and Attempts whatsoever, which shall be made against his Person, Crown, and Dignity; and I will do my utmost Endeavor to disclose and make known to his Majesty, his Heirs and Successors, all Treasons, and traitorous Conspiracies and Attempts, which I shall know to be against him, or any of them; and all this I do swear without any Equivocation, mental Evasion or secret Reservation, and renouncing all Pardons and Dispensations from any Power or Person whomsoever to the contrary. So help me GOD."

Persons refusing the Oath to be subject to the Penalties by Act 1 Eliz.

And every such Person, who shall neglect or refuse to take the said Oath before mentioned, shall incur and be liable to the same Penalties, Forfeitures, Disabilities and Incapacities as he would have incurred and been liable to for neglecting or refusing to take the Oath required by the said Statute passed in the first Year of the Reign of Queen Elizabeth.

His Majesty's
Canadian subjects
(religious Orders
excepted) may hold
all their Possessions,
&c.

VIII. And be it further enacted by the Authority aforesaid, That all his Majesty's Canadian Subjects within the Province of Quebec, the religious Orders and Communities only excepted, may also hold and enjoy their Property and Possessions, together with all Customs and Usages relative thereto, and all other their Civil Rights, in as large, ample and beneficial Manner, as if the said Proclamation, Commissions, Ordinances and other Acts and Instruments, had not been made, and as may consist with their Allegiance to his Majesty, and Subjection to the Crown and Parliament of Great Britain ; and that in all Matters of Controversy, relative to

and in Matters of
and in Matters of
Controversy Resort
may be had to the
Laws of Canada for
the decision

Property and Civil Rights, Resort shall be had to the Laws of Canada, as the Rule for the Decision of the same ; and all Causes that shall hereafter be instituted in any of the Courts of Justice, to be appointed within and for the said Province by his Majesty, his Heirs and Successors, shall, with respect to such Property and Rights, be determined agreeably to the said Laws and Customs of Canada, until they shall be varied or altered by any Ordinances that shall, from Time to Time, be passed in the said Province by the Governor, Lieutenant Governor or Commander in Chief, for the Time being, by and with the Advice and Consent of the Legislative Council of the same, to be appointed in Manner herein-after mentioned.

Not to extend to
Lands granted by
his Majesty in
common Soccage

IX. Provided always, That nothing in this Act contained shall extend, or be construed to extend, to any Lands that have been granted by his Majesty, or shall hereafter be granted by his Majesty, his Heirs and Successors, to be holden in free and common Soccage.

Owners of Goods
may alienate the
same by Will, &c.

X. Provided also, That it shall and may be lawful to and for every Person that is Owner of any Lands, Goods or Credits, in the said Province, and that has a Right to alienate the said Lands, Goods or Credits, in his or her Life-time, by Deed of Sale, Gift or otherwise, to devise or bequeath the same at his or her Death, by his or her last Will and Testament; any Law, Usage or Custom, heretofore or now prevailing in the Province, to

if executed according
to the Laws of Canada

the contrary hereof in any-wise notwithstanding; such Will being executed either according to the Laws of Canada, or according to the Forms prescribed by the Laws of England.

Criminal Law of
England to be
continued in the
Province

"XI. And whereas the Certainty and Lenity of the Criminal Law of England, and the Benefits and Advantages resulting from the Use of it, have been sensibly felt by the Inhabitants, from an Experience of more than nine Years, during which it has been uniformly administered;" be it therefore further enacted by the Authority aforesaid, That the same shall continue to be administered, and shall be observed as Law in the Province of Quebec, as well in the Description and Quality of the Offence as in the Method of Prosecution and Trial; and the Punishments and Forfeitures thereby inflicted to the Exclusion of every other Rule of Criminal Law or Mode of Proceeding thereon, which did or might prevail in the said Province before the Year of our Lord one thousand seven hundred and sixty-four; any Thing in this Act to the contrary thereof in any respect notwithstanding; subject nevertheless to such Alterations and Amendments as the Governor, Lieutenant-governor, or Commander in Chief for the Time being, by and with the Advice and Consent of the legislative Council of the said Province, hereafter to be appointed, shall, from Time to Time, cause to be made therein, in Manner hereinafter directed.

His Majesty may appoint a Council for the Affairs of the Province

"XII. And whereas it may be necessary to ordain many Regulations for the future Welfare and good Government of the Province of Quebec, the Occasions of which cannot now be foreseen, nor, without much Delay and Inconvenience, be provided for, without intrusting that Authority, for a certain Time, and under proper Restrictions, to Persons resident there: And whereas it is at present inexpedient to call an Assembly;" be it therefore enacted by the Authority aforesaid, That it shall and may be lawful for his Majesty, his Heirs and Successors, by Warrant under his or their Signet or Sign Manual, and with the Advice of the Privy Council, to constitute and appoint a Council for the Affairs of the Province of Quebec, to consist of such Persons resident there, not exceeding twenty-three, nor less than seventeen, as his Majesty, his Heirs and Successors, shall be pleased to appoint; and, upon the Death, Removal or Absence of any of the Members of the said Council, in like Manner to constitute and appoint such and so many other Person or Persons as shall

which Council may make Ordinances with consent of the Governor

be necessary to supply the Vacancy or Vacancies; which Council, so appointed and nominated, or the major Part thereof, shall have Power and Authority to make Ordinances for the Peace, Welfare and good Government, of the said Province, with the Consent of his Majesty's Governor, or, in his Absence, of the Lieutenant-governor, or Commander in Chief for the Time being.

[Note: Repealed by **The Constitutional Act, 1791**]

The Council are not impowered to lay Taxes

XIII. Provided always, That nothing in this Act contained shall extend to authorize or impower the said legislative Council to lay any Taxes or Duties within the said Province, such Rates and Taxes only excepted as the Inhabitants of any Town or District within the said Province may be authorized by the said Council to assess, levy and apply, within the said Town or District, for the Purpose of making Roads, erecting and repairing publick Buildings, or for any other Purpose respecting the local Convenience and Oeconomy of such Town or District.

publick Roads or Buildings excepted

Ordinances made to be laid before his Majesty for his Approbation

XIV. Provided also, and be it enacted by the Authority aforesaid, That every Ordinance so to be made, shall, within six Months, be transmitted by the Governor, or, in his Absence, by the Lieutenant-governor or Commander in Chief for the Time being, and laid before his Majesty for his Royal Approbation; and if his Majesty shall think fit to disallow thereof, the same shall cease and be void from the Time that his Majesty's Order in Council thereupon shall be promulgated at Quebec.

Ordinances touching Religion not to be in Force without his Majesty's Approbation

XV. Provided also, That no Ordinance touching Religion, or by which any Punishment may be inflicted greater than Fine or Imprisonment for three Months, shall be of any Force or Effect, until the same shall have received his Majesty's Approbation.

When Ordinances are to be passed by a Majority

XVI. Provided also, That no Ordinance shall be passed at any Meeting of the Council where less than a Majority of the whole Council is present, or at any Time except between the first Day of January and the first Day of May, unless upon some urgent Occasion, in which Case every Member thereof resident at Quebec, or within fifty miles thereof, shall be personally summoned by the Governor or, in his absence, by the Lieutenant-governor or Commander in Chief for the Time being, to attend the same.

Nothing to hinder his Majesty to constitute Courts of Criminal, Civil and Ecclesiastical Jurisdiction

XVII. And be it further enacted by the Authority aforesaid, That nothing herein contained shall extend, or be construed to extend, to prevent or hinder his Majesty, his Heirs and Successors, by his or their Letters Patent under the Great Seal of Great Britain, from erecting, constituting and appointing, such Courts of Criminal, Civil and Ecclesiastical Jurisdiction within and for the said Province of Quebec, and appointing, from Time to Time, the Judges and Officers thereof, as his Majesty, his Heirs and Successors, shall think necessary and proper for the Circumstances of the said Province.

All Acts formerly made are hereby in force within the Province

XVIII. Provided always, and it is hereby enacted, That nothing in this Act contained shall extend, or be construed to extend, to repeal or make void, within the said Province of Quebec, any Act or Acts of the Parliament of Great Britain heretofore made, for prohibiting, restraining or regulating, the Trade or Commerce of his Majesty's Colonies and Plantations in America; but that all and every the said Acts, and also all Acts of Parliament heretofore made concerning or respecting the said Colonies and Plantations, shall be, and are hereby declared to be, in Force, within the said Province of Quebec, and every Part thereof.

THE CONSTITUTIONAL ACT, 1791

31 George III, c. 31 (U.K.)

An Act to repeal certain Parts of an Act, passed in the fourteenth Year of his Majesty's Reign, intituled An Act for making more effectual Provision for the Government of the Province of Quebec, in North America; and to make further Provision for the Government of the said Province.

Preamble 14th Geo 3c. 83, recited

"WHEREAS an Act was passed in the fourteenth Year of the Reign of his present Majesty, intituled An Act for making more effectual Provision for the Government of the Province of Quebec in North America: And whereas the said Act is in many Respects inapplicable to the present Condition and Circumstances of the said Province: And whereas it is expedient and necessary that further Provision should now be made for the good Government and Prosperity thereof;" May it therefore please your most Excellent Majesty that it may be enacted; and be it enacted by the King's most Excellent Majesty, by and with the Advice and Consent of the Lords Spiritual and Temporal, and Commons, in this present Parliament assembled, and by the Authority of the same, That so much of the said Act as in any Manner relates to the Appointment of a Council for the Affairs of the said Province of Quebec, or to the Power given by the said Act to the said Council, or to the major Part of them, to make Ordinances for the Peace, Welfare and good Government of the said Province, with the Consent of his Majesty's Governor, Lieutenant Governor or Commander in Chief for the Time being, shall be, and the same is hereby repealed.

So much of recited Act as relates to the Appointment of a Council for Quebec, or its Powers, repealed

Within each of the intended Provinces a Legislative Council and Assembly to be constituted, by whose Advice his Majesty may make Laws for the Government of the Province

"*II. And whereas his Majesty has been pleased to signify, by his Message to both Houses of Parliament, his royal Intention to divide his Province of Quebec into two separate Provinces, to be called The Province of Upper Canada, and The Province of Lower Canada;* " be it enacted by the Authority aforesaid, That there shall be within each of the said Provinces respectively a Legislative Council, and an Assembly to be severally composed and constituted in the Manner hereinafter described; and that in each of the said Provinces respectively his Majesty, his Heirs or Successors, shall have Power, during the Continuance of this Act, by and with the Advice and Consent of the Legislative Council and Assembly of such Provinces respectively, to make Laws for the Peace, Welfare and good Government thereof, such Laws not being repugnant to this Act; and that all such Laws, being passed by the Legislative Council and

Assembly of either of the said Provinces respectively, and assented to by his Majesty, his Heirs or Successors, or assented to in his Majesty's Name, by such Person as his Majesty, his Heirs or Successors, shall from Time to Time appoint to be the Governor or Lieutenant Governor, of such Province, or by such Person as his Majesty, his Heirs and Successors, shall from Time to Time appoint to administer the Government within the same, shall be, and the same are hereby declared to be, by virtue of and under the Authority of this Act, valid and binding to all Intents and Purposes whatever, within the Province in which the same shall have been so passed.

His Majesty may authorize the Governor, or Lieutenant Governor, of each Province, to summon Members to the Legislative Council

III. And be it further enacted by the Authority aforesaid, That for the Purpose of constituting such Legislative Council as aforesaid in each of the said Provinces respectively, it shall and may be lawful for his Majesty, his Heirs or Successors, by an Instrument under his or their Sign Manual, to authorize and direct the Governor or Lieutenant Governor or Person administering the Government in each of the said Provinces respectively, within the Time hereinafter mentioned, in his Majesty's Name, and by an Instrument under the Great Seal of such Province, to summon to the said Legislative Council, to be established in each of the said Provinces respectively, a sufficient Number of discreet and proper Persons, being not fewer than seven to the Legislative Council for the Province of Upper Canada, and not fewer than fifteen to the Legislative Council for the Province of Lower Canada; and that it shall also be lawful for his Majesty, his Heirs or Successors, from Time to Time, by an Instrument under his or their Sign Manual, to authorize and direct the Governor or Lieutenant Governor or Person administering the Government in each of the said Provinces respectively, to summon to the Legislative Council of such Province, in like Manner, such other Person or Persons as his Majesty, his Heirs or Successors, shall think fit; and that every Person who shall be so summoned to the Legislative Council of either of the said Provinces respectively, shall thereby become a Member of such Legislative Council to which he shall have been so summoned.

No Person under 21 Years of Age, &c. to be summoned

IV. Provided always, and be it enacted by the Authority aforesaid, That no Person shall be summoned to the said Legislative Council, in either of the said Provinces, who shall not be of the full Age of twenty-one Years, and a natural-born Subject of his Majesty, or a Subject of his Majesty naturalized by Act of the British Parliament, or a Subject of his Majesty, having become such by the Conquest and Cession of the Province of Canada.

Members to hold their Seats for Life

V. And be it further enacted by the Authority aforesaid, That every Member of each of the said Legislative Councils shall hold his Seat therein for the Term of his Life, but subject nevertheless to the Provisions hereinafter contained for vacating the same, in the Cases hereinafter specified.

His Majesty may annex to hereditary Titles of Honour,

VI. And be it further enacted by the Authority aforesaid, That whenever his Majesty, his Heirs or Successors, shall think proper to confer upon any Subject of the Crown of Great Britain, by Letters Patent under the Great Seal of either of the said Provinces, any hereditary Title of Honour, Rank or Dignity of such Province, descendible according to any Course of Descent limited in such Letters Patent, it shall and may be lawful for his Majesty, his Heirs or Successors, to annex thereto, by the said Letters Patent, if his Majesty, his Heirs or Successors, shall so think fit, an *the Right of being summoned to the Legislative Council* hereditary Right of being summoned to the Legislative Council of such Province, descendible according to the Course of Descent so limited with respect to such Title, Rank or Dignity; and that every Person on whom such Right shall be so conferred, or to whom such Right shall severally so descend, shall thereupon be entitled to demand from the Governor, Lieutenant Governor or Person administering the Government of such Province, his Writ of Summons to such Legislative Council, at any Time after he shall have attained the Age of twenty-one Years, subject nevertheless to the Provisions hereinafter contained.

Such descendible Right forfeited, and

VII. Provided always, and be it further enacted by the Authority aforesaid, That when and so often as any Person to whom such hereditary Right shall have descended shall, without the Permission of his Majesty, his Heirs or Successors, signified to the Legislative Council of the Province by the Governor, Lieutenant Governor or Person administering the Government there, have been absent from the said Province for the Space of four Years continually, at any Time between the Date of his succeeding to such Right and the Time of his applying for such Writ of Summons, if he shall have been of the Age of twenty-one Years or upwards at the Time of his so succeeding, or at any Time between the Date of his attaining the said Age and the Time of his so applying, if he shall not have been of the said Age at the Time of his so succeeding; and also when and so often as any such Person shall at any Time, before his applying for such Writ of Summons, have taken any Oath of Allegiance or Obedience to any Foreign Prince or Power, in every such Case such Person shall not be entitled to receive any Writ of Summons to the Legislative Council by virtue of such hereditary Right, unless his Majesty, his Heirs or Successors, shall at any Time think fit, by Instrument under his or their Sign Manual, to direct that such Person shall be summoned to the said Council; and the Governor, Lieutenant Governor or Person administering the Government in the said Provinces respectively, is hereby authorized and required, previous to granting such Writ of Summons to any Person so applying for the same, to interrogate such Person upon Oath touching the said several Particulars, before such Executive Council as shall have been appointed by his Majesty, his Heirs or Successors, within such Province, for the affairs thereof.

Seats in Council vacated in certain Cases

VIII. Provided also, and be it further enacted by the Authority aforesaid, That if any Member of the Legislative Councils of either of the said Provinces respectively shall leave such Province, and shall reside out of the same for the Space of four Years continually, without the Permission of his Majesty, his Heirs or Successors, signified to such Legislative Council by the Governor or Lieutenant Governor or Person administering his Majesty's Government there, or for the Space of two Years continually, without the like Permission or the Permission of the Governor, Lieutenant Governor or Person administering the Government of such Province, signified to such Legislative Council in the Manner aforesaid; or if any such Member shall take any Oath of Allegiance or Obedience to any foreign Prince or Power; his Seat in such Council shall thereby become vacant.

Hereditary Rights and Seats to forfeited or vacated, to remain suspended during the Lives of of the Parties, but on their Deaths to go to the Persons next intitled thereto

IX. Provided also, and be it further enacted by the Authority aforesaid, That in every Case where a Writ of Summons to such Legislative Council shall have been lawfully withheld from any Person to whom such hereditary Right as aforesaid shall have descended, by Reason of such Absence from the Province as aforesaid, or of his having taken an Oath of Allegiance or Obedience to any foreign Prince or Power, and also in every Case where the Seat in such Council of any Member thereof, having such hereditary Right as aforesaid, shall have been vacated by Reason of any of the Causes hereinbefore specified, such hereditary Right shall remain suspended during the Life of such Person, unless his Majesty, his Heirs or Successors, shall afterwards think fit to direct that he be summoned to such Council; but that on the Death of such Person such Right, subject to the Provisions herein contained, shall descend to the Person who shall next be entitled thereto, according to the Course of Descent limited in the Letters Patent by which the same shall have been originally conferred.

Seats in Council forfeited, and hereditary Rights extinguished for Treason

X. Provided also, and be it further enacted by the Authority aforesaid, That if any Member of either of the said Legislative Councils shall be attainted for Treason in any Court of Law within any of his Majesty's Dominions, his Seat in such Council shall thereby become vacant, and any such hereditary Right as aforesaid then vested in such Person, or to be derived to any other Persons through him, shall be utterly forfeited and extinguished.

Questions respecting the Right to be Council, &c. to be determined as herein mentioned

XI. Provided also, and be it further enacted by the Authority aforesaid, That whenever any Question shall arise respecting the Right of any Person to be summoned to either of the said Legislative Councils respectively, or respecting the Vacancy of the Seat in such Legislative Council of any Person having been summoned thereto, every such Question shall, by the Governor or Lieutenant Governor of the Province, or by the Person administering the Government there, be referred to such Legislative Council, to be by the said Council heard and determined; and that it shall and may be lawful either for the Person desiring such Writ of Summons, or respecting whose Seat such Question shall have arisen, or for his Majesty's Attorney General of such Province in his Majesty's Name, to appeal from the Determination of the said Council, in such Case, to his Majesty in his Parliament of Great Britain; and that the Judgment thereon of his Majesty in his said Parliament shall be final and conclusive to all Intents and Purposes whatever.

The Governor of the Province may appoint and remove the Speaker

XII. And be it further enacted by the Authority aforesaid, That the Governor, or Lieutenant Governor of the said Provinces respectively or the Person administering his Majesty's Government therein respectively, shall have Power and Authority, from Time to Time, by an Instrument under the Great Seal of such Province, to constitute, appoint and remove the Speakers of the Legislative Councils of such Provinces respectively.

His Majesty may authorize the Governor to call together the Assembly

XIII. And be it further enacted by the Authority aforesaid, That, for the Purpose of constituting such Assembly as aforesaid, in each of the said Provinces respectively, it shall and may be lawful for his Majesty, his Heirs or Successors, by an Instrument under his or their Sign Manual, to authorize and direct the Governor or Lieutenant Governor or Person administering the Government in each of the said Provinces respectively, within the Time hereinafter mentioned, and thereafter from Time to Time, as Occasion shall require, in his Majesty's Name, and by an Instrument under the Great Seal of such Province, to summon and call together an Assembly in and for such Province.

and, for the Purpose of electing the Members, to issue a Proclamation dividing the Province into districts, &c.

XIV. And be it further enacted by the Authority aforesaid, That, for the Purpose of electing the Members of such Assemblies respectively, it shall and may be lawful for his Majesty, his Heirs or Successors, by an Instrument under his or their Sign Manual, to authorize the Governor or Lieutenant Governor, of each of the said Provinces respectively, or the Person administering the Government therein, within the Time hereinafter mentioned, to issue a Proclamation dividing such Province into Districts or Counties or Circles and Towns or Townships, and appointing the Limits thereof, and declaring and appointing the Number of Representatives to be chosen by each of such Districts or Counties or Circles and Towns or Townships respectively; and that it shall also be lawful for his Majesty, his Heirs or Successors, to authorize such Governor or Lieutenant Governor or Person administering the Government, from Time to Time, to nominate and appoint proper Persons to execute the Office of Returning Officer in each of the said Districts or Counties or Circles and Towns or Townships respectively; and that such Division of the said Provinces into Districts or Counties or Circles and Towns or Townships, and such Declaration and Appointment of the Number of Representatives to be chosen by each of the said Districts or Counties or Circles and Towns or Townships respectively, and also such Nomination and Appointment of Returning Officers in the same, shall be valid and effectual to all the Purposes of this Act, unless it shall at any Time be otherwise provided by any Act of the Legislative Council and Assembly of the Province, assented to by his Majesty, his Heirs or Successors.

Power of the Governor to appoint Returning Officers, to continue two Years from the Commencement of this Act

XV. Provided nevertheless, and be it further enacted by the Authority aforesaid, That the Provision hereinbefore contained, for impowering the Governor, Lieutenant Governor or Person administering the Government of the said Provinces respectively, under such Authority as aforesaid from his Majesty, his Heirs or Successors, from Time to Time, to nominate and appoint proper Persons to execute the Office of Returning Officer in the said Districts, Counties, Circles and Towns or Townships, shall remain and continue in force in each of the said Provinces respectively, for the

Term of two Years, from and after the Commencement of this Act, within such Province, and no longer; but subject nevertheless to be sooner repealed or varied by any Act of the Legislative Council and Assembly of the Province, assented to by his Majesty, his Heirs and Successors.

No Person obliged to serve as Returning Officer more than once, unless otherwise provided by an Act of the Province

XVI. Provided always, and be it further enacted by the Authority aforesaid, That no Person shall be obliged to execute the said Office of Returning Officer for any longer Time than one Year, or oftener than once, unless it shall at any Time be otherwise provided by any Act of the Legislative Council and Assembly of the Province, assented to by his Majesty, his Heirs or Successors.

Number of Members in each Province

XVII. Provided also, and be it enacted by the Authority aforesaid, That the whole Number of Members to be chosen in the Province of Upper Canada shall not be less than sixteen, and that the whole Number of Members to be chosen in the Province of Lower Canada shall not be less than fifty.

Regulations for issuing Writs for the Election of Members to serve in the Assemblies

XVIII. And be it further enacted by the Authority aforesaid, That Writs for the Election of Members to serve in the said Assemblies respectively shall be issued by the Governor, Lieutenant Governor or Person administering his Majesty's Government within the said Provinces respectively, within fourteen Days after the sealing of such Instrument as aforesaid for summoning and calling together such Assembly, and that such Writs shall be directed to the respective Returning Officers of the said Districts or Counties or Circles and Towns or Townships, and that such Writs shall be made returnable within fifty Days at farthest from the Day on which they shall bear Date, unless it shall at any Time be otherwise provided by any Act of the Legislative Council and Assembly of the Province, assented to by his Majesty, his Heirs or Successors; and that Writs shall in like Manner and Form be issued for the Election of Members in the Case of any Vacancy which shall happen by the Death of the Person chosen, or by his being summoned to the Legislative Council of either Province, and that such Writs shall be made returnable within fifty Days at farthest from the Day on which they shall bear Date, unless it shall at any Time be otherwise provided by any Act of the Legislative Council and Assembly of the Province, assented by his Majesty, his Heirs or Successors; and that in the Case of any such Vacancy which shall happen by the Death of the Person chosen or by Reason of his being so summoned as aforesaid, the Writ for the Election of a new Member shall be issued within six Days after the same shall be made known to the proper Office for issuing such Writs of Election.

Returning Officers to execute Writs

XIX. And be it further enacted by the Authority aforesaid, That all and every the Returning Officers so appointed as aforesaid, to whom any such Writs as aforesaid shall be directed, shall, and they are hereby authorized and required duly to execute such Writs.

By whom the Members are to be chosen

XX. And be it further enacted by the Authority aforesaid, That the Members for the several Districts or Counties or Circles of the said Provinces respectively, shall be chosen by the Majority of Votes of such

Persons as shall severally be possessed, for their own Use and Benefit, of Lands or Tenements within such District or County or Circle, as the Case shall be, such Lands being by them held in Freehold or in Fief or in Roture or by Certificate derived under the Authority of the Governor and Council of the Province of Quebec, and being of the yearly Value of forty Shillings Sterling or upwards, over and above all Rents and Charges payable out of or in respect of the same; and that the Members for the several Towns or Townships within the said Provinces respectively shall be chosen by the Majority of Votes of such Persons as either shall severally be possessed, for their own Use and Benefit, of a Dwelling House and Lot of Ground in such Town or Township, such Dwelling House and Lot of Ground being by them held in like Manner as aforesaid, and being of the yearly Value of five Pounds Sterling or upwards, or, as having been resident within the said Town or Township for the Space of twelve Calendar Months next before the Date of the Writ of Summons for the Election, shall bona fide have paid one Year's Rent for the Dwelling House in which they have so resided, at the Rate of ten Pounds Sterling per annum or upwards.

Certain Persons not eligible to the Assemblies

XXI. Provided always, and be it further enacted by the Authority aforesaid, That no Person shall be capable of being elected a Member to serve in either of the said Assemblies, or of sitting or voting therein, who shall be a Member of either of the said Legislative Councils to be established as aforesaid in the said two Provinces, or who shall be a Minister of the Church of England or a Minister, Priest, Ecclesiastic or Teacher, either according to the Rites of the Church of Rome or under any other Form or Profession of religious Faith or Worship.

No Person under 21 Years of Age, &c, capable of voting or being elected

XXII. Provided also, and be it further enacted by the Authority aforesaid, That no Person shall be capable of voting at any Election of a Member to serve in such Assembly, in either of the said Provinces, or of being elected at any such Election, who shall not be of the full Age of twenty-one Years and a natural-born Subject of his Majesty or a Subject of His Majesty naturalized by Act of the British Parliament or a Subject of his Majesty, having become such by the Conquest and Cession of the Province of Canada.

nor any Person attainted for Treason or Felony

XXIII. And be it also enacted by the Authority aforesaid, That no Person shall be capable of voting at any Election of a Member to serve in such Assembly, in either of the said Provinces, or of being elected at any such Election, who shall have been attainted for Treason or Felony in any Court of Law within any of his Majesty's Dominions, or who shall be within any Description of Persons disqualified by any Act of the Legislative Council and Assembly of the Province, assented to by his Majesty, his Heirs or Successors.

Voters, if required, to take the following

XXIV. Provided also, and be it further enacted by the Authority aforesaid, That every Voter, before he is admitted to give his Vote at any such Election, shall, if required by any of the Candidates or by the Returning Officer, take the following Oath, which shall be administered in the English or French Language, as the Case may require:

Oath

"I A.B. do declare and testify, in the Presence of Almighty God, That I am, to the best of my Knowledge and Belief, of the full Age of twenty-one Years, and that I have not voted before at this Election. "

and to make Oath to the Particularsh erein specified

And that every such person shall also, if so required as aforesaid, make Oath previous to his being admitted to vote, that he is, to the best of his Knowledge and Belief, duly possessed of such Lands and Tenements, or of such a Dwelling House and Lot of Ground, or that he has bona fide been so resident, and paid such Rent for his Dwelling House, as entitles him, according to the Provisions of this Act, to give his Vote at such Election for the County or District or Circle or for the Town or Township for which he shall offer the same.

His Majesty may authorize the Governor to fix the Time and Place of holding Elections

XXV. And be it further enacted by the Authority aforesaid, That it shall and may be lawful for his Majesty, his Heirs or Successors, to authorize the Governor or Lieutenant Governor or Person administering the Government within each of the said Provinces respectively, to fix the Time and Place of holding such Elections, giving not less than eight Days Notice of such Time, subject nevertheless to such Provisions as may hereafter be made in these Respects by any Act of the Legislative Council and Assembly of the Province, assented to by his Majesty, his Heirs or Successors.

and of holding the Sessions of the Council and Assembly, &c.

XXVI. And be it further enacted by the Authority aforesaid, That it shall and may be lawful for his Majesty, his Heirs or Successors, to authorize the Governor or Lieutenant Governor of each of the said Provinces respectively, or the Person administering the Government therein, to fix the Places and Times of holding the first and every other Session of the Legislative Council and Assembly of such Province, giving due and sufficient Notice thereof, and to prorogue the same, from Time to Time, and to dissolve the same, by Proclamation or otherwise, whenever he shall judge it necessary or expedient.

Council and Assembly to be called together once in twelve Months, &c.

XXVII. Provided always, and be it enacted by the Authority aforesaid, That the said Legislative Council and Assembly, in each of the said Provinces, shall be called together once at the least in every twelve Calendar Months, and that every Assembly shall continue for four Years from the Day of the Return of the Writs for choosing the same, and no longer, subject nevertheless to be sooner prorogued and dissolved by the Governor or Lieutenant Governor of the Province or Person administering his Majesty's Government therein.

and all Questions therein to be decided by the Majority of Votes

XXVIII. And be it further enacted by the Authority aforesaid, That all Questions which shall arise in the said Legislative Councils or Assemblies respectively shall be decided by the Majority of Voices of such Members as shall be present; and that in all Cases where the Voices shall be equal, the Speaker of such Council or Assembly, as the Case shall be, shall have a casting Voice.

No Member to sit or vote till he has taken the following

XXIX. Provided always, and be it enacted by the Authority aforesaid, That no Member, either of the Legislative Council or Assembly, in either of the said Provinces, shall be permitted to sit or to vote therein until he shall have taken and subscribed the following Oath, either before the Governor or Lieutenant Governor of such Province or Person administering the Government therein, or before some Person or Persons authorized by the said Governor or Lieutenant Governor or other Person as aforesaid, to administer such Oath, and that the same shall be administered in the English or French Language, as the Case shall require:

Oath

"*I A.B. do sincerely promise and swear, That I will be faithful, and bear true Allegiance to his Majesty King George, as lawful Sovereign of the Kingdom of Great Britain and of these Provinces dependant on and belonging to the said Kingdom; and that I will defend him to the utmost of my Power against all traitorous Conspiracies and Attempts whatever which shall be made against his Person, Crown and Dignity; and that I will do my utmost Endeavour to disclose and make known to his Majesty, his Heirs or Successors, all Treasons and traitorous Conspiracies and Attempts which I shall know to be against him or any of them: and all this I do swear without any Equivocation, mental Evasion or secret Reservation, and renouncing all Pardons and Dispensations from any Person or Power whatever to the contrary. So help me GOD.*"

Governor may give or withhold his Majesty's Assent to Bills passed by the Legislative Council and Assembly, or reserve them for his Majesty's Pleasure

XXX. And be it further enacted by the Authority aforesaid, That whenever any Bill which has been passed by the Legislative Council and by the House of Assembly, in either of the said Provinces respectively, shall be presented, for his Majesty's Assent, to the Governor or Lieutenant Governor of such Province or to the Person administering his Majesty's Government therein, such Governor or Lieutenant Governor or Person administering the Government shall, and he is hereby authorized and required to declare according to his Discretion, but subject nevertheless to the Provisions contained in this Act, and to such Instructions as may from Time to Time be given in that Behalf by his Majesty, his Heirs or Successors, that he assents to such Bill in his Majesty's Name, or that he withholds his Majesty's Assent from such Bill, or that he reserves such Bill for the Signification of his Majesty's Pleasure thereon.

Governor to transmit to the Secretary of State Copies of such Bills as have been assented to, which his Majesty in Council may declare his Disallowance of within two Years from the Receipt

XXXI. Provided always, and be it further enacted by the Authority aforesaid, That whenever any Bill, which shall have been so presented for his Majesty's Assent to such Governor, Lieutenant Governor or Person administering the Government, shall, by such Governor, Lieutenant Governor or Person administering the Government have been assented to in his Majesty's Name, such Governor, Lieutenant Governor, or Person as aforesaid shall, and he is hereby required, by the first convenient Opportunity, to transmit to one of his Majesty's principal Secretaries of State an authentic Copy of such Bill so assented to; and that it shall and may be lawful, at any Time within two years after such Bill shall have been so received by such Secretary of State, for his Majesty, his Heirs or Successors, by his or their Order in Council, to declare his or their Disallowance of such Bill, and that such Disallowance, together with a Certificate under the Hand and Seal of such Secretary of State, testifying the Day on which such Bill was received as aforesaid, being signified by such Governor, Lieutenant Governor or Person administering the Government, to the Legislative Council and Assembly of such Province, or by Proclamation, shall make void and annul the same, from and after the Date of such Signification.

Bills reserved for his Majesty's Pleasure not to have any Force till his Majesty's Assent be communicated to the Council and Assembly, &c.

XXXII. And be it further enacted by the Authority aforesaid, That no such Bill, which shall be so reserved for the Signification of his Majesty's Pleasure thereon, shall have any Force or Authority within either of the said Provinces respectively, until the Governor or Lieutenant Governor or Person administering the Government shall signify, either by Speech or Message, to the Legislative Council and Assembly of such Province, or by Proclamation, that such Bill has been laid before his Majesty in Council, and that his Majesty has been pleased to assent to the same; and that an Entry shall be made in the Journals of the said Legislative Council, of every such Speech, Message or Proclamation; and a Duplicate thereof, duly attested, shall be delivered to the proper Officer, to be kept amongst the public Records of the Province: And that no such Bill, which shall be so reserved as aforesaid, shall have any Force or Authority within either of the said Provinces respectively, unless his Majesty's Assent thereto shall have been so signified as aforesaid, within the Space of two Years from the Day on which such Bill shall have been presented for his Majesty's Assent to the Governor, Lieutenant Governor or Person administering the Government of such Province.

[Note: Paragraphs II to XXXII repealed by **The Union Act, 1840**]

Laws in force at the Commencement of this Act to continue so, except repealed or varied by it, &c.

XXXIII. And be it further enacted by the Authority aforesaid, That all Laws, Statutes and Ordinances, which shall be in force on the Day to be fixed in the Manner hereinafter directed for the Commencement of this Act, within the said Provinces or either of them, or in any Part thereof respectively, shall remain and continue to be of the same Force, Authority and Effect in each of the said Provinces respectively, as if this Act had not been made, and as if the said Province of Quebec had not been divided; except in so far as the same are expressly repealed or varied by this Act, or in so far as the same shall or may hereafter, by virtue of and under the Authority of this Act, be repealed or varied by his Majesty, his Heirs or Successors, by and with the Advice and Consent of the Legislative Councils and Assemblies of the said Provinces respectively, or in so far as the same may be repealed or varied by such temporary Laws or Ordinances as may be made in the Manner hereinafter specified.

Establishment of a Court of Civil Jurisdiction in each Province

"XXXIV. And whereas by an Ordinance passed in the Province of Quebec, the Governor and Council of the said Province were constituted a Court of Civil Jurisdiction for hearing and determining Appeals in certain Cases therein specified;" be it further enacted by the Authority aforesaid, That the Governor, or Lieutenant Governor or Person administering the Government of each of the said Provinces respectively, together with such Executive Council as shall be appointed by his Majesty for the Affairs of such Province, shall be a Court of Civil Jurisdiction within each of the said Provinces respectively, for hearing and determining Appeals within the same, in the like Cases and in the like

Manner and Form, and subject to such Appeal therefrom, as such Appeals might before the passing of this Act have been heard and determined by the Governor and Council of the Province of Quebec; but subject nevertheless to such further or other Provisions as may be made in this Behalf by any Act of the Legislative Council and Assembly of either of the said Provinces respectively, assented to by his Majesty, his Heirs or Successors.

14 Geo. 3 c. 83, and

Instructions of Jan. 3, 1775, to Sir Guy Carleton, &c. and

Instructions to Sir Frederick Haldimand and to Lord Dorchester, recited

"XXXV. And whereas, by the above-mentioned Act, passed in the fourteenth Year of the Reign of his present Majesty, it was declared That the Clergy of the Church of Rome, in the Province of Quebec, might hold, receive and enjoy, their accustomed Dues and Rights, with respect to such Persons only as should profess the said Religion; provided nevertheless, that it should be lawful for his Majesty, his Heirs or Successors, to make such Provision out of the rest of the said accustomed Dues and Rights, for the Encouragement of the Protestant Religion and for the Maintenance and Support of a Protestant Clergy within the said Province, as he or they should from Time to Time think necessary and expedient: And whereas by his Majesty's Royal Instructions, given under his Majesty's Royal Sign Manual on the third Day of January in the Year of our Lord one thousand seven hundred and seventy-five, to Guy Carleton, Esquire, now Lord Dorchester, at that Time his Majesty's Captain General and Governor in Chief in and over his Majesty's Province of Quebec, his Majesty was pleased, amongst other Things, to direct 'That no Incumbent professing the Religion of the Church of Rome, appointed to any Parish in the said Province, should be entitled to receive any Tythes for Lands or Possessions occupied by a Protestant, but that such Tythes should be received by such Persons as the said Guy Carleton, Esquire, his Majesty's Captain General and Governor in Chief in and over his Majesty's said Province of Quebec, should appoint, and should be reserved in the Hands of his Majesty's Receiver General of the said Province, for the Support of a Protestant Clergy in his Majesty's said Province, to be actually resident within the same, and not otherwise, according to such Directions as the said Guy Carleton, Esquire, his Majesty's Captain General and Governor in Chief in and over his Majesty's said Province, should receive from his Majesty in that Behalf; and that in like Manner all growing Rents and Profits of a vacant Benefice should, during such Vacancy, be reserved for and applied to the like Uses :' And whereas his Majesty's Pleasurehas likewise been signified to the same Effect in his Majesty's Royal Instructions, given in like Manner to Sir Frederick Haldimand, Knight of the Most Honourable Order of the Bath, late his Majesty's Captain General and Governor in Chief in and over his Majesty's said Province of Quebec, and also in his Majesty's Royal Instructions given in like Manner to the said Right Honourable Guy Lord Dorchester, now his Majesty's Captain General and Governor in Chief in and over his Majesty's said Province of Quebec;" be it enacted by the Authority aforesaid, That the said Declaration and Provision contained in

and the Declaration and Provisions therein respecting the Clergy of the Church of Rome to continue in force

the said above-mentioned Act, and also the said Provision so made by his Majesty in consequence thereof, by his Instructions above recited, shall remain and continue to be of full Force and Effect in each of the said two Provinces of Upper Canada and Lower Canada respectively, except in so far as the said Declaration or provisions respectively, or any Part thereof, shall be expressly varied or repealed by any Act or Acts which may be passed by the Legislative Council and Assembly of the said Provinces respectively, and assented to by his Majesty, his Heirs or Successors, under the Restriction hereinafter provided.

His Majesty's Message to Parliament recited

"XXXVI. And whereas his Majesty has been graciously pleased, by Message to both Houses of Parliament, to express his Royal Desire to be enabled to make a permanent Appropriation of Lands in the said Provinces, for the Support and Maintenance of a Protestant Clergy within the same, in Proportion to such Lands as have been already granted within the same by his Majesty: And whereas his Majesty has been graciously pleased, by his said Message, further to signify his Royal Desire that such Provision may be made, with respect to all future Grants of Land within the said Provinces respectively, as may best conduce to the due and sufficient Support and Maintenance of a Protestant Clergy within the said Provinces, in Proportion to such Increase as may happen in the Population and Cultivation thereof:" Therefore, for the Purpose of more effectually fulfilling his Majesty's gracious Intentions as aforesaid, and of providing for the due Execution of the same in all Time to come, be it enacted by

His Majesty may authorize the Governor to make Allotments of Lands, for the Support of a Protestant Clergy in each Province

the Authority aforesaid, That it shall and may be lawful for his Majesty, his Heirs or Successors, to authorize the Governor or Lieutenant Governor of each of the said Provinces respectively, or the Person administering the Government therein, to make, from and out of the Lands of the Crown within such Provinces, such Allotment and Appropriation of Lands, for the Support and Maintenance of a Protestant Clergy within the same, as may bear a due Proportion to the Amount of such Lands within the same as have at any Time been granted by or under the Authority of his Majesty; and that whenever any Grant of Lands within either of the said Provinces shall hereafter be made, by or under the Authority of his Majesty, his Heirs or Successors, there shall at the same Time be made, in respect of the same, a proportionable Allotment and Appropriation of Lands for the above-mentioned Purpose, within the Township or Parish to which such Lands so to be granted shall appertain or be annexed, or as nearly adjacent thereto as Circumstances will admit; and that no such Grant shall be valid or effectual unless the same shall contain a Specification of the Lands so allotted and appropriated, in respect of the Lands to be thereby granted; and that such Lands, so allotted and appropriated, shall be, as nearly as the Circumstances and Nature of the Case will admit, of the Like Quality as the Lands in respect of which the same are so allotted and appropriated, and shall be, as nearly as the same can be estimated at the Time of making such Grant, equal in Value to the seventh Part of the Lands so granted.

and the Rents arising
from such Allotments
to be applicable to
that Purpose solely

XXXVII. And be it further enacted by the Authority aforesaid, That all and every the Rents, Profits or Emoluments, which may at any Time arise from such Lands so allotted and appropriated as aforesaid, shall be applicable solely to the Maintenance and Support of a Protestant Clergy within the Province in which the same shall be situated, and to no other Use or Purpose whatever.

His Majesty may
authorize the
Governor, with the
Advice of the
Executive Council, to
erect Parsonages, and
endow them

XXXVIII. And be it further enacted by the Authority aforesaid, That it shall and may be lawful for his Majesty, his Heirs or Successors, to authorize the Governor or Lieutenant Governor of each of the said Provinces respectively, or the Person administering the Government therein, from Time to Time, with the Advice of such Executive Council as shall have been appointed by his Majesty, his Heirs or Successors, within such Province, for the Affairs thereof, to constitute and erect, within every Township or Parish which now is or hereafter may be formed, constituted or erected within such Province, one or more Parsonage or Rectory, or Parsonages or Rectories, according to the Establishment of the Church of England; and, from Time to Time, by an Instrument under the Great Seal of such Province, to endow every such Parsonage or Rectory with so much or such Part of the Lands so allotted and appropriated as aforesaid, in respect of any Lands within such Township or Parish, which shall have been granted subsequent to the Commencement of this Act, or of such Lands as may have been allotted and appropriated for the same Purpose, by or in virtue of any Instruction which may be given by his Majesty, in respect of any Lands granted by his Majesty before the Commencement of this Act, as such Governor, Lieutenant Governor or Person administering the Government shall, with the Advice of the said Executive Council, judge to be expedient under the then existing Circumstances of such Township or Parish.

And the Governor to
present Incumbents
tothem, who are to
enjoy the same as
Incumbents in
England

XXXIX. And be it further enacted by the Authority aforesaid, That it shall and may be lawful for his Majesty, his Heirs or Successors, to authorize the Governor, Lieutenant Governor or Person administering the Government of each of the said Provinces respectively, to present to every such Parsonage or Rectory an Incumbent or Minister of the Church of England, who shall have been duly ordained according to the rites of the said Church, and to supply from Time to Time such Vacancies as may happen therein; and that every Person so presented to any such Parsonage or Rectory, shall hold and enjoy the same and all Rights, Profits and Emoluments thereunto belonging or granted, as fully and amply and in the same Manner and on the same Terms and Conditions and liable to the Performance of the same Duties, as the Incumbent of a Parsonage or Rectory in England.

Presentations to
Parsonages, and the
Enjoyment of them,
to be subject to the
Jurisdiction granted
to the Bishop of Nova
Scotia, &c.

XL. Provided always, and be it further enacted by the Authority aforesaid, That every such Presentation of an Incumbent or Minister to any such Parsonage or Rectory, and also the Enjoyment of any such Parsonage or Rectory, and of the Rights, Profits and Emoluments thereof by any such Incumbent or Minister, shall be subject and liable to all Rights of Institution, and all other Spiritual and Ecclesiastical Jurisdiction and Authority, which have been lawfully granted by his Majesty's Royal Letters Patent to the Bishop of Nova Scotia or which may hereafter, by his Majesty's Royal Authority, be lawfully granted or appointed to be administered and executed within the said Provinces, or either of them respectively, by the said Bishop of Nova Scotia, or by any other Person or Persons, according to the Laws and Canons of the Church of England, which are lawfully made and received in England.

Provisions respecting the Allotment of Lands for the Support of a Protestant Clergy, &c. may be varied or repealed by the Legislative Council and Assembly

XLI. Provided always, and be it further enacted by the Authority aforesaid, That the several Provisions hereinbefore contained, respecting the Allotment and Appropriation of Lands for the Support of a Protestant Clergy within the said Provinces, and also respecting the constituting, erecting and endowing Parsonages or Rectories within the said Provinces, and also respecting the Presentation of Incumbents or Ministers to the same and also respecting the Manner in which such Incumbents or Ministers shall hold and enjoy the same, shall be subject to be varied or repealed by any express Provisions for that Purpose, contained in any Act or Acts which may be passed by the Legislative Council and Assembly of the said Provinces respectively, and assented to by his Majesty, his Heirs or Successors, under the Restriction herein-after provided.

Acts of the Legislative Council and Assembly, containing Provisions to the Effect herein mentioned, to be laid before Parliament, previous to receiving his Majesty's Assent, &c.

XLII. Provided nevertheless, and be it further enacted by the Authority aforesaid, That whenever any Act or Acts shall be passed by the Legislative Council and Assembly of either of the said Provinces, containing any Provisions to vary or repeal the above-recited Declaration and Provision contained in the said Act passed in the fourteenth Year of the Reign of his present Majesty; or to vary or repeal the above-recited Provision contained in his Majesty's Royal Instructions, given on the third Day of January in the Year of our Lord one thousand seven hundred and seventy-five, to the said Guy Carleton, Esquire, now Lord Dorchester; or to vary or repeal Provisions hereinbefore contained for continuing the Force and Effect of the said Declaration and Provisions; or to vary or repeal any of the several Provisions hereinbefore contained respecting the Allotment and Appropriation of Lands for the Support of a Protestant Clergy within the said Provinces; or respecting the constituting, erecting or endowing Parsonages or Rectories within the said Provinces; or respecting the Presentation of Incumbents or Ministers to the same; or respecting the Manner in which such Incumbents or Ministers shall hold and enjoy the same: And also that whenever any Act or Acts shall be so passed, containing any Provisions which shall in any Manner relate to or affect the Enjoyment or Exercise of any religious Form or Mode of Worship; or shall impose or create any Penalties, Burthens, Disabilities or Disqualifications in respect of the same; or shall in any Manner relate to or affect the Payment, Recovery or Enjoyment of any of the accustomed Dues or Rights hereinbefore mentioned; or shall in any Manner relate to the granting, imposing or recovering any other Dues or Stipends or Emoluments whatever to be paid to or for the Use of any Minister, Priest, Ecclesiastic or Teacher, according to any religious Form or Mode of Worship, in respect of his said Office or Function; or shall in any Manner relate to or affect the Establishment or Discipline of the Church of England, amongst the Ministers and Members thereof within the said Provinces; or shall in any Manner relate to or affect the King's Prerogative touching the granting the Waste Lands of the Crown within the said Provinces; every such Act or Acts shall, previous to any Declaration or Signification of the King's Assent thereto, be laid before both Houses of Parliament in Great Britain; and that it shall not be lawful for his Majesty, his Heirs or Successors, to signify his or their Assent to any such Act or Acts, until thirty Days after the same shall have been laid before the said Houses, or to assent to any such Act or Acts, in case either House of Parliament shall, within the said thirty Days, address his Majesty, his Heirs or Successors, to withhold his or their Assent from such Act or Acts; and that no such Act shall be valid or effectual to any of the said Purposes, within either of the said Provinces, unless the Legislative Council and Assembly of such Province shall, in the Session in which the same shall have been passed by them, have presented to the Governor, Lieutenant Governor or Person administering the Government of such Province, an Address or Addresses, specifying that such Act contains Provisions for some of the said Purposes hereinbefore specially described, and desiring that, in order to give Effect to the same, such Act should be transmitted to England without Delay, for the Purpose of being laid before Parliament previous to the Signification of his Majesty's Assent thereto.

Lands in Upper Canada to be granted in Free and Common Soccage, and also in Lower Canada if desired

XLIII. And be it further enacted by the Authority aforesaid, That all Lands which shall be hereafter granted within the said Province of Upper Canada shall be granted in Free and Common Soccage, in like Manner as Lands are now holden in Free and Common Soccage, in that Part of Great Britain called England; and that in every Case where Lands shall be hereafter granted within the said Province of Lower Canada, and where the Grantee thereof shall desire the same to be granted in Free and Common Soccage, the same shall be so granted; but subject nevertheless to such Alterations, with respect to the Nature and Consequences of such Tenure of Free and Common Soccage, as may be established by any Law or Laws which may be made by his Majesty, his Heirs or Successors, by and with the Advice and Consent of the Legislative Council and Assembly of the Province.

Persons holding Lands in Upper Canada may have fresh Grants

XLIV. And be it further enacted by the Authority aforesaid, That if any Person or Persons holding any Lands in the said Province of Upper Canada, by virtue of any Certificate of Occupation derived under the Authority of the Governor and Council of the Province of Quebec, and having Power and Authority to alienate the same, shall at any Time, from and after the Commencement of this Act, surrender the same into the Hands of his Majesty, his Heirs or Successors, by Petition to the Governor or Lieutenant Governor or Person administering the Government of the said Province, setting forth that he, she, or they is or are desirous of holding the same in Free and Common Soccage, such Governor or Lieutenant Governor or Person administering the Government, shall thereupon cause a fresh Grant to be made to such Person or Persons of such Lands, to be holden in Free and Common Soccage.

Such fresh Grants not to bar any Right or Title to the Lands

XLV. Provided nevertheless, and be it further enacted by the Authority aforesaid, That such Surrender and Grant shall not avoid or bar any Right or Title to any such Lands so surrendered, or any Interest in the same, to which any Person or Persons, other than the Person or Persons surrendering the same, shall have been entitled, either in Possession, Remainder or Reversion or otherwise, at the time of such Surrender; but that every such Surrender and Grant shall be made subject to every such Right, Title and Interest, and that every such Right, Title or Interest shall be as valid and effectual as if such Surrender and Grant had never been made.

18 Geo. 3, c. 12 recited

"XLVI. And whereas by an Act passed in the eighteenth Year of the Reign of his present Majesty, intituled An Act for removing all Doubts and Apprehensions concerning Taxation by the Parliament of Great Britain, in any of the Colonies, Provinces and Plantations in North America and the West Indies; and for repealing so much of an Act, made in the seventh Year of the Reign of his present Majesty, as imposes a Duty on Tea imported from Great Britain into any Colony or Plantation in America, or relates thereto, it has been declared, 'That the King and Parliament of Great Britain will not impose any Duty, Tax or Assessment whatever payable in any of his Majesty's Colonies, Provinces and Plantations in North America or the West Indies, except only such Duties as it may be expedient to impose for the Regulation of Commerce, the net Produce of such Duties to be always paid and applied to and for the Use of the Colony, Province or Plantation in which the same shall be respectively levied in such Manner as other Duties collected by the Authority of the respective General Courts or General Assemblies of such Colonies, Provinces or Plantations, are ordinarily paid and applied:' And whereas it is necessary, for the general Benefit of the British Empire, that

This Act not to prevent the Operation of any Act of Parliament, establishing Prohibitions or imposing Duties for the Regulation of Navigation and Commerce, &c.

such Power of Regulation of Commerce should continue to be exercised by his Majesty, his Heirs or Successors and the Parliament of Great Britain, subject nevertheless to the Condition hereinbefore recited, with respect to the Application of any Duties which may be imposed for that Purpose:" Be it therefore enacted by the Authority aforesaid, That nothing in this Act contained shall extend, or be construed to extend, to prevent or affect the Execution of any Law which hath been or shall at any Time be made by his Majesty, his Heirs or Successors and the Parliament of Great Britain, for establishing Regulations or Prohibitions, or for imposing, levying or collecting Duties for the Regulation of Navigation, or for the Regulation of the Commerce to be carried on between the said two Provinces, or between either of the said Provinces and any other Part of his Majesty's Dominions, or between either of the said Provinces and any foreign County or State, or for appointing and directing the Payment of Drawbacks of such Duties so imposed, or to give to his Majesty, his Heirs or Successors, any Power or Authority, by and with the Advice and Consent of such Legislative Councils and Assemblies respectively, to vary or repeal any such Law or Laws or any Part thereof, or in any Manner to prevent or obstruct the Execution thereof.

Such Duties to be applied to the Use of the respective Provinces

XLVII. Provided always, and be it enacted by the Authority aforesaid, That the net Produce of all Duties which shall be so imposed shall at all Times hereafter be applied to and for the Use of each of the said Provinces respectively, and in such Manner only as shall be directed by any Law or Laws which may be made by his Majesty, his Heirs or Successors, by and with the Advice and Consent of the Legislative Council and Assembly of such Province.

His Majesty in Council to fix and declare the Commencement of this Act, &c.

"XLVIII. And whereas, by Reason of the Distance of the said Provinces from this Country and of the Change to be made by this Act in the Government thereof, it may be necessary that there should be some Interval of Time between the Notification of this Act to the said Provinces respectively, and the Day of its Commencement within the said Provinces respectively:" Be it therefore enacted by the Authority aforesaid, That it shall and may be lawful for his Majesty, with the Advice of his Privy Council, to fix and declare or to authorise the Governor or Lieutenant Governor of the Province of Quebec or the Person administering the Government there, to fix and declare the Day of the Commencement of this Act within the said Provinces respectively, provided that such Day shall not be later than the thirty-first Day of December in the Year of our Lord one thousand seven hundred and ninety-one.

Time for issuing the Writs of Summons and Election, &c. not to be later than December 31, 1792

XLIX. And be it further enacted by the Authority aforesaid, That the Time to be fixed by his Majesty, his Heirs or Successors or under his or their Authority, by the Governor, Lieutenant Governor or Person administering the Government in each of the said Provinces respectively, for issuing the Writs of Summons and Election, and calling together the Legislative Councils and Assemblies of each of the said Provinces respectively, shall not be later than the thirty-first Day of December in the Year of our Lord one thousand seven hundred and ninety-two.

Between the Commencement of this Act, and the first Meeting of the Legislative Council and Assembly, temporary Laws may be made

L. Provided always, and be it further enacted by the Authority aforesaid, That during such Interval as may happen between the Commencement of this Act, within the said Provinces respectively, and the first Meeting of the Legislative Council and Assembly of each of the said Provinces respectively, it shall and may be lawful for the Governor or Lieutenant Governor of such Province or for the Person administering the Government therein, with the Consent of the major Part of such Executive Council as shall be appointed by his Majesty for the Affairs of such Province, to make temporary Laws and Ordinances for the good Government, Peace and Welfare of such Province, in the same Manner, and under the same Restrictions, as such Laws or Ordinances might have been made by the Council for the Affairs of the Province of Quebec, constituted by virtue of the above-mentioned Act of the fourteenth Year of the Reign of his present Majesty; and that such temporary Laws or Ordinances shall be valid and binding within such Province, until the Expiration of six Months after the Legislative Council and Assembly of such Province shall have been first assembled by virtue of and under the Authority of this Act; subject nevertheless to be sooner repealed or varied by any Law or Laws which may be made by his Majesty, his Heirs or Successors, by and with the Advice and Consent of the said Legislative Council and Assembly.

THE UNION ACT, 1840

3-4 Victoria, c. 35 (U.K.)

An Act to re-unite the Provinces of Upper and Lower Canada, and for the Government of Canada

[23d July 1840]

"Whereas it is necessary that Provision be made for the good Government of the Provinces of Upper Canada and Lower Canada, in such Manner as may secure the Rights and Liberties and promote the Interests of all Classes of Her Majesty's Subjects within the same: And whereas to this end it is expedient that the said Provinces be re-united and form One Province for the Purposes of Executive Government and Legislation:" Be it therefore enacted by the Queen's most Excellent Majesty, by and with the Advice and Consent of the Lords Spiritual and Temporal, and Commons, in this present parliament assembled, and by the Authority of the same, That it shall be lawful for Her Majesty, with **Declaration** the Advice of Her Privy Council, to declare, or to authorize the Governor **of Union** General of the said Two Provinces of Upper and Lower Canada to declare, by Proclamation, that the said Provinces, upon, from, and after a certain Day in such Proclamation to be appointed, which Day shall be within Fifteen Calendar Months next after the passing of this Act, shall form and be One Province, under the Name of the Province of Canada, and thenceforth the said Provinces shall constitute and be One Province, under the Name aforesaid, upon, from, and after the Day so appointed as aforesaid.

Repeal of Acts, 31 G. II. And be it enacted, That so much of an Act passed in the Session of **3. c. 31** Parliament held in the Thirty-first Year of the Reign of King George the Third, intituled An Act to repeal certain Parts of an Act passed in the Fourteenth Year of His Majesty's Reign, intituled "An Act for making more effectual Provision for the Government of the Province of Quebec in North America," and to make further Provision for the Government of the said Province, as provides for constituting and composing a **1 & 2 Vict. c. 9** Legislative Council and Assembly within each of the said Provinces respectively, and for the making of Laws; and also the whole of an Act passed in the Session of Parliament held in the First and Second Years of **2 & 3 Vict. c. 53** the Reign of Her present Majesty, intituled An Act to make temporary Provision for the Government of Lower Canada; and also the whole of an Act passed in the Session of Parliament held in the Second and Third Years of the Reign of Her present Majesty, intituled An Act to amend an

Act of the last Session of Parliament, for making temporary Provision for the Government of Lower Canada; and also the whole of an Act passed in the Session of Parliament held in the First and Second Years of the Reign of His late Majesty King William the Fourth, intituled An Act to amend an Act of the Fourteenth Year of His Majesty King George the Third, for establishing a fund towards defraying the Charges of the Administration of Justice and the Support of Civil Government in the Province of Quebec in America, shall continue and remain in force until the Day on which it shall be declared, by Proclamation as aforesaid, that the said Two Provinces shall constitute and be One Province as aforesaid, and shall be repealed on, from, and after such Day: Provided always, that the Repeal of the said several Acts of Parliament and Parts of Acts of Parliament shall not be held to revive or give any Force or Effect to any Enactment which has by the said Acts, or any of them, been repealed or determined.

1 & 2 W. 4 c. 23

14 G 3. c. 88

Composition and Powers of Legislature

III. And be it enacted, That from and after the Re-union of the said Two Provinces there shall be within the Province of Canada One Legislative Council and One Assembly, to be severally constituted and composed in the Manner herein-after prescribed, which shall be called "The Legislative Council and Assembly of Canada;" and that, within the Province of Canada, Her Majesty shall have Power, by and with the Advice and Consent of the said Legislative Council and Assembly, to make Laws for the Peace, Welfare, and good Government of the Province of Canada, such laws not being repugnant to this Act, or to such Parts of the said Act passed in the Thirty-first Year of the Reign of His said late Majesty as are not hereby repealed, or to any Act of Parliament made or to be made, and not hereby repealed, which does or shall, by express Enactment or by necessary Intendment, extend to the Provinces of Upper and Lower Canada, or to either of them, or to the Province of Canada; and that all such Laws being passed by the said Legislative Council and Assembly, and assented to by Her Majesty, or assented to in Her Majesty's Name by the Governor of the Province of Canada, shall be valid and binding to all Intents and Purposes within the Province of Canada.

Appointment of Legislative Councillors

IV. And be it enacted, That for the Purpose of composing the Legislative Council of the Province of Canada it shall be lawful for Her Majesty, before the Time to be appointed for the First Meeting of the said Legislative Council and Assembly, by an Instrument under the Sign Manual, to authorize the Governor, in Her Majesty's Name, by an Instrument under the Great Seal of the said Province, to summon to the said Legislative Council of the said Province such Persons, being not fewer than Twenty, as Her Majesty shall think fit; and that it shall also be lawful for Her Majesty from Time to Time to authorize the Governor in like Manner to summon to the said Legislative Council such other Person or Persons as Her Majesty shall think fit, and that every Person who shall be so summoned shall thereby become a Member of the Legislative Council of the Province of Canada: Provided always, that no Person shall be summoned to the said Legislative Council of the Province of Canada who shall not be of the full Age of Twenty-one Years, and a natural-born Subject of Her Majesty, or a Subject of Her Majesty

Qualification of Legislative Councillors

naturalized by Act of the Parliament of Great Britain, or by Act of the Parliament of the United Kingdom of Great Britain and Ireland, or by an Act of the Legislature of either of the Provinces of Upper or Lower Canada, or by an Act of the Legislature of the Province of Canada.

Tenure of Office of Councillor

V. And be it enacted, That every Member of the Legislative Council of the Province of Canada shall hold his Seat therein for the Term of his Life, but subject nevertheless to the Provisions herein-after contained for vacating the same.

Resignation of Legislative Councillor

VI. And be it enacted, That it shall be lawful for any Member of the Legislative Council of the Province of Canada to resign his Seat in the said Legislative Council, and upon such Resignation the Seat of such Legislative Councillor shall become vacant.

Vacating Seat by Absence

VII. And be it enacted, That if any Legislative Councillor of the Province of Canada shall for Two successive Sessions of the Legislature of the said Province fail to give his Attendance in the said Legislative Council, without the Permission of Her Majesty or of the Governor of the said Province, signified by the said Governor to the Legislative Council, or shall take any Oath or make any Declaration or Acknowledgment of Allegiance, Obedience, or Adherence to any Foreign Prince or Power, or shall do, concur in, or adopt any Act whereby he may become a Subject or Citizen of any Foreign State or Power, or whereby he may become entitled to the Rights, Privileges, or Immunities of a Subject or Citizen of any Foreign State or Power, or shall become bankrupt, or take the Benefit of any Law relating to Insolvent Debtors, or become a public Defaulter, or be attainted of Treason, or be convicted of Felony or of any infamous Crime, his Seat in such Council shall thereby become vacant.

Trial of Questions

VIII. And be it enacted, That any Question which shall arise respecting any Vacancy in the Legislative Council of the Province of Canada, on occasion of any of the Matters aforesaid, shall be referred by the Governor of the Province of Canada to the said Legislative Council, to be by the said Legislative Council heard and determined: Provided always, that it shall be lawful, either for the Person respecting whose Seat such Question shall have arisen, or for Her Majesty's Attorney General for the said Province on Her Majesty's Behalf, to appeal from the Determination of the said Council in such Case to Her Majesty, and that the Judgment of Her Majesty given with the Advice of Her Privy Council thereon shall be final and conclusive to all Intents and Purposes.

Appointment of Speaker

IX. And be it enacted, That the Governor of the Province of Canada shall have Power and Authority from Time to Time, by an Instrument under the Great Seal of the said Province, to appoint One Member of the said Legislative Council to be Speaker of the said Legislative Council, and to remove him, and appoint another in his Stead.

Quorum

Division

Casting Vote

X. And be it enacted, That the Presence of at least Ten Members of the said Legislative Council, including the Speaker, shall be necessary to constitute a Meeting for the Exercise of its Powers; and that all Questions which shall arise in the said Legislative Council shall be decided by a Majority of Voices of the Members present other than the Speaker, and when the Voices shall be equal the Speaker shall have the casting Vote.

Convoking the
Assembly

XI. And be it enacted, That for the Purpose of constituting the Legislative Assembly of the Province of Canada it shall be lawful for the Governor of the said Province, within the Time herein-after mentioned, and thereafter from Time to Time as Occasion shall require, in Her Majesty's Name and by an Instrument or Instruments under the Great Seal of the said Province, to summon and call together a Legislative Assembly in and for the said Province.

Representatives
for each Province

XII. And be it enacted, That in the Legislative Assembly of the Province of Canada to be constituted as aforesaid the Parts of the said Province which now constitute the Provinces of Upper and Lower Canada respectively shall, subject to the Provisions herein-after contained, be represented by an equal Number of Representatives, to be elected for the Places and in the Manner herein-after mentioned.

County of Halton

XIII. And be it enacted, That the County of Halton in the Province of Upper Canada shall be divided into Two Ridings, to be called respectively the East Riding and the West Riding; and that the East Riding of the said county shall consist of the following Townships, namely, Trafalgar, Nelson, Esquesing, Nassagawega, East Flamborough, West Flamborough, Ering, Beverley; and that the West Riding of the said County shall consist of the following Townships, namely, Garafraxa, Nichol, Woolwich, Guelph, Waterloo, Wilmot, Dumfries, Puslinch, Eramosa; and that the East Riding and West Riding of the said County shall each be represented by One Member in the Legislative Assembly of the Province of Canada.

County of
Northumberland

XIV. And be it enacted, That the County of Northumberland in the Province of Upper Canada shall be divided into Two Ridings, to be called respectively the North Riding and the South Riding; and that the North Riding of the last-mentioned County shall consist of the following Townships, namely, Monaghan, Otonabee, Asphodel, Smith, Douro, Dummer, Belmont, Methuen, Burleigh, Harvey, Emily, Gore, Ennismore; and that the South Riding of the last-mentioned County shall consist of the following Townships, namely, Hamilton, Haldimand, Cramak, Murray, Seymour, Percy; and that the North Riding and South Riding of the last-mentioned County shall each be represented by One Member in the Legislative Assembly of the Province of Canada.

County of Lincoln

XV. And be it enacted, That the County of Lincoln in the Province of Upper Canada shall be divided into Two Ridings, to be called respectively the North Riding and the South Riding; and that the North Riding shall be formed by uniting the First Riding and Second Riding of the said County, and the South Riding by uniting the Third Riding and Fourth Riding of the said County; and that the North and South Riding of the last-mentioned County shall each be represented by One Member in the Legislative Assembly of the Province of Canada.

**Other County
Constituency
of Upper Canada**

XVI. And be it enacted, That every County and Riding, other than those herein-before specified, which at the Time of the passing of this Act was by Law entitled to be represented in the Assembly of the Province of Upper Canada, shall be represented by One Member in the Legislative Assembly of the Province of Canada.

**Town Constituency
of Upper Canada**

XVII. And be it enacted, That the City of Toronto shall be represented by Two Members, and the Towns of Kingston, Brockville, Hamilton, Cornwall, Niagara, London, and Bytown shall each be represented by One Member in the Legislative Assembly of the Province of Canada.

**County Constituency
of Lower Canada**

1 & 2 Vict. c. 9

XVIII. And be it enacted, That every County which before and at the Time of the passing of the said Act of Parliament, intituled An Act to make temporary Provision for the Government of Lower Canada, was entitled to be represented in the Assembly of the Province of Lower Canada, except the Counties of Montmorency, Orleans, L'Assomption, La Chesnaye, L'Acadie, Laprairie, Dorchester, and Beauce, herein-after mentioned, shall be represented by One Member in the Legislative Assembly of the Province of Canada.

**Further Provision
as to Constituency
of Lower Canada**

XIX. And be it enacted, That the said Counties of Montmorency and Orleans shall be united into and form One County, to be called the County of Montmorency; and that the said Counties of L'Assomption and La Chesnaye shall be united into and form One County, to be called the County of Leinster; and that the said Counties of L'Acadie and Laprairie shall be united into and form One County, to be called the County of Huntingdon; and that the Counties of Dorchester and Beauce shall be united into and form One County, to be called the County of Dorchester; and that each of the said Counties of Montmorency, Leinster, Huntingdon, and Dorchester shall be represented by One Member in the Legislative Assembly of the said Province of Canada.

**Town Constituency
of Lower Canada**

XX. And be it enacted, That the Cities of Quebec and Montreal shall each be represented by Two Members, and the Towns of Three Rivers and Sherbrooke shall each be represented by One Member in the Legislative Assembly of the Province of Canada.

**Boundaries of Cities
and Towns to be
settled by Governor**

XXI. And be it enacted, That for the Purpose of electing their several Representatives to the said Legislative Assembly, the Cities and Towns herein-before mentioned shall be deemed to be bounded and limited in such Manner as the Governor of the Province of Canada, by Letters Patent under the Great Seal of the Province, to be issued within Thirty Days after the Union of the said Provinces of Upper Canada and Lower Canada, shall set forth and describe; and such Parts of any such City or Town (if any) which shall not be included within the Boundary of such City or Town respectively by such Letters Patent, for the Purposes of this Act shall be taken to be a Part of the adjoining County or Riding, for the Purpose of being represented in the said Legislative Assembly.

Returning Officers

XXII. And be it enacted, That for the Purpose of electing the Members of the Legislative Assembly of the Province of Canada, it shall be lawful for the Governor of the said Province, from Time to Time, to nominate proper Persons to execute the Office of Returning Officer in each of the Counties, Ridings, Cities, and Towns which shall be represented in the Legislative Assembly of the Province of Canada, subject nevertheless to the Provisions herein-after contained.

Term of Office
of Returning Officer

XXIII. And be it enacted, That no Person shall be obliged to execute the said Office of Returning Officer for any longer Term than One Year, or oftener than once, unless it shall be at any Time otherwise provided by some Act or Acts of the Legislature of the Province of Canada.

Writs of Election

XXIV. And be it enacted, That Writs for the Election of Members to serve in the Legislative Assembly of the Province of Canada shall be issued by the Governor of the said Province, within Fourteen Days after the sealing of such Instrument as aforesaid, for summoning and calling together such Legislative Assembly; and that such Writs shall be directed to the Returning Officers of the said Counties, Ridings, Cities, and Towns respectively; and that such Writs shall be made returnable within Fifty Days at farthest from the Day on which they shall bear Date, unless it shall at any Time be otherwise provided by any Act of the Legislature of the said Province; and that Writs shall in like Manner and Form be issued for the Election of Members in the Case of any Vacancy which shall happen by the Death or Resignation of the Person chosen, or by his being summoned to the Legislative Council of the said Province, or from any other legal Cause; and that such Writs shall be made returnable within Fifty Days at farthest from the Day on which they shall bear Date, unless it shall be at any Time otherwise provided by any Act of the Legislature of the said Province; and that in any Case of any such Vacancy which shall happen by the Death of the Person chosen, or by reason of his being so summoned as aforesaid, the Writ for the Election of a new Member shall be issued within Six Days after Notice thereof shall have been delivered to or left at the Office of the proper Officer for issuing such Writs of Election.

Time and Place
of holding
Elections

XXV. And be it enacted, That it shall be lawful for the Governor of the Province of Canada for the Time being to fix the Time and Place of holding Elections of Members to serve in the Legislative Assembly of the said Province, until otherwise provided for as herein-after is mentioned, giving not less than Eight Days Notice of such Time and Place.

Power to alter
System of
Representation

XXVI. And be it enacted, That it shall be lawful for the Legislature of the Province of Canada, by any Act or Acts to be hereafter passed, to alter the Divisions and Extent of the several Counties, Ridings, Cities, and Towns which shall be represented in the Legislative Assembly of the Province of Canada, and to establish new and other Divisions of the same, and to alter the Apportionment of Representatives to be chosen by the said Counties, Ridings, Cities, and Towns respectively, and make a new and different Apportionment of the Number of Representatives to be chosen in and for those Parts or the Province of Canada which now constitute the said Provinces of Upper and Lower Canada respectively, and in and for the several Districts, Counties, Ridings, and Towns in the same, and to alter and regulate the Appointment of Returning Officers in and for the same, and make Provision, in such Manner as they may deem expedient, for the issuing and Return of Writs for the Election of Members to serve in the said Legislative Assembly, and the Time and Place of holding such Elections: Provided always, that it shall not be lawful to present to the Governor of the Province of Canada for Her Majesty's Assent any Bill of the Legislative Council and Assembly of the said Province by which the Number of Representatives in the Legislative Assembly may be altered, unless the Second and Third Reading of such Bill in the Legislative Council and the Legislative Assembly shall have been passed with the Concurrence of Two Thirds of the Members for the Time being of the said Legislative Council, and of Two Thirds of the Members for the Time being of the said Legislative Assembly respectively, and the Assent of Her Majesty shall not be given to any such Bill unless Addresses shall have been presented by the Legislative Council and the Legislative Assembly respectively to the Governor, stating that such Bill has been so passed.

XXVII. And be it enacted, That until Provisions shall otherwise be made by an Act or Acts of the Legislature of the Province of Canada all the Laws which at the Time of the passing of this Act are in force in the Province of Upper Canada, and all the Laws which at the Time of the passing of the said Act of Parliament, intituled An Act to make temporary Provision for the Government of Lower Canada, were in force in the Province of Lower Canada, relating to the Qualification and Disqualification of any Person to be elected or to sit or vote as a Member of the Assembly in the said Provinces respectively, (except those which require a Qualification of Property in Candidates for Election, for which Provision is herein-after made,) and relating to the Qualification and Disqualification of Voters at the Election of Members to serve in the Assemblies of the said Provinces respectively, and to the Oaths to be taken by any such Voters, and to the Powers and Duties of Returning Officers, and the Proceedings at such Elections, and the Period during which such Elections may be lawfully continued, and relating to the Trial of controverted Elections, and the Proceedings incident thereto, and to the vacating of Seats of Members, and the issuing and Execution of new Writs in case of any Seat being vacated otherwise than by a Dissolution of the Assembly, shall respectively be applied to Elections of Members to serve in the Legislative Assembly of the Province of Canada for Places situated in those Parts of the Province of Canada for which such Laws were passed.

XXVIII. And be it enacted, That no Person shall be capable of being elected a Member of the Legislative Assembly of the Province of Canada who shall not be legally or equitably seised as of Freehold, for his own Use and Benefit, of Lands or Tenements held in Free and Common Socage, or seised or possessed, for his own Use and Benefit, of Lands or Tenements held in Fief or in Roture, within the said Province of Canada, of the Value of Five hundred Pounds of Sterling Money of Great Britain, over and above all Rents, Charges, Mortgages, and Incumbrances charged

Proviso

The present Election Laws of the Two Provinces to apply until altered

1 & 2 Vict. c. 9

Qualification of Members

upon and due and payable out of or affecting the same; and that every Candidate at such Election, before he shall be capable of being elected, shall, if required by any other Candidate, or by any Elector, or by the Returning Officer, make the following Declaration:

Declaration of Candidates for Election

"I, A.B. do declare and testify, That I am duly seised at Law or in Equity as of Freehold, for my own Use and Benefit, of Lands or Tenements held in Free and Common Socage, [or duly seised or possessed, for my own Use and Benefit, of Lands or Tenements held in Fief or in Roture (as the Case may be),] in the Province of Canada, of the Value of Five hundred Pounds of Sterling Money of Great Britain, over and above all Rents, Mortgages, Charges, and Incumbrances charged upon or due and payable out of or affecting the same; and that I have not collusively or colourably obtained a Title to or become possessed of the said Lands and Tenements, or any Part thereof, for the Purpose of qualifying or enabling me to be returned a Member of the Legislative Assembly of the Province of Canada."

Persons making false Declaration liable to the Penalties of Perjury

XXIX. And be it enacted, That if any Person shall knowingly and wilfully make a false Declaration respecting his Qualification as a Candidate at any Election as aforesaid, such Person shall be deemed to be guilty of a Misdemeanor, and being thereof lawfully convicted shall suffer the like Pains and Penalties as by Law are incurred by Persons guilty of wilful and corrupt Perjury in the Place in which such false Declaration shall have been made.

Place and Times of holding Parliament

XXX. And be it enacted, That it shall be lawful for the Governor of the Province of Canada for the Time being to fix such Place or Places within any Part of the Province of Canada, and such Times for holding the First and every other Session of the Legislative Council and Assembly of the said Province as he may think fit, such Times and Places to be afterwards changed or varied as the Governor may judge advisable and most consistent with general Convenience and the Public Welfare, giving sufficient Notice thereof; and also to prorogue the said Legislative Council and Assembly from Time to Time, and dissolve the same, by Proclamation or otherwise, whenever he shall deem it expedient.

Duration of Parliament

XXXI. And be it enacted, That there shall tbe a Session of the Legislative Council and Assembly of the Province of Canada once at least in every Year, so that a Period of Twelve Calendar Months shall not intervene between the last Sitting of the Legislative Council and Assembly in One Session and the First Sitting of the Legislative Council and Assembly in the next Session; and that every Legislative Assembly of the said Province hereafter to be summoned and chosen shall continue for Four Years from the Day of the Return of the Writs for choosing the same, and no longer, subject nevertheless to be sooner prorogued or dissolved by the Governor of the said Province.

First calling together of the Legislature

XXXII. And be it enacted, That the Legislative Council and Assembly of the Province of Canada shall be called together for the first Time at some Period not later than Six Calendar Months after the Time at which the Provinces of Upper and Lower Canada shall become re-united as aforesaid.

Election of
the Speaker

XXXIII. And be it enacted, That the Members of the Legislative Assembly of the Province of Canada shall, upon the First Assembling after every General Election, proceed forthwith to elect One of their Number to be Speaker; and in case of his Death, Resignation, or Removal by a Vote of the said Legislative Assembly, the said Members shall forthwith proceed to elect another of such Members to be such Speaker; and the Speaker so elected shall preside at all Meetings of the said Legislative Assembly.

Quorum

Division

Casting Vote

XXXIV. And be it enacted, That the Presence of at least Twenty Members of the Legislative Assembly of the Province of Canada, including the Speaker, shall be necessary to constitute a Meeting of the said Legislative Assembly for the Exercise of its Powers; and that all Questions which shall arise in the said Assembly shall be decided by the Majority of Voices of such Members as shall be present, other than the Speaker, and when the Voices shall be equal the Speaker shall have the casting Voice.

No Member to sit or
vote until he has
taken the following
Oath of Allegiance

XXXV. And be it enacted, That no Member, either of the Legislative Council or of the Legislative Assembly of the Province of Canada, shall be permitted to sit or vote therein until he shall have taken and subscribed the following Oath before the Governor of the said Province, or before some Person or Persons authorized by such Governor to administer such Oath:

Oath of Allegiance

"I A.B. do sincerely promise and swear, That I will be faithful and bear true Allegiance to Her Majesty Queen Victoria, as lawful Sovereign of the United Kingdom of Great Britain and Ireland, and of this Province of Canada, dependent on and belonging to the said United Kingdom; and that I will defend Her to the utmost of my Power against all traitorous Conspiracies and Attempts whatever which shall be made against Her Person, Crown, and Dignity; and that I will do my utmost Endeavour to disclose and make known to Her Majesty, Her Heirs and Successors, all Treasons and traitorous Conspiracies and Attempts which I shall know to be against Her or any of them; and all this I do swear without any Equivocation, mental Evasion, or secret Reservation, and renouncing all Pardons and Dispensations from any Person or Persons whatever to the contrary. So help me GOD."

Affirmation
instead of Oath

XXXVI. And be it enacted, That every Person authorized by Law to make an Affirmation instead of taking an Oath may make such Affirmation in every Case in which an Oath is herein-before required to be taken.

Giving or
withholding Assent to
Bills

XXXVII. And be it enacted, That whenever any Bill which has been passed by the Legislative Council and Assembly of the Province of Canada shall be presented for Her Majesty's Assent to the Governor of the said Province, such Governor shall declare, according to his Discretion, but subject nevertheless to the Provisions contained in this

Act, and to such Instructions as may from Time to Time be given in that Behalf by Her Majesty, Her Heirs or Successors, that he assents to such Bill in Her Majesty's Name, or that he withholds Her Majesty's Assent, or that he reserves such Bill for the Signification of Her Majesty's Pleasure thereon.

Disallowance of Bills assented to

XXXVIII. And be it enacted, That whenever any Bill which shall have been presented for Her Majesty's Assent to the Governor of the said Province of Canada shall by such Governor have been assented to in Her Majesty's Name, such Governor shall by the first convenient Opportunity transmit to One of Her Majesty's Principal Secretaries of State an authentic Copy of such Bill so assented to; and that it shall be lawful, at any Time within Two Years after such Bill shall have been so received by such Secretary of State, for Her Majesty, by Order in Council, to declare Her Disallowance of such Bill; and that such Disallowance, together with a Certificate under the Hand and Seal of such Secretary of State, certifying the Day on which such Bill was received as aforesaid, being signified by such Governor to the Legislative Council and Assembly of Canada, by Speech or Message to the Legislative Council and Assembly of the said Province, or by Proclamation, shall make void and annul the same from and after the Day of such Signification.

Assent to Bills reserved

XXXIX. And be it enacted, That no Bill which shall be reserved for the Signification of Her Majesty's Pleasure thereon shall have any Force or Authority within the Province of Canada until the Governor of the said Province shall signify, either by Speech or Message to the Legislative Council and Assembly of the said Province, or by Proclamation, that such Bill has been laid before Her Majesty in Council and that Her Majesty has been pleased to assent to the same; and that an Entry shall be made in the Journals of the said Legislative Council of every such Speech, Message, or Proclamation, and a Duplicate thereof, duly attested, shall be delivered to the proper Officer, to be kept among the Records of the said Province; and that no Bill which shall be so reserved as aforesaid shall have any Force or Authority in the said Province unless Her Majesty's Assent thereto shall have been so signified as aforesaid within the Space of Two Years from the Day on which such Bill shall have been presented for Her Majesty's Assent to the Governor as aforesaid.

Authority of the Governor

XL. Provided always, and be it enacted, That nothing herein contained shall be construed to limit or restrain the Exercise of Her Majesty's Prerogative in authorizing, and that notwithstanding this Act, and any other Act or Acts passed in the Parliament of Great Britain, or in the Parliament of the United Kingdom of Great Britain and Ireland, or of the Legislature of the Province of Quebec, or of the Provinces of Upper or Lower Canada respectively, it shall be lawful for Her Majesty to authorize the Lieutenant Governor of the Province of Canada to exercise and execute, within such Parts of the said Province as Her Majesty shall think fit, notwithstanding the Presence of the Governor within the Province, such of the Powers, Functions, and Authority, as well judicial as other, which before and at the Time of passing of this Act were and are vested in the Governor, Lieutenant Governor, or Person administering the Government of the Provinces of Upper Canada and Lower Canada respectively, or of either of them, and which from and after the said Re-union of the said Two Provinces shall become vested in the Governor of the Province of Canada; and to authorize the Governor of the Province of Canada to assign, depute, substitute, and appoint any Person or Persons, jointly or severally, to be his Deputy or Deputies within any Part or Parts of the Province of Canada, and in that Capacity to exercise, perform, and execute during the Pleasure of the said Governor such of the Powers, Functions, and Authorities, as well judicial as other, as before and at the Time of the passing of this Act were and are vested in the Governor, Lieutenant Governor, or Person administering the Government of the Provinces of Upper and Lower Canada respectively, and which from and after the Union of the said Provinces shall become vested in the Governor of the Province of Canada, as the Governor of the Province of Canada shall deem to be necessary or expedient: Provided always, that by the Appointment of a Deputy or Deputies as aforesaid the Power and Authority of the Governor of the Province of Canada shall not be abridged, altered, or in any way affected otherwise than as Her Majesty shall think proper to direct.

Language of
Legislative Records

XLI. And be it enacted, That from and after the said Re-union of the said Two Provinces all Writs, Proclamations, Instruments for summoning and calling together the Legislative Council and Legislative Assembly of the Province of Canada, and for proroguing and dissolving the same, and all Writs of Summons and Election, and all Writs and public Instruments whatsoever relating to the said Legislative Council and Legislative Assembly, or either of them, and all Returns to such Writs and Instruments, and all Journals, Entries, and written or printed Proceedings, of what Nature soever, of the said Legislative Council and Legislative Assembly, and of each of them respectively, and all written or printed Proceedings and Reports of Committees of the said Legislative Council and Legislative Assembly respectively, shall be in the English Language only: Provided always, that this Enactment shall not be construed to prevent translated Copies of any such Documents being made, but no such Copy shall be kept among the Records of the Legislative Council or Legislative Assembly, or be deemed in any Case to have the Force of an original Record.

Ecclesiastical
and Crown Rights

14 G. 3. c. 83

XLII. And be it enacted, That whenever any Bill or Bills shall be passed by the Legislative Council and Assembly of the Province of Canada, containing any Provisions to vary or repeal any of the Provisions now in force contained in an Act of the Parliament of Great Britain passed in the Fourteenth Year of the Reign of His late Majesty King George the Third, intituled An Act for making more effectual Provision for the Government of the Province of Quebec in North America, or in the aforesaid Acts of Parliament passed in the Thirty-first Year of the same Reign, respecting the accustomed Dues and Rights of the Clergy of the Church of Rome; or to vary or repeal any of the several Provisions contained in the said last-mentioned Act, respecting the Allotment and Appropriation of Lands for the Support of the Protestant Clergy within the Province of Canada, or respecting the constituting, erecting, or endowing of Parsonages or Rectories within the Province of Canada, or respecting the Presentation of Incumbents or Ministers of the same, or respecting the Tenure on which such Incumbents or Ministers shall hold or enjoy the same; and also that whenever any Bill or Bills shall be passed containing any Provisions which shall in any Manner relate to or affect the Enjoyment or Exercise of any Form or Mode of Religious Worship, or shall impose or create any Penalties, Burdens, Disabilities, or Disqualifications in respect of the same, or shall in any Manner relate to or affect the Payment, Recovery, or Enjoyment of any of the accustomed Dues or Rights herein-before mentioned, or shall in any Manner relate to the granting, imposing, or recovering of any other Dues, or Stipends, or Emoluments, to be paid to or for the Use of any Minister, Priest, Ecclesiastic, or Teacher, according to any Form or Mode of Religious Worship, in respect of his said Office or Function; or shall in any Manner relate to or affect the Establishment or Discipline of the United Church of England and Ireland among the Members thereof within the said Province; or shall in any Manner relate to or affect Her Majesty's Prerogative touching the granting of Waste Lands of the Crown within the said Province; every such Bill or Bills shall, previously to any Declaration or Signification of Her Majesty's Assent thereto, be laid before both Houses of Parliament of the United Kingdom of Great Britain and Ireland; and that it shall not be lawful for Her Majesty to signify Her Assent to any such Bill or Bills until Thirty Days after the same shall have been laid before the said Houses, or to assent to any such Bill or Bills in case either House of Parliament shall, within the said Thirty Days, address Her Majesty to withhold Her Assent from any such Bill or Bills; and that no such Bill shall be valid or effectual to any of the said Purposes within the said Province of Canada unless the Legislative Council and Assembly of such Province shall, in the Session in which the same shall have been passed by them, have presented to the Governor of the said Province an Address or Addresses specifying that such Bill or Bills contains Provisions for some of the Purposes herein-before specially described, and desiring that, in order to give Effect to the same, such Bill or Bills may be transmitted to England without Delay, for the Purpose of its being laid before Parliament previously to the Signification of Her Majesty's Assent thereto.

Colonial Taxation

18 G. 3. c. 12

XLIII. "And whereas by an Act passed in the Eighteenth Year of the Reign of His late Majesty King George the Third, intituled An Act for removing all Doubts and Apprehensions concerning Taxation by the Parliament of Great Britain in any of the Colonies, Provinces, and Plantations in North America and the West Indies; and for repealing so much of an Act made in the Seventh Year of the Reign of His present Majesty as imposes a Duty on Tea imported from Great Britain into any Colony or Plantation in America, or relating thereto, it was declared, that 'the King and Parliament of Great Britain would not impose any Duty, Tax, or Assessment whatever, payable in any of His Majesty's Colonies, Provinces, and Plantations in North America or the West Indies, except only such Duties as it might be expedient to impose for the Regulation of Commerce, the net Produce of such Duties to be always paid and applied to and for the Use of the Colony, Province, or Plantation in which the same shall be respectively levied, in such Manner as other Duties collected by the Authority of the respective General Courts or General

Assemblies of such Colonies, Provinces, or Plantations were ordinarily paid and applied:" And whereas it is necessary, for the General Benefit of the Empire, that such Power of Regulation of Commerce should continue to be exercised by Her Majesty and the Parliament of the United Kingdom of Great Britain and Ireland, subject nevertheless to the Conditions herein-before recited with respect to the Application of any Duties which may be imposed for that Purpose;' be it therefore enacted, That nothing in this Act contained shall prevent or affect the Execution of any Law which hath been or shall be made in the Parliament of the said United Kingdom for establishing Regulations and Prohibitions, or for the imposing, levying, or collecting Duties for the Regulation of Navigation, or for the Regulation of the Commerce between the Province of Canada and any other Part of Her Majesty's Dominions, or between the said Province of Canada or any Part thereof and any Foreign Country or State, or for appointing and directing the Payment of Drawbacks of such Duties so imposed, or to give to Her Majesty any Power or Authority, by and with the Advice and Consent of such Legislative Council and Assembly of the said Province of Canada, to vary or repeal any such Law or Laws, or any Part thereof, or in any Manner to prevent or obstruct the Execution thereof: Provided always, that the net Produce of all Duties which shall be so imposed shall at all Times hereafter be applied to and for the Use of the said Province of Canada, and (except as herein-after provided) in such Manner only as shall be directed by any Law or Laws which may be made by Her Majesty, by and with the Advice and Consent of the Legislative Council and Assembly of such Province.

Courts of Appeal, Probate, Queen's Bench, and Chancery, in Upper Canada; and Court of Appeal in Lower Canada

XLIV. "And whereas by the Laws now in force in the said Province of Upper Canada the Governor, Lieutenant Governor, or Person administering the Government of the said Province, or the Chief Justice of the said Province, together with any Two or more of the Members of the Executive Council of the said Province, constitute and are a Court of Appeal for hearing and determining all Appeals from such Judgments or Sentences as may lawfully be brought before them: And whereas by an Act of the Legislature of the said Province of Upper Canada, passed in the Thirty-third Year of the Reign of His late Majesty King George the Third, intituled An Act to establish a Court of Probate in the said Province, and also a Surrogate Court in every District thereof, there was and is established a Court of Probate in the said Province, in which Act it was enacted that the Governor, Lieutenant Governor, or Person administering the Government of the said last-mentioned Province should preside, and that he should have the Powers and Authorities in the said Act specified: And whereas by an Act of the Legislature of the said Province of Upper Canada, passed in the Second Year of the Reign of His late Majesty King William the Fourth, intituled An Act respecting the Time and Place of sitting of the Court of King's Bench, it was among other things enacted, that His Majesty's Court of King's Bench in that Province should be holden in a Place certain; that is, in the City, Town, or Place which should be for the Time being the Seat of the Civil Government of the said Province or within One Mile therefrom; And whereas by an Act of the Legislature of the said Province of Upper

(Laws of Upper Canada, 33 G. 3 sess. 2. c. 8)

(Laws of Upper Canada, 2 W. 4. c. 8)

(Laws of Upper
Canada,
7 W. 4. c. 2)

Canada, passed in the Seventh Year of the Reign of His late Majesty King William the Fourth, intituled An Act to Establish a Court of Chancery in this Province, it was enacted that there should be constituted and established a Court of Chancery, to be called and known by the Name and Style of 'The Court of Chancery for the Province of Upper Canada,' of which Court the Governor, Lieutenant Governor, or Person administering the Government of the said Province should be Chancellor; and which Court, it was also enacted, should be holden at the Seat of Government in the said Province, or in such other Place as should be appointed by Proclamation of the Governor, Lieutenant Governor, or Person administering the Government of the said Province: And whereas by an Act of the Legislature of the Province of Lower Canada, passed in the Thirty-fourth Year of the Reign of His late Majesty King George the Third, intituled An Act for the Division of the Province of Lower Canada, for amending the Judicature thereof, and for repealing certain Laws therein mentioned, it was enacted, that the Governor, Lieutenant Governor, or the Person administering the Government, the Members of the Executive Council of the said Province, the Chief Justice thereof, and the Chief Justice to be appointed for the Court of King's Bench at Montreal, or any Five of them, the Judges of the Court of the District wherein the Judgment appealed from was given excepted, should constitute a Superior Court of Civil Jurisdiction, or Provincial Court of Appeals, and should take cognizance of, hear, try, and determine all Causes, Matters, and Things appealed from all Civil Jurisdictions and Courts wherein an Appeal is by Law allowed;" be it enacted, That until otherwise provided by an Act of the Legislature of the Province of Canada, all judicial and ministerial Authority which before and at the Time of passing this Act was vested in or might be exercised by the Governor, Lieutenant Governor, or Person administering the Government of the said Province of Upper Canada, or the Members or any Number of the Members of the Executive Council of the same Province, or was vested in or might be exercised by the Governor, Lieutenant Governor, or the Person administering the Government of the Province of Lower Canada, and the Members of the Executive Council of that Province, shall be vested in and may be exercised by the Governor, Lieutenant Governor, or Person administering the Government of the Province of Canada, and in the Members or the like Number of the Members of the Executive Council of the Province of Canada respectively; and that until otherwise provided by Act or Acts of the Legislature of the Province of Canada, the said Court of King's Bench, now called the Court of Queen's Bench of Upper Canada, shall from and after the Union of the Provinces of Upper and Lower Canada be holden at the City of Toronto, or within One Mile from the Municipal Boundary of the said City of Toronto: Provided always, that, until otherwise provided by Act or Acts of the Legislature of the Province of Canada, it shall be lawful for the Governor of the Province of Canada, by and with the Advice and Consent of the Executive Council of the same Province, by his Proclamation to fix and appoint such other Place as he may think fit within that Part of the last-mentioned Province which now constitutes the Province of Upper Canada for the holding of the said Court of Queen's Bench.

(Laws of Lower
Canada,
34 G. 3)

Powers to be
exercised by
Governor, with the
Executive Council,
or alone

XLV. And be it enacted, That all Powers, Authorities, and Functions which by the said Act passed in the Thirty-first Year of the Reign of His late Majesty King George the Third, or by any other Act of Parliament, or by any Act of the Legislature of the Provinces of Upper and Lower Canada respectively, are vested in or are authorized or required to be exercised by the respective Governors or Lieutenant Governors of the said Provinces, with the Advice or with the Advice and Consent of the Executive Council of such Provinces respectively, or in conjunction with such Executive Council, or with any Number of the Members thereof, or by the said Governors or Lieutenant Governors individually and alone, shall, in so far as the same are not repugnant to or inconsistent with the Provision of this Act, be vested in and may be exercised by the Governor of the Province of Canada, with the Advice or with the Advice and Consent of, or in conjunction, as the Case may require, with such Executive Council, or any Members thereof, as may be appointed by Her Majesty for the Affairs of the Province of Canada, or by the said Governor of the Province of Canada individually and alone in Cases where the Advice, Consent, or Concurrence of the Executive Council is not required.

Existing Laws saved

XLVI. And be it enacted, That all Laws, Statutes, and Ordinances, which at the Time of the Union of the Provinces of Upper Canada and Lower Canada shall be in force within the said Provinces or either of them, or any Part of the said Provinces respectively, shall remain and continue to be of the same Force, Authority, and Effect in those Parts of the Province of Canada which now constitute the said Provinces respectively as if this Act had not been made, and as if the said Two Provinces had not been united as aforesaid, except in so far as the same are repealed or varied by this Act, or in so far as the same shall or may hereafter, by virtue and under the Authority of this Act, be repealed or varied by any Act or Acts of the Legislature of the Province of Canada.

Courts of Justice,
Commissions,
Officers, &c.

XLVII. And be it enacted, That all the Courts of Civil and Criminal Jurisdiction within the Provinces of Upper and Lower Canada at the Time of the Union of the said Provinces, and all legal Commissions, Powers, and Authorities, and all Officers, judicial, administrative, or ministerial, within the said Provinces respectively, except in so far as the same may be abolished, altered, or varied by or may be inconsistent with the Provisions of this Act, or shall be abolished, altered, or varied by any Act or Acts of the Legislature of the Province of Canada, shall continue to subsist within those Parts of the Province of Canada which now constitute the said Two Provinces respectively, in the same Form and with the same Effect as if this Act had not been made, and as if the said Two Provinces had not been re-united as aforesaid.

Provision respecting
temporary Acts

XLVIII. "And whereas the Legislatures of the said Provinces of Upper and Lower Canada have from Time to Time passed Enactments, which Enactments were to continue in force for a certain Number of Years after the passing thereof, 'and from thence to the End of the then next ensuing Session of the Legislature of the Province in which the same were passed;'" be it therefore enacted, That whenever the Words "and from thence to the End of the then next ensuing Session of the Legislature," or

Words to the same Effect, have been used in any temporary Act of either of the said Two Provinces which shall not have expired before the Re-union of the said Two Provinces, the said Words shall be construed to extend and apply to the next Session of the Legislature of the Province of Canada.

Repeal of Part of
3 G. 4. c. 119

XLIX. "And whereas by a certain Act passed in the Third Year of the Reign of His late Majesty King George the Fourth, intituled An Act to regulate the Trade of the Provinces of Lower and Upper Canada, and for other Purposes relating to the said Provinces, certain Provisions were made for appointing Arbitrators, with Power to hear and determine certain Claims of the Province of Upper Canada upon the Province of Lower Canada, and to hear any Claim which might be advanced on the Part of the Province of Upper Canada to a Proportion of certain Duties therein mentioned, and for prescribing the Course of Proceeding to be pursued by such Arbitrators;" be it enacted, That the said recited Provisions of the said last-mentioned Act, and all Matters in the same Act contained which are consequent to or dependent upon the said Provisions of any of them, shall be repealed.

Revenues of the Two
Provinces to form a
Consolidated
Revenue Fund

L. And be it enacted, That upon the Union of the Provinces of Upper and Lower Canada all Duties and Revenues over which the respective Legislatures of the said Provinces before and at the Time of the passing of this Act had and have Power of Appropriation shall form one Consolidated Revenue Fund, to be appropriated for the Public Service of the Province of Canada, in the Manner and subject to the Charges herein-after mentioned.

Consolidated
Revenue Fund to be
charged with
Expence of
Collection, &c.

LI. And be it enacted, That the said Consolidated Revenue Fund of the Province of Canada shall be permanently charged with all the Costs, Charges, and Expences incident to the Collection, Management, and Receipt thereof, such Costs, Charges, and Expences being subject nevertheless to be reviewed and audited in such Manner as shall be directed by any Act of the Legislature of the Province of Canada.

45,000L. to be
granted permanently,
for the Services in
Schedule A. and
30,000L. for the Life
of Her Majesty and
Five Years following,
for those in
Schedule B

LII. And be it enacted, That out of the Consolidated Revenue Fund of the Province of Canada there shall be payable in every Year to Her Majesty, Her Heirs and Successors, the Sum of Forty-five thousand Pounds, for defraying the Expence of the several Services and Purposes named in the Schedule marked A. to this Act annexed; and during the Life of Her Majesty, and for Five Years after the Demise of Her Majesty, there shall be payable to Her Majesty, Her Heirs and Successors, out of the said Consolidated Revenue Fund, a further Sum of Thirty thousand Pounds, for defraying the Expence of the several Services and Purposes named in the Schedule marked B. to this Act annexed; the said Sums of Forty-five thousand Pounds and Thirty thousand Pounds to be issued by the Receiver General in discharge of such Warrant or Warrants as shall be from Time to Time directed to him under the Hand and Seal of the Governor; and the said Receiver General shall account to Her Majesty for the same, through the Lord High Treasurer or Lords Commissioners of Her Majesty's Treasury, in such Manner and Form as Her Majesty shall be graciously pleased to direct.

How the
Appropriation
of Sums granted may
be varied

LIII. And be it enacted, That, until altered by any Act of the Legislature of the Province of Canada, the Salaries of the Governor and of the Judges shall be those respectively set against their several Offices in the said Schedule A.; but that it shall be lawful for the Governor to abolish any of the Offices named in the said Schedule B., or to vary the Sums appropriated to any of the Services or Purposes named in the said Schedule B.; and that the Amount of Saving which may accrue from any such Alteration in either of the said Schedules shall be appropriated to such Purposes connected with the Administration of the Government of the said Province as to Her Majesty shall seem fit; and that Accounts in detail of the Expenditure of the several Sums of Forty-five thousand Pounds and Thirty thousand Pounds herein-before granted, and of every Part thereof, shall be laid before the Legislative Council and Legislative Assembly of the said Province within Thirty Days next after the Beginning of the Session after such Expenditure shall have been made: Provided always, that not more than Two thousand Pounds shall be payable at the same Time for Pensions to the Judges out of the said Sum of Forty-five thousand Pounds, and that not more than Five thousand Pounds shall be payable at the same Time for Pensions out of the said Sum of Thirty thousand Pounds; and that a List of all such Pensions, and of the Persons to whom the same shall have been granted, shall be laid in every Year before the said Legislative Council and Legislative Assembly.

Surrender of
Hereditary Revenues
of the Crown

LIV. And be it enacted, That during the Time for which the said several Sums of Forty-five thousand Pounds and Thirty thousand Pounds are severally payable the same shall be accepted and taken by Her Majesty by way of Civil List, instead of all Territorial and other Revenues now at the Disposal of the Crown, arising in either of the said Provinces of Upper Canada or Lower Canada, or in the Province of Canada, and that Three Fifths of the net Produce of the said Territorial and other Revenues now at the Disposal of the Crown within the Province of Canada shall be paid over to the Account of the said Consolidated Revenue Fund; and also during the Life of Her Majesty, and for Five Years after the Demise of Her Majesty, the remaining Two Fifths of the net Produce of the said Territorial and other Revenues now at the Disposal of the Crown within the Province of Canada shall be also paid over in like Manner to the Account of the said Consolidated Revenue Fund.

Charges already
created in either
Province

LV. And be it enacted, That the Consolidation of the Duties and Revenues of the said Province shall not be taken to affect the Payment out of the said Consolidated Revenue Fund of any Sum or Sums heretofore charged upon the Rates and Duties already raised, levied, and collected, or to be raised, levied, and collected, to and for the Use of either of the said Provinces of Upper Canada or Lower Canada, or of the Province of Canada, for such Time as shall have been appointed by the several Acts of the Legislature of the Province by which such Charges were severally authorized.

The Order of Charges
on the Consolidated
Fund to be
—1st. Expence of
Collection;
2d. Interest of the
Debt;
3d. Payments to the
Clergy;
4th. and 5th. Civil
List;
6th. Other Charges
already made on the
Public Revenue

LVI. And be it enacted, That the Expences of the Collection, Management, and Receipt of the said Consolidated Revenue Fund shall form the First Charge thereon; and that the annual Interest of the Public Debt of the Provinces of Upper and Lower Canada, or of either of them, at the Time of the Re-union of the said Provinces, shall form the Second Charge thereon; and that the Payments to be made to the Clergy of the United Church of England and Ireland, and to the Clergy of the Church of Scotland, and to Ministers of other Christian Denominations, pursuant to any Law or Usage whereby such Payments, before or at the Time of passing this Act, were or are legally or usually paid out of the Public or Crown Revenue of either of the Provinces of Upper and Lower Canada, shall form the Third Charge upon the said Consolidated Revenue Fund; and that the said Sum of Forty-five thousand Pounds shall form the Fourth Charge thereon; and that the said Sum of Thirty thousand Pounds, so long as the same shall continue to be payable, shall form the Fifth Charge thereon; and that the other Charges upon the Rates and Duties levied within the said Province of Canada herein-before reserved shall form the Sixth Charge thereon, so long as such Charges shall continue to be payable.

Subject to the above
Charges, the
Consolidated
Revenue Fund to be
appropriated by the
Provincial Legislature

by Bills, &c.

LVII. And be it enacted, That, subject to the several Payments hereby charged on the said Consolidated Revenue Fund, the same shall be appropriated by the Legislature of the Province of Canada for the Public Service, in such Manner as they shall think proper: Provided always, that all Bills for appropriating any Part of the Surplus of the said Consolidated Revenue Fund, or for imposing any new Tax or Impost, shall originate in the Legislative Assembly of the said Province of Canada: Provided also, that it shall not be lawful for the said Legislative Assembly to originate or pass any Vote, Resolution, or Bill for the Appropriation of any Part of the Surplus of the said Consolidated Revenue Fund, or of any other Tax or Impost, to any Purpose which shall not have been first recommended by a Message of the Governor to the said Legislative Assembly during the Session in which such Vote, Resolution, or Bill shall be passed.

Townships
to be constituted

LVIII. And be it enacted, That it shall be lawful for the Governor, by an Instrument or Instruments to be issued by him for that Purpose under the Great Seal of the Province, to constitute Townships in those Parts of the Province of Canada in which Townships are not already constituted, and to fix the Metes and Bounds thereof, and to provide for the Election and Appointment of Township Officers therein, who shall have and exercise the like Powers as are exercised by the like Officers in the Townships already constituted in that Part of the Province of Canada now called Upper Canada; and every such Instrument shall be published by Proclamation, and shall have the Force of Law from a Day to be named in each Case in such Proclamation.

Powers of Governor,
how to be exercised

LIX. And be it enacted, That all Powers and Authorities expressed in this Act to be given to the Governor of the Province of Canada shall be exercised by such Governor in conformity with and subject to such Orders, Instructions, and Directions as Her Majesty shall from Time to Time see fit to make or issue.

Magdalen Islands
may be annexed to
the Island of
Prince Edward

14 G. 3. c. 83

LX. "And whereas His late Majesty King George the Third, by His Royal Proclamation, bearing Date the Seventh Day of October in the Third Year of His Reign, was pleased to declare that he had put the Coast of Labrador, from the River Saint John to Hudson's Straits, with the Islands of Anticosti and Madelaine, and all other smaller Islands lying on the said Coast, under the Care and Inspection of the Governor of Newfoundland: And whereas by an Act passed in the Fourteenth Year of the Reign of His said late Majesty, intituled An Act for the making more effectual Provision for the Government of the Province of Quebec in North America, all such Territories, Islands, and Counties which had, since the Tenth Day of February in the Year One thousand seven hundred and sixty-three, been made Part of the Government of Newfoundland, were during His Majesty's Pleasure annexed to and made Part and Parcel of the Province of Quebec, as created and established by the said Royal Proclamation;" be it declared and enacted, That nothing in this or any other Act contained shall be construed to restrain Her Majesty, if She shall be so pleased, from annexing the Magdalen Islands in the Gulf of Saint Lawrence to Her Majesty's Island of Prince Edward.

Interpretation
Clause

LXI. And be it enacted, That in this Act, unless otherwise expressed therein, the Words "Act of the Legislature of the Province of Canada" are to be understood to mean "Act of Her Majesty, Her Heirs or Successors, enacted by Her Majesty, or by the Governor on behalf of Her Majesty, with the Advice and Consent of the Legislative Council and Assembly of the Province of Canada;" and the Words "Governor of the Province of Canada" are to be understood as comprehending the Governor, Lieutenant Governor, or Person authorized to execute the Office or the Functions of Governor of the said Province.

Act may be
amended, &c.

LXII. And be it enacted, That this Act may be amended or repealed by any Act to be passed in the present Session of Parliament.

SCHEDULES

SCHEDULE A

		(STERLING)
Governor		7,000
Lieutenant Governor		1,000

UPPER CANADA

1	Chief Justice	1,500
4	Puisne Judges, at 900L. each	3,600
1	Vice Chancellor	1,125

LOWER CANADA

1	Chief Justice, Quebec	1,500
3	Puisne Judges, Quebec, at 900L. each	2,700
1	Chief Justice, Montreal	1,100
3	Puisne Judges, Montreal, at 900L. each	2,700
1	Resident Judge at Three Rivers	900
1	Judge of the Inferior District of St. Francis	500
1	Judge of the Inferior District of Gaspé	500

Pensions to the Judges, Salaries of the Attornies and Solicitors General, and Contingent and Miscellaneous Expenses of Administration of Justice throughout the Province of Canada 20,875

(STERLING) 45,000

SCHEDULE B

	(STERLING)
Civil Secretaries and their Offices	8,000
Provincial Secretaries and their Offices	3,000
Receiver General and his Office	3,000
Inspector General and his Office	2,000
Executive Council	3,000
Board of Works	2,000
Emigrant Agent	700
Pensions	5,000
Contingent Expenses of Public Offices	3,300

(STERLING) 30,000

CONSTITUTION ACT, 1867

(THE BRITISH NORTH AMERICA ACT, 1867)

30 & 31 Victoria, c. 3 (U.K.)

{Note: This text contains the amendments made to the *British North America Act, 1867* since its enactment. The present short title was substituted for the original short title in italics by the **Constitution Act, 1982.**}

An Act for the Union of Canada, Nova Scotia, and New Brunswick, and the Government thereof; and for Purposes connected therewith

[29th March 1867]

Whereas the Provinces of Canada, Nova Scotia, and New Brunswick have expressed their Desire to be federally united into One Dominion under the Crown of the United Kingdom of Great Britain and Ireland, with a Constitution similar in Principle to that of the United Kingdom:

And whereas such a Union would conduce to the Welfare of the Provinces and promote the Interests of the British Empire:

And whereas on the Establishment of the Union by Authority of Parliament it is expedient, not only that the Constitution of the Legislative Authority in the Dominion be provided for, but also that the Nature of the Executive Government therein be declared:

And whereas it is expedient that Provision be made for the eventual Admission into the Union of other Parts of British North America:

I. PRELIMINARY

Short title

1. This Act may be cited as the **Constitution Act, 1867.**

2. Repealed.

II. UNION

Declaration of Union

3. It shall be lawful for the Queen, by and with the Advice of Her Majesty's Most Honourable Privy Council, to declare by Proclamation that, on and after a Day therein appointed, not being more than Six Months after the passing of this Act, the Provinces of Canada, Nova Scotia, and New Brunswick shall form and be One Dominion under the Name of Canada; and on and after that Day those Three Provinces shall form and be One Dominion under that Name accordingly.

Construction of subsequent Provisions of Act

4. Unless it is otherwise expressed or implied, the Name Canada shall be taken to mean Canada as constituted under this Act.

Four Provinces

5. Canada shall be divided into Four Provinces, named Ontario, Quebec, Nova Scotia, and New Brunswick.

{Note: Canada now consists of ten provinces (Ontario, Quebec, Nova Scotia, New Brunswick, Manitoba, British Columbia, Prince Edward Island, Alberta, Saskatchewan and Newfoundland) and two territories (the Yukon Territory and the Northwest Territories).

Provinces of Ontario and Quebec

6. The Parts of the Province of Canada (as it exists at the passing of this Act) which formerly constituted respectively the Provinces of Upper Canada and Lower Canada shall be deemed to be severed, and shall form Two separate Provinces. The Part which formerly constituted the Province of Upper Canada shall constitute the Province of Ontario; and the Part which formerly constituted the Province of Lower Canada shall constitute the Province of Quebec.

Provinces of Nova Scotia and New Brunswick

7. The Provinces of Nova Scotia and New Brunswick shall have the same Limits as at the passing of this Act.

Decennial Census

8. In the general Census of the Population of Canada which is hereby required to be taken in the Year One thousand eight hundred and seventy-one, and in every Tenth Year thereafter, the respective Populations of the Four Provinces shall be distinguished.

III. EXECUTIVE POWER

Declaration of Executive Power in the Queen

9. The Executive Government and Authority of and over Canada is hereby declared to continue and be vested in the Queen.

Application of Provisions referring to Governor General

10. The Provisions of this Act referring to the Governor General extend and apply to the Governor General for the Time being of Canada, or other the Chief Executive Officer or Administrator for the Time being carrying on the Government of Canada on behalf and in the Name of the Queen, by whatever Title he is designated.

Constitution of Privy Council for Canada

11. There shall be a Council to aid and advise in the Government of Canada, to be styled the Queen's Privy Council for Canada; and the Persons who are to be Members of that Council shall be from Time to

Time chosen and summoned by the Governor General and sworn in as Privy Councillors, and Members thereof may be from Time to Time removed by the Governor General.

All Powers under Acts to be exercised by Governor General with Advice of Privy Council, or alone

12. All Powers, Authorities, and Functions which under any Act of the Parliament of Great Britain, or of the Parliament of the United Kingdom of Great Britain and Ireland, or of the Legislature of Upper Canada, Lower Canada, Canada, Nova Scotia, or New Brunswick, are at the Union vested in or exerciseable by the respective Governors or Lieutenant Governors of those Provinces, with the Advice, or with the Advice and Consent, of the respective Executive Councils thereof, or in conjunction with those Councils, or with any Number of Members thereof, or by those Governors or Lieutenant Governors individually, shall, as far as the same continue in existence and capable of being exercised after the Union in relation to the Government of Canada, be vested in and exerciseable by the Governor General, with the Advice or with the Advice and Consent of or in conjunction with the Queen's Privy Council for Canada, or any Members thereof, or by the Governor General individually, as the Case requires, subject nevertheless (except with respect to such as exist under Acts of the Parliament of Great Britain or of the Parliament of the United Kingdom of Great Britain and Ireland) to be abolished or altered by the Parliament of Canada.

Application of Provisions referring to Governor General in Council

13. The Provisions of this Act referring to the Governor General in Council shall be construed as referring to the Governor General acting by and with the Advice of the Queen's Privy Council for Canada.

Power to Her Majesty to authorize Governor General to appoint Deputies

14. It shall be lawful for the Queen, if Her Majesty thinks fit, to authorize the Governor General from Time to Time to appoint any Person or any Persons jointly or severally to be his Deputy or Deputies within any Part of Parts of Canada, and in that Capacity to exercise during the Pleasure of the Governor General such of the Powers, Authorities, and Functions of the Governor General as the Governor General deems it necessary or expedient to assign to him or them, subject to any Limitations or Directions expressed or given by the Queen; but the Appointment of such a Deputy or Deputies shall not affect the Exercise by the Governor General himself of any Power, Authority, or Function.

Command of Armed Forces to continue to be vested in the Queen

15. The Command-in-Chief of the Land and Naval Militia, and of all Naval and Military Forces, of and in Canada, is hereby declared to continue and be vested in the Queen.

Seat of Government of Canada

16. Until the Queen otherwise directs, the Seat of Government of Canada shall be Ottawa.

IV. LEGISLATIVE POWER

Constitution of Parliament of Canada

17. There shall be One Parliament for Canada, consisting of the Queen, an Upper House styled the Senate, and the House of Commons.

Privileges, etc., of Houses

18. The privileges, immunities, and powers to be held, enjoyed, and exercised by the Senate and by the House of Commons, and by the members therefor respectively, shall be such as are from time to time defined by Act of the Parliament of Canada, but so that any Act of the Parliament of Canada defining such privileges, immunities, and powers shall not confer any privileges, immunities, or powers exceeding those at the passing of such Act held, enjoyed, and exercised by the Commons House of Parliament of the United Kingdom of Great Britain and Ireland, and by the members thereof.

First Session of the Parliament of Canada

19. The Parliament of Canada shall be called together not later than Six Months after the Union.

20. Repealed.

Number of Senators

21. *The Senate* shall, subject to the Provisions of this Act, consist of One Hundred and four Members, who shall be styled Senators.

Representation of Provinces in Senate

22. In relation to the Constitution of the Senate Canada shall be deemed to consist of Four Divisions: —

1. Ontario;

2. Quebec;

3. The Maritime Provinces, Nova Scotia and New Brunswick, and Prince Edward Island;

4. The Western Provinces of Manitoba, British Columbia, Saskatchewan, and Alberta;

which Four Divisions shall (subject to the Provisions of this Act) be equally represented in the Senate as follows: Ontario by twenty-four senators; Quebec by twenty-four senators; the Maritime Provinces and Prince Edward Island by twenty-four senators, ten thereof representing Nova Scotia, ten thereof representing New Brunswick, and four thereof representing Prince Edward Island; the Western Provinces by twenty-four senators, six thereof representing Manitoba, six thereof representing British Columbia, six thereof representing Saskatchewan, and six thereof representing Alberta; Newfoundland shall be entitled to be represented in the Senate by six members; the Yukon Territory and the Northwest Territories shall be entitled to be represented in the Senate by one member each.

In the Case of Quebec each of the Twenty-four Senators representing that Province shall be appointed for One of the Twenty-four Electoral Divisions of Lower Canada specified in Schedule A. to Chapter One of the Consolidated Statutes of Canada.

Qualifications of Senator

23. The Qualifications of a Senator shall be as follows:

(1) He shall be of the full age of Thirty Years:

(2) He shall be either a natural-born Subject of the Queen, or a Subject of the Queen naturalized by an Act of the Parliament of

Great Britain, or of the Parliament of the United Kingdom of Great Britain and Ireland, or of the Legislature of One of the Provinces of Upper Canada, Lower Canada, Canada, Nova Scotia, or New Brunswick, before the Union, or of the Parliament of Canada after the Union:

(3) He shall be legally or equitably seised as of Freehold for his own Use and Benefit of Lands or Tenements held in Free and Common Socage, or seised or possessed for his won Use and Benefit of Lands or Tenements held in Franc-alleu or in Roture, within the Province for which he is appointed, of the Value of Four thousand Dollars, over and above all Rents, Dues, Debts, Charges, Mortgages, and Incumbrances due or payable out of or charged on or affecting the same:

(4) His Real and Personal Property shall be together worth Four thousand Dollars over and above his Debts and Liabilities:

(5) He shall be resident in the Province for which he is appointed:

(6) In the Case of Quebec he shall have his Real Property Qualification in the Electoral Division for which he is appointed, or shall be resident in that Division.

Summons of Senator

24. The Governor General shall from Time to Time, in the Queen's Name, by Instrument under the Great Seal of Canada, summon qualified Persons to the Senate; and, subject to the Provisions of this Act, every Person so summoned shall become and be a Member of the Senate and a Senator.

25. Repealed.

Addition of Senators in certain cases

26. If at any Time on the Recommendation of the Governor General the Queen thinks fit to direct that Four or Eight Members be added to the Senate, the Governor General may by Summons to Four or Eight qualified Persons (as the Case may be), representing equally the Four Divisions of Canada, add to the Senate accordingly.

Reduction of Senate to normal Number

27. In case of such Addition being at any Time made, the Governor General shall not summon any Person to the Senate, except on a further like Direction by the Queen on the like Recommendation, to represent one of the Four Divisions until such Division is represented by Twenty-four Senators and no more.

Maximum Number of Senators

28. The Number of Senators shall not at any Time exceed One Hundred and twelve.

Tenure of Place in Senate

29. (1) Subject to subsection (2), a Senator shall, subject to the provisions of this Act, hold his place in the Senate for life.

Retirement upon attaining age of seventy-five years

(2) A Senator who is summoned to the Senate after the coming into force of this subsection shall, subject to this Act, hold his place in the Senate until he attains the age of seventy-five years.

{Note: As enacted by the **Constitution Act, 1965** which came into force on June 1, 1965}.

Resignation of Place in Senate

30. A Senator may by Writing under his Hand addressed to the Governor General resign his Place in the Senate, and thereupon the same shall be vacant.

Disqualification of Senators

31. The Place of a Senator shall become vacant in any of the following Cases:

(1) If for Two consecutive Sessions of the Parliament he fails to give his Attendance in the Senate:

(2) If he takes an Oath or makes a Declaration or Acknowledgment of Allegiance, Obedience, or Adherence to a Foreign Power, or does an Act whereby he become a Subject or Citizen, or entitled to the Rights or Privileges of a Subject or Citizen, of a Foreign Power:

(3) If he is adjudged Bankrupt or Insolvent, or applies for the Benefit of any Law relating to Insolvent Debtors, or becomes a public Defaulter:

(4) If he is attainted of Treason or convicted of Felony or of any infamous Crime:

(5) If he ceases to be qualified in respect of Property or of Residence; provided, that a Senator shall not be deemed to have ceased to be qualified in respect of Residence by reason only of his residing at the Seat of the Government of Canada while holding an Office under that Government requiring his Presence there.

Summons on Vacancy in Senate

32. When a Vacancy happens in the Senate by Resignation, Death, or otherwise, the Governor General shall by Summons to a fit and qualified Person fill the Vacancy.

Questions as to Qualifications and Vacancies in Senate

33. If any Question arises respecting the Qualification of a Senator or a Vacancy in the Senate the same shall be heard and determined by the Senate.

Appointment of Speaker of Senate

34. The Governor General may from Time to Time, by Instrument under the Great Seal of Canada, appoint a Senator to be Speaker of the Senate, and may remove him and appoint another in his Stead.

Quorum of Senate

35. Until the Parliament of Canada otherwise provides, the Presence of a least Fifteen Senators, including the Speaker, shall be necessary to constitute a Meeting of the Senate for the Exercise of its Powers.

Voting in Senate

36. Questions arising in the Senate shall be decided by a Majority of Voices, and the Speaker shall in all Cases have a Vote, and when the voices are equal the Decision shall be deemed to be in the Negative.

The House of Commons

Constitution of House of Commons in Canada

37. The House of Commons shall, subject to the Provisions of this Act, consist of two hundred and ninety-five members of whom ninety-nine shall be elected for Ontario, seventy-five for Quebec, eleven for Nova Scotia, ten for New Brunswick, fourteen for Manitoba, thirty-two for British Columbia, four for Prince Edward Island, twenty-six for Alberta, fourteen for Saskatchewan, seven for Newfoundland, one for the Yukon Territory and two for the Northwest Territories.

Summoning of House of Commons

38. The Governor General shall from Time to Time, in the Queen's Name, by Instrument under the Great Seal of Canada, summon and call together the House of Commons.

Senators not to sit in House of Commons

39. A Senator shall not be capable of being elected or of sitting or voting as a Member of the House of Commons.

Electoral districts of the four Provinces

40. Until the Parliament of Canada otherwise provides, Ontario, Quebec, Nova Scotia, and New Brunswick shall, for the Purposes of the Election of Members to serve in the House of Commons, be divided into Electoral Districts as follows:

1. – ONTARIO

Ontario shall be divided into the Counties, Ridings of Counties, Cities, Parts of Cities, and Towns enumerated in the First Schedule to this Act, each whereof shall be an Electoral District, each such District as numbered in that Schedule being entitled to return One Member.

2. – QUEBEC

Quebec shall be divided into Sixty-five Electoral Districts, composed of the Sixty-five Electoral Divisions into which Lower Canada is at the passing of this Act divided under Chapter Two of the Consolidated Statutes of Canada, Chapter Seventy-five of the Consolidated Statutes for Lower Canada, and the Act of the Province of Canada of the Twenty-third Year of the Queen, Chapter One, or any other Act amending the same in force at the Union, so that each such Electoral Division shall be for the Purposes of this Act an Electoral District entitled to return One Member.

3. – NOVA SCOTIA

Each of the Eighteen Counties of Nova Scotia shall be an Electoral District. The County of Halifax shall be entitled to return Two Members, and each of the other Counties One Member.

4. – NEW BRUNSWICK

Each of the Fourteen Counties into which New Brunswick is divided, including the City and County of St. John, shall be an Electoral District.

The City of St. John shall also be a separate Electoral District. Each of those Fifteen Electoral Districts shall be entitled to return One Member.

Continuance of existing Election Laws until Parliament of Canada otherwise provides

41. Until the Parliament of Canada otherwise provides, all Laws in force in the several Provinces at the Union relative to the following Matters or any of them, namely, — the Qualifications and Disqualifications of Persons to be elected or to sit or vote as Members of the House of Assembly or Legislative Assembly in the several Provinces, the Voters at Elections of such Members, the Oaths to be taken by Voters, the Returning Officers, their Powers and Duties, the Proceedings at Elections, the Periods during which Elections may be continued, the Trial of controverted Elections, and Proceedings incident thereto, the vacating of Seats of Members, and the Execution of new Writs in case of Seats vacated otherwise than by Dissolution, — shall respectively apply to Elections of Members to serve in the House of Commons for the same several Provinces.

Provided that, until the Parliament of Canada otherwise provides, at any Election for a Member of the House of Commons for the District of Algoma, in addition to Persons qualified by the Law of the Province of Canada to vote, every Male British Subject, aged Twenty-one Years or upwards, being a Householder, shall have a Vote.

42. Repealed.

43. Repealed.

As to Election of Speaker of House of Commons

44. The House of Commons on its first assembling after a General Election shall proceed with all practicable Speed to elect One of its Members to be Speaker.

As to filling up Vacancy in Office of Speaker

45. In case of a Vacancy happening in the Office of Speaker by Death, Resignation, or otherwise, the House of Commons shall with all practicable Speed proceed to elect another of its Members to be Speaker.

Speaker to preside

46. The Speaker shall preside at all Meeting of the House of Commons.

Provision in case of Absence of Speaker

47. Until the Parliament of Canada otherwise provides, in case of the Absence for any Reason of the Speaker from the Chair of the House of Commons for a Period of Forty-eight consecutive Hours, the House may elect another of its Members to act as Speaker, and the Member so elected shall during the Continuance of such Absence of the Speaker have and execute all the Powers, Privileges, and Duties of Speaker.

Quorum of House of Commons

48. The Presence of at least Twenty Members of the House of Commons shall be necessary to constitute a Meeting of the House for the Exercise of its Powers, and for that Purpose the Speaker shall be reckoned as a Member.

Voting in House of Commons

49. Questions arising in the House of Commons shall be decided by a Majority of Voices other than that of the Speaker, and when the Voices are equal, but not otherwise, the Speaker shall have a Vote.

Duration of House of
Commons

50. Every House of Commons shall continue for Five Years from the Day of the Return of the Writs for choosing the House (subject to be sooner dissolved by the Governor General), and no longer.

Readjustment of
representation in
Commons

51. (1) The number of members of the House of Commons and the representation of the provinces therein shall, on the coming into force of this subsection and thereafter on the completion of each decennial census, be readjusted by such authority, in such manner, and from such time as the Parliament of Canada from time to time provides, subject and according to the following rules:

Rules

1. There shall be assigned to each of the provinces a number of members equal to the number obtained by dividing the total population of the provinces by two hundred and seventy-nine and by dividing the population of each province by the quotient so obtained, counting any remainder in excess of 0.50 as one after the said process of division.

2. If the total number of members that would be assigned to a province by the application of rule 1 is less than the total number assigned to that province on the date of coming into force of this subsection, there shall be added to the number of members so assigned such number of members as will result in the province having the same number of members as were assigned on that date.

Yukon Territory and
Northwest Territories

(2) The Yukon Territory as bounded and described in the schedule to chapter Y-2 of the Revised Statutes of Canada, 1970, shall be entitled to one member, and the Northwest Territories as bounded and described in section 2 of chapter N-22 of the Revised Statutes of Canada, 1970, shall be entitled to two members.

Constitution of House
of Commons

51A. Notwithstanding anything in this Act a province shall always be entitled to a number of members in the House of Commons not less than the number of senators representing such province.

Increase of
Number of House of
Commons

52. The Number of Members of the House of Commons may be from Time to Time increased by the Parliament of Canada, provided the proportionate Representation of the Provinces prescribed by this Act is not thereby disturbed.

Money Votes; Royal Assent

Appropriation and
Tax Bills

53. Bills for appropriating any Part of the Public Revenue, or for imposing any Tax or Impost, shall originate in the House of Commons.

Recommendation of
Money Votes

54. It shall not be lawful for the House of Commons to adopt or pass any Vote, Resolution, Address, or Bill for the Appropriation of any Part of the Public Revenue, or of any Tax or Impost, to any Purpose that has not been first recommended to that House by Message of the Governor General in the Session in which such Vote, Resolution, Address, or Bill is proposed.

Royal Assent to Bills,
etc.

55. Where a Bill passed by the Houses of the Parliament is presented to the Governor General for the Queen's Assent, he shall declare,

according to his Discretion, but subject to the Provisions of this Act and to Her Majesty's Instructions, either that he assents thereto in the Queen's Name, or that he withholds the Queen's Assent, or that he reserves the Bill for the Signification of the Queen's Pleasure.

Disallowance by Order in Council of Act assented to by Governor General

56. Where the Governor General assents to a Bill in the Queen's Name, he shall by the first convenient Opportunity send an authentic Copy of the Act to One of Her Majesty's Principal Secretaries of State, and if the Queen in Council within Two Years after Receipt thereof by the Secretary of State thinks fit to disallow the Act, such Disallowance (with a Certificate of the Secretary of State of the Day on Which the Act was received by him) being signified by the Governor General, by Speech or Message to each of the House of the Parliament or by Proclamation, shall annul the Act from and after the Day of such Signification.

Signification of Queen's Pleasure on Bill reserved

57. A Bill reserved for the Signification of the Queen's Pleasure shall not have any Force unless and until, within Two Years from the Day on which it was presented to the Governor General for the Queen's Assent, the Governor General signifies, by Speech or Message to each of the Houses of the Parliament or by Proclamation, that it has received the Assent of the Queen in Council.

An Entry of every such Speech, Message, or Proclamation shall be made in the Journal of each House, and a Duplicate thereof duly attested shall be delivered to the proper Officer to be kept among the Records of Canada.

V. PROVINCIAL CONSTITUTIONS

Executive Power

Appointment of Lieutenant Governors of Provinces

58. For each Province there shall be an Officer, styled the Lieutenant Governor, appointed by the Governor General in Council by Instrument under the Great Seal of Canada.

Tenure of Office of Lieutenant Governor

59. A Lieutenant Governor shall hold Office during the Pleasure of the Governor General; but any Lieutenant Governor appointed after the Commencement of the First Session of the Parliament of Canada shall not be removeable within Five Years from his Appointment, except for Cause assigned, which shall be communicated to him in Writing within One Month after the Order for his Removal is made, and shall be communicated by Message to the Senate and to the House of Commons within One Week thereafter if the Parliament is then sitting, and if not then within One Week after the Commencement of the next Session of the Parliament.

Salaries of Lieutenant Governors

60. The Salaries of the Lieutenant Governors shall be fixed and provided by the Parliament of Canada.

Oaths, etc., of Lieutenant Governor

61. Every Lieutenant Governor shall, before assuming the Duties of his Office, make and subscribe before the Governor General or some Person authorized by him Oaths of Allegiance and Office similar to those taken by the Governor General.

Application of
Provisions referring
to Lieutenant
Governor

62. The Provisions of this Act referring to the Lieutenant Governor extend and apply to the Lieutenant Governor for the Time being of each Province, or other the Chief Executive Officer or Administrator for the Time being carrying on the Government of the Province, by whatever Title he is designated.

Appointment of
Executive Officers
for Ontario and
Quebec

63. The Executive Council of Ontario and of Quebec shall be composed of such Persons as the Lieutenant Governor from Time to Time thinks fit, and in the first instance of the following Officers, namely, — the Attorney General, the Secretary and Registrar of the Province, the Treasurer of the Province, the Commissioner of Crown Lands, and the Commissioner of Agriculture and Public Words, with in Quebec the Speaker of the Legislative Council and the Solicitor General.

Executive
Government of
Nova Scotia and New
Brunswick

64. The Constitution of the Executive Authority in each of the Provinces of Nova Scotia and New Brunswick shall, subject to the Provisions of this Act, continue as it exists at the Union until altered under the Authority of this Act.

Powers to be
exercised by
Lieutenant Governor
of Ontario or Quebec
with Advice, or alone

65. All Powers, Authorities, and Functions which under any Act of the Parliament of Great Britain, or of the Parliament of the United Kingdom of Great Britain and Ireland, or of the Legislature of Upper Canada, Lower Canada, or Canada, were or are before or at the Union vested in or exerciseable by the respective Governors or Lieutenant Governors of those Provinces, with the Advice or with the Advice and Consent of the respective Executive Councils thereof, or in conjunction with those Councils, or with any Number of Members thereof, or by those Governors or Lieutenant Governors individually, shall, as far as the same are capable of being exercised after the Union in relation to the Government of Ontario and Quebec respectively, be vested in and shall or may be exercised by the Lieutenant Governor of Ontario and Quebec respectively, with the Advice or with the Advice and Consent of or in conjunction with the respective Executive Councils, or any Members thereof, or by the Lieutenant Governor individually, as the Case requires, subject nevertheless (except with respect to such as exist under Acts of the Parliament of Great Britain, or of the Parliament of the United Kingdom of Great Britain, and Ireland,) to be abolished or altered by the respective Legislatures of Ontario and Quebec.

Application of
Provisions referring
to Lieutenant
Governor in Council

66. The provisions of this Act referring to the Lieutenant Governor in Council shall be construed as referring to the Lieutenant Governor of the Province acting by and with the Advice of the Executive Council thereof.

Administration in
Absence, etc., of
Lieutenant Governor

67. The Governor General in Council may from Time to Time appoint an Administrator to execute the Office and Functions of Lieutenant Governor during his Absence, Illness, or other Inability.

Seats of Provincial
Governments

68. Unless and until the Executive Government of any Province otherwise directs with respect to that Province, the Seats of Government of the Provinces shall be as follows, namely, — of Ontario, the City of Toronto; of Quebec, the City of Quebec; of Nova Scotia, the City of Halifax; and of New Brunswick, the City of Fredericton.

Legislative Power

1. – ONTARIO

Legislature for
Ontario

69. There shall be a Legislature for Ontario consisting of the Lieutenant Governor and of One House, styled the Legislative Assembly of Ontario.

Electoral districts

70. The Legislative Assembly of Ontario shall be composed of Eighty-two Members, to be elected to represent the Eighty-two Electoral Districts set forth in the First Schedule to this Act.

2. – QUEBEC

Legislature for
Quebec

71. There shall be a Legislature for Quebec consisting of the Lieutenant Governor and of Two Houses, styled the Legislative Council of Quebec and the Legislative Assembly of Quebec.

Constitution of
Legislative Council

72. The Legislative Council of Quebec shall be composed of Twenty-four Members, to be appointed by the Lieutenant Governor, in the Queen's Name, by Instrument under the Great Seal of Quebec, one being appointed to represent each of the Twenty-four Electoral Divisions of Lower Canada in this Act referred to, and each holding Office for the Term of his Life, unless the Legislature of Quebec otherwise provides under the Provisions of this Act.

Qualification of
Legislative
Councillors

73. The Qualifications of the Legislative Councillors of Quebec shall be the same as those of the Senators for Quebec.

Resignation,
Disqualification, etc.

74. The Place of a Legislative Councillor of Quebec shall become vacant in the Cases, *mutatis mutandis*, in which the Place of Senator becomes vacant.

Vacancies

75. When a Vacancy happens in the Legislative Council of Quebec by Resignation, Death, or otherwise, the Lieutenant Governor, in the Queen's Name, by Instrument under the Great Seal of Quebec, shall appoint a fit and qualified Person to fill the Vacancy.

Questions as to
Vacancies, etc.

76. If any Question arises respecting the Qualification of a Legislative Councillor of Quebec, or a Vacancy in the Legislative Council of Quebec, the same shall be heard and determined by the Legislative Council.

Speaker of
Legislative Council

77. The Lieutenant Governor may from Time to Time, by Instrument under the Great Seal of Quebec, appoint a Member of the Legislative Council of Quebec to be Speaker thereof, and may remove him and appoint another in his Stead.

Quorum of
Legislative Council

78. Until the Legislature of Quebec otherwise provides, the Presence of at least Ten Members of the Legislative Council, including the speaker, shall be necessary to constitute a Meeting for the Exercise of its Powers.

Voting in Legislative
Council

79. Questions arising in the Legislative Council of Quebec shall be decided by a Majority of Voices, and the Speaker shall in all Cases have

a Vote, and when the Voices are equal the Decision shall be deemed to be in the Negative.

Constitution of Legislative Assembly of Quebec

80. The Legislative Assembly of Quebec shall be composed of Sixty-five Members, to be elected to represent the Sixty-five Electoral Divisions or Districts of Lower Canada in this Act referred to, subject to Alteration thereof by the Legislature of Quebec: Provided that it shall not be lawful to present to the Lieutenant governor of Quebec for Assent any Bill for altering the Limits of any of the Electoral Divisions or Districts mentioned in the Second Schedule to this Act, unless the Second and Third Readings of such Bill have been passed in the Legislative Assembly with the Concurrence of the Majority of the Members representing all those Electoral Divisions or Districts, and the Assent shall not be given to such Bill unless an Address has been presented by the Legislative Assembly to the Lieutenant Governor stating that it has been so passed.

3. – ONTARIO AND QUEBEC

81. Repealed.

Summoning of Legislative Assemblies

82. The Lieutenant Governor of Ontario and of Quebec shall from Time to Time, in the Queen's Name, by Instrument under the Great Seal of the Province, summon and call together the Legislative Assembly of the Province.

Restriction on election of Holders of Offices

83. Until the Legislature of Ontario or of Quebec otherwise provides, a Person accepting or holding in Ontario or in Quebec any Office, Commission, or Employment, permanent or temporary, at the Nomination of the Lieutenant Governor, to which an annual Salary, or any Fee, Allowance, Emolument, or Profit of any Kind or Amount whatever from the Province is attached, shall not be eligible as a Member of the Legislative Assembly of the respective Province, nor shall be sit or vote as such; but nothing in this Section shall make ineligible any Person being a Member of the Executive Council of the respective Province, or holding any of the following Offices, that is to say, the Offices of Attorney General, Secretary and Registrar of the Province, Treasurer of the Province, Commissioner of Crown Lands, and Commissioner of Agriculture and Public Works, and in Quebec Solicitor General, or shall disqualify him to sit or vote in the House for which he is elected, provided he is elected while holding such Office.

Continuance of existing Election Laws

84. Until the legislatures of Ontario and Quebec respectively otherwise provide, all Laws which at the Union are in force in those Provinces respectively, relative to the following Matters, or any of them, namely, — the Qualifications and Disqualifications of Persons to be elected or to sit or vote as Members of the Assembly of Canada, the Qualifications or Disqualifications of Voters, the Oaths to be taken by Voters, the Returning Officers, their Powers and Duties, the Proceedings at Elections, the Periods during which such Elections may be continued, and the Trial of controverted Elections and the Proceedings incident thereto, the vacating of the Seats of Members and the issuing and execution of new Writs in case of Seats vacated otherwise than by Dissolution, — shall

respectively apply to Elections of Members to serve in the respective Legislative Assemblies of Ontario and Quebec.

Provided that, until the Legislature of Ontario otherwise provides, at any Election for a Member of the Legislative Assembly of Ontario for the District of Algoma, in addition to Persons qualified by the Law of the Province of Canada to vote, every Male British Subject, aged Twenty-one Years or upwards, being a Householder, shall have a Vote.

Duration of
Legislative
Assemblies

85. Every Legislative Assembly of Ontario and every Legislative Assembly of Quebec shall continue for Four Years from the Day of the Return of the Writs for choosing the same (subject nevertheless to either the Legislative Assembly of Ontario or the Legislative Assembly of Quebec being sooner dissolved by the Lieutenant Governor of the Province), and no longer.

Yearly Session of
Legislature

86. There shall be a Session of the Legislature of Ontario and of that of Quebec once at least in every Year, so that Twelve Months shall not intervene between the last Sitting of the Legislature in each Province in one Session and its first Sitting in the next Session.

Speaker, Quorum, etc.

87. The following Provisions of this Act respecting the House of Commons of Canada shall extend and apply to the Legislative Assemblies of Ontario and Quebec, that is to say, — the Provisions relating to the Election of a Speaker originally and on Vacancies, the Duties of the Speaker, the Absence of the Speaker, the Quorum, and the Mode of voting, as if those Provisions were here re-enacted and made applicable in Terms to each such Legislative Assembly.

4. – NOVA SCOTIA AND NEW BRUNSWICK

Constitution of
Legislatures of Nova
Scotia and New
Brunswick

88. The Constitution of the Legislature of each of the Provinces of Nova Scotia and New Brunswick shall, subject to the Provisions of this Act, continue as it exists at the Union until altered under the Authority of this Act.

5. – ONTARIO, QUEBEC, AND NOVA SCOTIA

89. Repealed.

6. – THE FOUR PROVINCES

Application to
Legislatures of
Provisions
respecting Money
Votes, etc.

90. The following Provisions of this Act respecting the Parliament of Canada, namely, — the Provisions relating to Appropriation and Tax Bills, the Recommendation of Money Votes, the Assent to Bills, the Disallowance of Acts, and the Signification of Pleasure on Bills reserved, — shall extend and apply to the Legislatures of the several Provinces as if those Provisions were here re-enacted and made applicable in Terms to the respective Provinces and the Legislatures thereof, with the Substitution of the Lieutenant Governor of the Province for the Governor General, of the governor General for the Queen and for a Secretary of State, of One Year for Two Years, and of the Province for Canada.

VI. DISTRIBUTION OF LEGISLATIVE POWERS

Powers of the Parliament

Legislative Authority of Parliament of Canada

91. It shall be lawful for the Queen, by and with the Advice and Consent of the Senate and House of Commons, to make Laws for the Peace, Order, and good Government of Canada, in Relation to all Matters not coming within the Classes of Subjects by this Act assigned exclusively to the Legislatures of the Provinces; and for greater Certainty, but not so as to restrict the Generality of the foregoing Terms of this Section, it is hereby declared that (notwithstanding anything in this Act) the exclusive Legislative Authority of the Parliament of Canada extends to all Matters coming within the Classes of Subjects next hereinafter enumerated; that is to say, —

1. Repealed.

1A. The Public Debt and Property.

2. The Regulation of Trade and Commerce.

2A. Unemployment insurance.

3. The raising of Money by any Mode or System of Taxation.

4. The borrowing of Money on the Public Credit.

5. Postal Service.

6. The Census and Statistics.

7. Militia, Military and Naval Service, and Defence.

8. The fixing of and providing for the Salaries and Allowances of Civil and other Officers of the Government of Canada.

9. Beacons, Buoys, Lighthouses, and Sable Island.

10. Navigation and Shipping.

11. Quarantine and the Establishment and Maintenance of Marine Hospitals.

12. Sea Coast and Inland Fisheries.

13. Ferries between a Province and any British or Foreign Country or between Two Provinces.

14. Currency and Coinage.

15. Banking, Incorporation of Banks, and the Issue of Paper Money.

16. Savings Banks.

17. Weights and Measures.

18. Bills of Exchange and Promissory Notes.

19. Interest.

20. Legal Tender.

21. Bankruptcy and Insolvency.

22. Patents of Invention and Discovery.

23. Copyrights.

24. Indians, and Lands reserved for the Indians.

25. Naturalization and Aliens.

26. Marriage and Divorce.

27. The Criminal Law, except the Constitution of Courts of Criminal Jurisdiction, but including the Procedure in Criminal Matters.

28. The Establishment, Maintenance, and Management of Penitentiaries.

29. Such Classes of Subjects as are expressly excepted in the Enumeration of the Classes of Subjects by this Act assigned exclusively to the Legislatures of the Provinces.

And any Matter coming within any of the Classes of Subjects enumerated in this Section shall not be deemed to come within the Class of Matters of a local or private Nature comprised in the Enumeration of the Classes of Subjects by this Act assigned exclusively to the Legislatures of the Provinces.

Exclusive Powers of Provincial Legislatures

Subjects of exclusive Provincial Legislation

92. In each Province the Legislature may exclusively make Laws in relation to Matters coming within the Classes of Subjects next hereinafter enumerated; that is to say, —

1. Repealed.

2. Direct Taxation within the Province in order to the raising of a Revenue for Provincial Purposes.

3. The borrowing of Money on the sole Credit of the Province.

4. The Establishment and Tenure of Provincial Offices and the Appointment and Payment of Provincial Officers.

5. The Management and Sale of the Public Lands belonging to the Province and of the Timber and Wood thereon.

6. The Establishment, Maintenance, and Management of Public and Reformatory Prisons in and for the Province.

7. The Establishment, Maintenance, and Management of Hospitals, Asylums, Charities, and Eleemosynary Institutions in and for the Province, other than Marine Hospitals.

8. Municipal Institutions in the Province.

9. Shop, Saloon, Tavern, Auctioneer, and other Licences in order to the raising of a Revenue for Provincial, Local, or Municipal Purposes.

10. Local Works and Undertakings other than such as are of the following Classes : —

(a) Lines of Steam or other Ships, Railways, Canals, Telegraphs, and other Works and Undertakings connecting the Province with any other or others of the Provinces, or extending beyond the Limits of the Province:

(b) Lines of Steam Ships between the Province and any British or Foreign Country:

(c) Such Works as, although wholly situate within the Province, are before or after their Execution declared by the Parliament of Canada to be for the general Advantage of Canada or for the Advantage of Two or more of the Provinces.

11. The Incorporation of Companies with Provincial Objects.

12. The Solemnization of Marriage in the Province.

13. Property and Civil Rights in the Province.

14. The Administration of Justice in the Province, including the Constitution, Maintenance, and Organization of Provincial Courts, both of Civil and of Criminal Jurisdiction, and including Procedure in Civil Matters in those Courts.

15. The Imposition of Punishment by Fine, Penalty, or Imprisonment for enforcing any Law of the Province made in relation to any Matter coming within any of the Classes of Subjects enumerated in this Section.

16. Generally all Matters of a merely local or private Nature in the Province.

Non-Renewable Natural Resources,
Forestry Resources and Electrical Energy

Laws respecting non-renewable natural resources, forestry resources and electrical energy

92A. (1) In each province, the legislature may exclusively make laws in relation to

(a) exploration for non-renewable natural resources in the province;

(b) development, conservation and management of non-renewable natural resources and forestry resources in the province, including laws in relation to the rate of primary production therefrom; and

(c) development, conservation and management of sites and facilities in the province for the generation and production of electrical energy.

Export from provinces of resources

(2) In each province, the legislature may make laws in relation to the export from the province to another part of Canada of the primary production from non-renewable natural resources and forestry resources in the province and the production from facilities in the province for the generation of electrical energy, but such laws may not authorize or provide for discrimination in prices or in supplies exported to another part of Canada.

Authority of Parliament

(3) Nothing in subsection (2) derogates from the authority of Parliament to enact laws in relation to the matters referred to in that subsection and, where such a law of Parliament and a law of a province conflict, the law of Parliament prevails to the extent of the conflict.

Taxation of resources

(4) In each province, the legislature may make laws in relation to the raising of money by any mode or system of taxation in respect of

(a) non-renewable natural resources and forestry resources in the province and the primary production therefrom, and

(b) sites and facilities in the province for the generation of electrical energy and the production therefrom,

whether or not such production is exported in whole or in part from the province, but such laws may not authorize or provide for taxation that differentiates between production exported to another part of Canada and production not exported from the province.

"Primary production"

(5) The expression "primary production" has the meaning assigned by the Sixth Schedule.

Existing powers or rights

(6) Nothing in subsections (1) to (5) derogates from any powers or rights that a legislature or government of a province had immediately before the coming into force of this section.

Education

Legislation respecting Education

93. In and for each Province the Legislature may exclusively make Laws in relation to Education, subject and according to the following Provisions: —

(1) Nothing in any such Law shall prejudicially affect any Right or Privilege with respect to Denominational Schools which any Class of Persons have by Law in the Province at the Union:

(2) All the Powers, Privileges, and Duties at the Union by Law conferred and imposed in Upper Canada on the Separate Schools and School Trustees of the Queen's Roman Catholic Subjects shall be and the same are hereby extended to the Dissentient Schools of the Queen's Protestant and Roman Catholic Subjects in Quebec:

(3) Where in any Province a System of Separate or Dissentient Schools exists by Law at the Union or is thereafter established by the Legislature of the Province, an Appeal shall lie to the Governor General in Council from any Act or Decision of any Provincial Authority affecting any Right or Privilege of the Protestant or Roman Catholic Minority of the Queen's Subjects in relation to Education:

(4) In case any such Provincial Law as from Time to Time seems to the Governor General in Council requisite for the due Execution of the Provisions of this Section is not made, or in case any Decision of the Governor General in Council on any Appeal under this Section is not duly executed by the proper Provincial Authority in that Behalf, then and in every such Case, and as far only as the Circumstances of each Case require, the Parliament of Canada may make remedial Laws for the due Execution of the Provisions of this Section and of any Decision of the Governor General in Council under this Section.

Uniformity of Laws in Ontario, Nova Scotia and New Brunswick

Legislation for Uniformity of Laws in Three Provinces

94. Notwithstanding anything in this Act, the Parliament of Canada may make Provision for the Uniformity of all or any of the Laws relative to Property and Civil Rights in Ontario, Nova Scotia, and New Brunswick, and of the Procedure of all or any of the Courts in those Three Provinces, and from and after the passing of any Act in that Behalf the Power of the Parliament of Canada to make Laws in relation to any Matter comprised in any such Act shall, notwithstanding anything in this Act, be unrestricted; but any Act of the Parliament of Canada making Provision for such Uniformity shall not have effect in any Province unless and until it is adopted and enacted as Law by the Legislature thereof.

Old Age Pensions

Legislation respecting old age pensions and supplementary benefits

94A. The Parliament of Canada may make laws in relation to old age pensions and supplementary benefits, including survivors' and disability benefits irrespective of age, but no such law shall affect the operation of any law present or future of a provincial legislature in relation to any such matter.

Agriculture and Immigration

Concurrent Powers of Legislation respecting Agriculture, etc.

95. In each Province the Legislature may make Laws in relation to Agriculture in the Province, and to Immigration into the Province; and it is hereby declared that the Parliament of Canada may from Time to Time make Laws in relation to Agriculture in all or any of the Provinces, and to Immigration into all or any of the Provinces; and any Law of the Legislature of a Province relative to Agriculture or to Immigration shall have effect in and for the Province as long and as far only as it is not repugnant to any Act of the Parliament of Canada.

VII. JUDICATURE

Appointment of
Judges

96. The Governor General shall appoint the Judges of the Superior, District, and County Courts in each Province, except those of the Courts of Probate in Nova Scotia and New Brunswick.

Selection of Judges in
Ontario, etc.

97. Until the Laws relative to Property and Civil Rights in Ontario, Nova Scotia, and New Brunswick, and the Procedure of the Courts in those Provinces, are made uniform, the Judges of the Courts of those Provinces appointed by the Governor General shall be selected from the respective Bars of those Provinces.

Selection of Judges in
Quebec

98. The Judges of the Courts of Quebec shall be selected from the Bar of that Province.

Tenure of office of
Judges

99. (1) Subject to subsection two of this section, the Judges of the Superior Courts shall hold office during good behaviour, but shall be removable by the Governor General on Address of the Senate and House of Commons.

Termination at age 75

(2) A Judge of a Superior Court, whether appointed before or after the coming into force of this section, shall cease to hold office upon attaining the age of seventy-five years, or upon the coming into force of this section if at that time he has already attained that age.

Salaries, etc., of
Judges

100. The Salaries, Allowances, and Pensions of the Judges of the Superior, District, and County Courts (except the Courts of Probate in Nova Scotia and New Brunswick), and of the Admiralty Courts in Cases where the Judges thereof are for the Time being paid by Salary, shall be fixed and provided by the Parliament of Canada.

General Court of
Appeal, etc.

101. The Parliament of Canada may, notwithstanding anything in this Act, from Time to Time provide for the Constitution, Maintenance, and Organization of a General Court of Appeal for Canada, and for the Establishment of any additional Courts for the better Administration of the Laws of Canada.

VIII. REVENUES; DEBTS; ASSETS; TAXATION

Creation of
Consolidated
Revenue Fund

102. All Duties and Revenues over which the respective Legislatures of Canada, Nova Scotia, and New Brunswick before and at the Union had and have Power of Appropriation, except such Portions thereof as are by this Act reserved to the respective Legislatures of the Provinces, or are raised by them in accordance with the special Powers conferred on them by this Act, shall form One Consolidated Revenue Fund, to be appropriated for the Public Service of Canada in the Manner and subject to the Charges in this Act provided.

Expenses of
Collection, etc.

103. The Consolidated Revenue Fund of Canada shall be permanently charged with the Costs, Charges, and Expenses incident to the Collections, Management, and Receipt thereof, and the same shall form the First Charge thereon, subject to be reviewed and audited in such Manner as shall be ordered by the Governor General in Council until the Parliament otherwise provides.

Interest of Provincial
Public Debts

104. The annual Interest of the Public Debts of the several Provinces of Canada, Nova Scotia, and New Brunswick at the Union shall form the Second Charge on the Consolidated Revenue of Canada.

Salary of Governor
General

105. Unless altered by the Parliament of Canada, the Salary of the Governor General shall be Ten thousand Pounds Sterling Money of the United Kingdom of Great Britain and Ireland, payable out of the Consolidated Revenue Fund of Canada, and the same shall form the Third Charge thereon.

Appropriation from
Time to Time

106. Subject to the several Payments by this Act charged on the Consolidated Revenue Fund of Canada, the same shall be appropriated by the Parliament of Canada for the Public Service.

Transfer of Stocks,
etc.

107. All Stocks, Cash, Banker's Balances, and Securities for Money belonging to each Province at the Time of the Union, except as in this Act mentioned, shall be the Property of Canada, and shall be taken in Reduction of the Amount of the respective Debts of the Provinces at the Union.

Transfer of Property
in Schedule

108. The Public Works and Property of each Province, enumerated in the Third Schedule to this Act, shall be the Property of Canada.

Property in Lands,
Mines, etc.

109. All Lands, Mines, Minerals, and Royalties belonging to the several Provinces of Canada, Nova Scotia, and New Brunswick at the Union, and all Sums then due or payable for such Lands, Mines, Minerals, or Royalties, shall belong to the several Provinces of Ontario, Quebec, Nova Scotia, and New Brunswick in which the same are situate or arise, subject to any Trusts existing in respect thereof, and to any Interest other than that of the Province in the same.

Assets connected
with Provincial Debts

110. All Assets connected with such Portions of the Public Debt of each Province as are assumed by that Province shall belong to that Province.

Canada to be liable
for Provincial Debts

111. Canada shall be liable for the Debts and Liabilities of each Province existing at the Union.

Debts of Ontario and
Quebec

112. Ontario and Quebec conjointly shall be liable to Canada for the Amount (if any) by which the Debt of the Province of Canada exceeds at the Union Sixty-two million five hundred thousand Dollars, and shall be charged with Interest at the Rate of Five per Centum per Annum thereon.

Assets of Ontario and
Quebec

113. The Assets enumerated in the Fourth Schedule to this Act belonging at the Union to the Province of Canada shall be the Property of Ontario and Quebec conjointly.

Debt of Nova
Scotia

114. Nova Scotia shall be liable to Canada for the Amount (if any) by which its Public Debt exceeds at the Union Eight million Dollars, and shall be charged with Interest at the Rate of Five per Centum per Annum thereon.

Debt of New
Brunswick

115. New Brunswick shall be liable to Canada for the Amount (if any) by which its Public Debt exceeds at the Union Seven million Dollars, and

shall be charged with Interest at the Rate of Five per Centum per Annum thereon.

Payment of interest to Nova Scotia and New Brunswick

116. In case the Public Debts of Nova Scotia and New Brunswick do not at the Union amount to Eight million and Seven million Dollars respectively, they shall respectively receive by half-yearly Payments in advance from the Government of Canada Interest at Five per Centum per Annum on the Difference between the actual Amounts of their respective Debts and such stipulated Amounts.

Provincial Public Property

117. The several Provinces shall retain all their respective Public Property not otherwise disposed of in this Act, subject to the Right of Canada to assume any Lands or Public Property required for Fortifications or for the Defence of the Country.

118. Repealed.

Further Grant to New Brunswick

119. New Brunswick shall receive by half-yearly Payments in advance from Canada for the Period of Ten Years from the Union and additional Allowance of sixty-three thousand Dollars per Annum; but as long as the Public Debt of that Province remains under Seven million Dollars, a Deduction equal to the Interest at Five per Centum per Annum on such Deficiency shall be made from that Allowance of Sixty-three thousand Dollars.

Form of Payments

120. All Payments to be made under this Act, or in discharge of Liabilities created under any Act of the Provinces of Canada, Nova Scotia, and New Brunswick respectively, and assumed by Canada, shall, until the Parliament of Canada otherwise directs, be made in such Form and Manner as may from Time to Time be ordered by the Governor General in Council.

Canadian Manufactures, etc.

121. All Articles of the Growth, Produce, or Manufacture of any one of the Provinces shall, from and after the Union, be admitted free into each of the other Provinces.

Continuance of Customs and Excise Laws

122. The Customs and Excise Laws of each Province shall, subject to the Provisions of this Act, continue in force until altered by the Parliament of Canada. Exportation and

Importation as between Two Provinces

123. Where Customs Duties are, at the Union, leviable on any Goods, Wares, or Merchandises in any Two Provinces, those Goods, Wares, and Merchandises may, from and after the Union, be imported from one of those Provinces into the other of them on Proof of Payment of the Customs Duty leviable thereon in the Province of Exportation, and on Payment of such further Amount (if any) of Customs Duty as is leviable thereon in the Province of Importation.

Lumber Dues in New Brunswick

124. Nothing in this Act shall affect the Right of New Brunswick to levy the Lumber Dues provided in Chapter Fifteen of Title Three of the Revised Statutes of New Brunswick, or in any Act amending that Act before or after the Union, and not increasing the Amount of such Dues; but the Lumber of any of the Provinces other than New Brunswick shall not be subject to such Dues.

Exemption of Public
Lands, etc.

125. No Lands or Property belonging to Canada or any Province shall be liable to Taxation.

Provincial
Consolidated
Revenue Fund

126. Such Portions of the Duties and Revenues over which the respective Legislatures of Canada, Nova Scotia, and New Brunswick had before the Union Power of Appropriation as are by this Act reserved to the respective Governments or Legislatures of the Provinces, and all Duties and Revenues raised by them in accordance with the special Powers conferred upon them by this Act, shall in each Province form One Consolidated Revenue Fund to be appropriated for the Public Service of the Province.

IX. MISCELLANEOUS PROVISIONS

General

127. Repealed.

Oath of
Allegiance, etc.

128. Every Member of the Senate or House of Commons of Canada shall before taking his Seat therein take and subscribe before the Governor General or some Person authorized by him, and every Member of a Legislative Council or Legislative Assembly of any Province shall before taking his Seat therein take and subscribe before the Lieutenant Governor of the Province or some Person authorized by him, the Oath of Allegiance contained in the Fifth Schedule to this Act; and every Member of the Senate of Canada and every Member of the Legislative Council of Quebec shall also, before taking his Seat therein, take and subscribe before the Governor General, or some Person authorized by him, the Declaration of Qualification contained in the same Schedule.

Continuance of
existing Laws,
Courts, Officers, etc.

129. Except as otherwise provided by this Act, all Laws in force in Canada, Nova Scotia, or New Brunswick at the Union, and all Courts of Civil and Criminal Jurisdiction, and all legal Commissions, Powers, and Authorities, and all Officers, Judicial, Administrative, and Ministerial, existing therein at the Union, shall continue in Ontario, Quebec, Nova Scotia, and New Brunswick respectively, as if the Union had not been made; subject nevertheless (except with respect to such as are enacted by or exist under Acts of the Parliament of Great Britain or of the Parliament of the United Kingdom of Great Britain and Ireland), to be repealed, abolished, or altered by the Parliament of Canada, or by the Legislature of the respective Province, according to the Authority of the Parliament or of that Legislature under this Act.

Transfer of
Officers to Canada

130. Until the Parliament of Canada otherwise provides, all Officers of the several Provinces having Duties to discharge in relation to Matters other than those coming within the Classes of Subjects by this Act assigned exclusively to the Legislatures of the Provinces shall be Officers of Canada, and shall continue to discharge the Duties of their respective Offices under the same Liabilities, Responsibilities, and Penalties as if the Union had not been made.

Appointment of new Officers

131. Until the Parliament of Canada otherwise provides, the Governor General in Council may from Time to Time appoint such Officers as the Governor General in Council deems necessary or proper for the effectual Execution of this Act.

Treaty Obligations

132. The Parliament and Government of Canada shall have all Powers necessary or proper for performing the Obligations of Canada or of any Province thereof, as Part of the British Empire, towards Foreign Countries, arising under Treaties between the Empire and such Foreign Countries.

Use of English and French Languages

133. Either the English or the French Language may be used by any Person in the Debates of the Houses of the Parliament of Canada and of the Houses of the Legislature of Quebec; and both those Languages shall be used in the respective Records and Journals of those Houses; and either of those Languages may be used by any Person or in any Pleading or Process in or issuing from any Court of Canada established under this Act, and in or from all or any of the Courts of Quebec.

The Acts of the Parliament of Canada and of the Legislature of Quebec shall be printed and published in both those Languages.

{Note: Similar provisions were enacted by Section 33 of the **Manitoba Act, 1870** and also by Sections 17 to 19 of the **Constitution Act, 1982** in respect of the Legislature and the courts of New Brunswick}.

Ontario and Quebec

Appointment of Executive Officers for Ontario and Quebec

134. Until the Legislature of Ontario or of Quebec otherwise provides, the Lieutenant Governors of Ontario and Quebec may each appoint under the Great Seal of the Province the following Officers, to hold Office during Pleasure, that is to say, — the Attorney General, the Secretary and Registrar of the Province, the Treasurer of the Province, the Commissioner of Crown Lands, and the Commissioner of Agriculture and Public Works, and in the Case of Quebec the Solicitor General, and may, by Order of the Lieutenant Governor in Council, from Time to Time prescribe the Duties of those Officers, and of the several Departments over which they shall preside or to which they shall belong, and of the Officers and Clerks thereof, and may also appoint other and additional Officers to hold Office during Pleasure, and may from Time to Time prescribe the Duties of those Officers, and of the several Departments over which they shall preside or to which they shall belong, and of the Officers and Clerks thereof.

Powers, Duties, etc. of Executive Officers

135. Until the Legislature of Ontario or Quebec otherwise provides, all Rights, Powers, Duties, Functions, Responsibilities, or Authorities at the passing of this Act vested in or imposed on the Attorney General, Solicitor General, Secretary and Registrar of the Province of Canada, Minister of Finance, Commissioner of Crown Lands, Commissioner of Public Works, and Minister of Agriculture and Receiver General, by any Law, Statute, or Ordinance of Upper Canada, Lower Canada, or Canada, and not repugnant to this Act, shall be vested in or imposed on any Officer

to be appointed by the Lieutenant Governor for the Discharge of the same or any of them; and the Commissioner of Agriculture and Public Works shall perform the Duties and Functions of the Office of Minister of Agriculture at the passing of this Act imposed by the Law of the Province of Canada, as well as those of the Commissioner of Public Works.

Great Seals

136. Until altered by the Lieutenant Governor in Council, the Great Seals of Ontario and Quebec respectively shall be the same, or of the same Design, as those used in the Provinces of Upper Canada and Lower Canada respectively before their Union as the Province of Canada.

Construction of temporary Acts

137. The words "and from thence to the End of the then next ensuing Session of the Legislature," or Words to the same Effect, used in any temporary Act of the Province of Canada not expired before the Union, shall be construed to extend and apply to the next Session of the Parliament of Canada if the Subject Matter of the Act is within the Powers of the same as defined by this Act, or to the next Sessions of the Legislatures of Ontario and Quebec respectively if the Subject Matter of the Act is within the Powers of the same as defined by this Act.

As to Errors in Names

138. From and after the Union the Use of the Words "Upper Canada" instead of "Ontario," or "Lower Canada" instead of "Quebec," in any Deed, Writ, Process, Pleading, Document, Matter, or Thing shall not invalidate the same.

As to issue of Proclamations before Union, to commence after Union

139. Any Proclamation under the Great Seal of the Province of Canada issued before the Union to take effect at a Time which is subsequent to the Union, whether relating to that Province, or to Upper Canada, or to Lower Canada, and the several Matters and Things therein proclaimed, shall be and continue of like Force and Effect as if the Union had not been made.

As to issue of Proclamations after Union

140. Any Proclamation which is authorized by any Act of the Legislature of the Province of Canada to be issued under the Great Seal of the Province of Canada, whether relating to that Province, or to Upper Canada, or to Lower Canada, and which is not issued before the Union, may be issued by the Lieutenant Governor of Ontario or of Quebec, as its Subject Matter requires, under the Great Seal thereof; and from and after the Issue of such Proclamation the same and the several Matters and Things therein proclaimed shall be and continue of the like Force and Effect in Ontario or Quebec as if the Union had not been made.

Penitentiary

141. The Penitentiary of the Province of Canada shall, until the Parliament of Canada otherwise provides, be and continue the Penitentiary of Ontario and of Quebec.

Arbitration respecting Debts, etc.

142. The Division and Adjustment of the Debts, Credits, Liabilities, Properties, and Assets of Upper Canada and Lower Canada shall be referred to the Arbitrament of Three Arbitrators, One chosen by the Government of Ontario, One by the Government of Quebec, and One by the Government of Canada; and the Selection of the Arbitrators shall not be made until the Parliament of Canada and the Legislatures of Ontario

and Quebec have met; and the Arbitrator chosen by the Government of Canada shall not be a Resident either in Ontario or in Quebec.

Division of
Records

143. The Governor General in Council may from Time to Time order that such and so many of the Records, Books, and Documents of the Province of Canada as he thinks fit shall be appropriated and delivered either to Ontario or to Quebec, and the same shall thenceforth be the Property of that Province; and any Copy thereof or Extract therefrom, duly certified by the Officer having charge of the Original thereof, shall be admitted as Evidence.

Constitution of
Townships in Quebec

144. The Lieutenant Governor of Quebec may from Time to Time, by Proclamation under the Great Seal of the Province, to take effect from a Day to be appointed therein, constitute Townships in those Parts of the Province of Quebec in which Townships are not then already constituted, and fix the Metes and Bounds thereof.

X. INTERCOLONIAL RAILWAY

145. Repealed.

XI. ADMISSION OF OTHER COLONIES

Power to admit
Newfoundland, etc.,
into the Union

146. It shall be lawful for the Queen, by and with the Advice of Her Majesty's Most Honourable Privy Council, on Addresses from the Houses of the Parliament of Canada, and from the Houses of the respective Legislatures of the Colonies or Provinces of Newfoundland, Prince Edward Island, and British Columbia, to admit those Colonies or Provinces, or any of them, into the Union, and on Address from the Houses of the Parliament of Canada to admit Rupert's Land and the North-western Territory, or either of them, into the Union, on such Terms and Conditions in each Case as are in the Addresses expressed and as the Queen thinks fit to approve, subject to the Provisions of this Act; and the Provisions of any Order in Council in that Behalf shall have effect as if they had been enacted by the Parliament of the United Kingdom of Great Britain and Ireland.

As to Representation
of Newfoundland and
Prince Edward Island
in Senate

147. In case of the Admission of Newfoundland and Prince Edward Island, or either of them, each shall be entitled to a Representation in the Senate of Canada of Four Members, and (notwithstanding anything in this Act) in case of the Admission of Newfoundland the normal Number of Senators shall be Seventy-six and their maximum Number shall be Eighty-two; but Prince Edward Island when admitted shall be deemed to be comprised in the third of the Three Division into which Canada is, in relation to the Constitution of the Senate, divided by this Act, and accordingly, after the Admission of Prince Edward Island, whether Newfoundland is admitted or not, the Representation of Nova Scotia and New Brunswick in the Senate shall, as Vacancies occur, be reduced from Twelve to Ten Members respectively, and the Representation of each of those Provinces shall not be increased at any Time beyond Ten, except under the Provisions of this Act for the Appointment of Three or Six additional Senators under the Direction of the Queen.

SCHEDULES

THE FIRST SCHEDULE

Electoral Districts of Ontario

A.
EXISTING ELECTORAL DIVISIONS

COUNTIES

1.	Prescott.	6.	Carleton.
2.	Glengarry.	7.	Prince Edward.
3.	Stormont.	8.	Halton.
4.	Dundas.	9.	Essex.
5.	Russell.		

RIDINGS OF COUNTIES

10. North Riding of Lanark.
11. South Riding of Lanark.
12. North Riding of Leeds and North Riding of Grenville.
13. South Riding of Leeds.
14. South Riding of Grenville.
15. East Riding of Northumberland.
16. West Riding of Northumberland (excepting therefrom the Township of South Monaghan).
17. East Riding of Durham.
18. West Riding of Durham.
19. North Riding of Ontario.
20. South Riding of Ontario.
21. East Riding of York.
22. West Riding of York.
23. North Riding of York.
24. North Riding of Wentworth.
25. South Riding of Wentworth.
26. East Riding of Elgin.
27. West Riding of Elgin.
28. North Riding of Waterloo.
29. South Riding of Waterloo.
30. North Riding of Brant.
31. South Riding of Brant.
32. North Riding of Oxford.
33. South Riding of Oxford.
34. East Riding of Middlesex.

CITIES, PARTS OF CITIES, AND TOWNS

35. West Toronto.
36. East Toronto.
37. Hamilton.
38. Ottawa.
39. Kingston.
40. London.
41. Town of Brockville, with the Township of Elizabethtown thereto attached.
42. Town of Niagara, with the Township of Niagara thereto attached.
43. Town of Cornwall, with the Township of Cornwall thereto attached.

B.
NEW ELECTORAL DIVISIONS

44. The Provisional Judicial District of ALGOMA.

The County of BRUCE, divided into Two ridings, to be called respectively the North and South Ridings: —

45. The North Riding of Bruce to consist of the Townships of Bury, Lindsay, Eastnor, Albermarle, Amable, Arran, Bruce, Elderslie, and Saugeen, and the Village of Southampton.

46. The South Riding of Bruce to consist of the Townships of Kincardine (including the Village of Kincardine), Greenock, Brant, Huron, Kinloss, Culross, and Carrick.

The County of HURON, divided into Two Ridings, to be called respectively the North and South Ridings: —

47. The North Riding to consist of the Townships of Ashfield, Wawanosh, Turnberry, Howick, Morris, Grey, Colborne, Hullett, including the Village of Clinton, and McKillop.

48. The South Riding to consist of the Town of Goderich and the Townships of Goderich, Tuckersmith, Stanley, Hay, Usborne, and Stephen.

The County of MIDDLESEX, divided into three Ridings, to be called respectively the North, West, and East Ridings: —

49. The North Riding to consist of the Townships of McGillivray and Biddulph (taken from the County of Huron), and Williams East, Williams West, Adelaide, and Lobo.

50. The West Riding to consist of the Townships of Delaware, Carradoc, Metcalfe, Mosa and Ekfrid, and the Village of Strathroy.

(The East Riding to consist of the Townships now embraced therein, and be bounded as it is at present.)

51. The County of LAMBTON to consist of the Townships of Bosanquet, Warwick, Plympton, Sarnia, Moore, Enniskillen, and Brooke, and the Town of Sarnia.

52. The County of KENT to consist of the Townships of Chatham, Dover, East Tilbury, Romney, Raleigh, and Harwich, and the Town of Chatham.

53. The County of BOTHWELL to consist of the Townships of Sombra, Dawn, and Eupehmia (taken from the County of Lambton), and the Townships of Zone, Camden with the Gore thereof, Orford, and Howard (taken from the County of Kent).

The County of GREY divided in Two Ridings to be called respectively South and North Ridings: —

54. The South Riding to consist of the Townships of Bentick, Glenelg, Artemesia, Osprey, Normanby, Egremont, Proton, and Melancthon.

55. The North Riding to consist of the Townships of Collingwood, Euphrasia, Holland, Saint-Vincent, Sydenham, Sullivan, Derby, and Keppel, Sarawak and Brooke, and the Town of Owen Sound.

The County of PERTH divided into Two Ridings, to be called respectively the South and North Ridings: —

56. The North Riding to consist of the Townships of Wallace, Elma, Logan, Ellice, Morning-ton, and North Easthope, and the Town of Stratford.

57. The South Riding to consist of the Townships of Blanchard, Downie, South Easthope, Fullarton, Hibbert, and the Villages of Mitchell and Ste. Marys.

The County of WELLINGTON divided into Three Ridings to be called respectively North, South and Centre Ridings: —

58. The North Riding to consist of the Townships of Amaranth, Arthur, Luther, Minto, Maryborough, Peel, and the Village of Mount Forest.

59. The Centre Riding to consist of the Townships of Garafraxa, Erin, Eramosa, Nichol, and Pilkington, and the Villages of Fergus and Elora.

60. The South Riding to consist of the Town of Guelph, and the Townships of Guelph and Puslinch.

The County of NORFOLK, divided into Two Ridings, to be called respectively the South and North Ridings: —

61. The South Riding to consist of the Townships of Charlotteville, Houghton, Walsingham, and Woodhouse, and with the Gore thereof.

62. The North Riding to consist of the Townships of Middleton, Townsend, and Windham, and the Town of Simcoe.

63. The County of HALDIMAND to consist of the Townships of Oneida, Seneca, Cayuga North, Cayuga South, Raynham, Walpole, and Dunn.

64. The County of MONCK to consist of the Townships of Canborough and Moulton, and Sherbrooke, and the Village of Dunnville (taken from the County of Haldimand), the Townships of Caister and Gainsborough (taken from the County of Lincoln), and the Townships of Pelham and Wainfleet (taken from the County of Welland).

65. The County of LINCOLN to consist of the Townships of Clinton, Grantham, Grimsby, and Louth, and the Town of St. Catherines.

66. The County of WELLAND to consist of the Townships of Berti, Crowland, Humberstone, Stamford, Thorold, and Willoughby, and the Villages of Chippewa, Clifton, Fort Erie, Thorold, and Welland.

67. The County of PEEL to consist of the Townships of Chinguacousy, Toronto, and the Gore of Toronto, and the Villages of Brampton and Streetsville.

68. The County of CARDWELL to consist of the Townships of Albion and Caledon (taken from the County of Peel), and the Townships of Adjala and Mono (taken from the County of Simcoe).

The County of SIMCOE, divided into Two Ridings, to be called respectively the South and North Ridings: —

69. The South Riding to consist of the Townships of West Gwillimbury, Tecumseth, Innisfil, Essa, Tosorontio, Mulmur, and the Village of Bradford.

70.   The North Riding to consist of the Townships of Nottawasaga, Sunnidale, Vespra, Flos, Oro, Medonte, Orillia and Matchedash, Tiny and Tay, Balaklava and Robinson, and the Towns of Barrie and Collingwood.

The County of VICTORIA, divided into Two Ridings, to be called respectively the South and North Ridings: —

71.   The South Riding to consist of the Townships of Ops, Mariposa, Emily, Verulam, and the Town of Lindsay.

72.   The North Riding to consist of the Townships of Anson, Bexley, Carden, Dalton, Digby, Eldon, Fenelon, Hindon, Laxton, Lutterworth, Macaulay and Draper, Sommerville, and Morrison, Muskoka, Monck and Watt (taken from the County of Simcoe), and any other surveyed Townships lying to the North of the said North Riding.

The County of PETERBOROUGH, divided into Two Ridings, to be called respectively the West and East Ridings: —

73.   The West Riding to consist of the Townships of South Monaghan (taken from the County of Northumberland), North Monaghan, Smith, and Ennismore, and the Town of Peterborough.

74.   The East Riding to consist of the Townships of Asphodel, Belmont and Methuen, Douro, Dummer, Galway, Harvey, Minden, Stanhope and Dysart, Otonabee, and Snowden, and the Village of Ashburnham, and any other surveyed Townships lying to the North of the said East Riding.

The County of HASTINGS, divided into Three Ridings, to be called respectively the West, East, and North Ridings: —

75.   The West Riding to consist of the Town of Belleville, the Township of Sydney, and the Village of Trenton.

76.   The East Riding to consist of the Townships of Thurlow, Tyendinaga, and Hungerford.

77.   The North Riding to consist of the Townships of Rawdon, Huntingdon, Madoc, Elzevir, Tudor, Marmora, and Lake, and the Village of Stirling, and any other surveyed Townships lying to the North of the said North Riding.

78.   The County of LENNOX to consist of the Townships of Richmond, Adolphustown, North Fredericksburg, South Fredericksburg, Ernest Town, and Amherst Island, and the Village of Napanee.

79.   The County of ADDINGTON to consist of the Townships of Camden, Portland, Sheffield, Hinchinbrooke, Kaladar, Kennebec, Olden, Oso, Anglesea, Barrie, Clarendon, Parmerston, Effingham, Abinger, Miller, Canonto, Denbigh, Loughborough, and Bedford.

80.   The County of FRONTENAC to consist of the Townships of Kingston, Wolfe Island, Pittsburg and Howe Island, and Storrington.

The County of RENFREW, divided into Two Ridings, to be called respectively the South and North Ridings: —

81.   The South Riding to consist of the Townships of McNab, Bagot, Blithfield, Brougham, Horton, Admaston, Grattan, Matawatchan, Griffith, Lyndoch, Raglan, Radcliffe, Brudenell, Sebastopol, and the Villages of Arnprior and Renfrew.

82.   The North Riding to consist of the Townships of Ross, Bromley, Westmeath, Stafford, Pembroke, Wilberforce, Alice, Petawawa, Buchanan, South Algona, North Algona, Fraser, McKay, Wylie, Rolph, Head, Maria, Clara, Haggerty, Sherwood, Burns, and Richards, and any other surveyed Townships lying North-westerly of the said North Riding.

Every Town and incorporated Village existing at the Union, not especially mentioned in this Schedule, is to be taken as Part of the County or Riding within which it is locally situate.

THE SECOND SCHEDULE

Electoral Districts of Quebec specially fixed

COUNTIES OF —

Pontiac.	Missisquoi.	Compton.
Ottawa.	Brome.	Wolfe
Argenteuil.	Shefford.	and Richmond.
Huntingdon.	Stanstead.	Megantic.
	Town of Sherbrooke.	

THE THIRD SCHEDULE

Provincial Public Works and Property to be the Property of Canada

1. Canals, with Lands and Water Power connected therewith.
2. Public Harbours.
3. Lighthouses and Piers, and Sable Island.
4. Steamboats, Dredges, and public Vessels.
5. Rivers and Lake Improvements.
6. Railways and Railway Stocks, Mortgages, and other Debts due by Railway Companies.
7. Military Roads.
8. Custom Houses, Post Offices, and all other Public Buildings, except such as the Government of Canada appropriate for the Use of the Provincial Legislatures and Governments.
9. Property transferred by the Imperial Government, and known as Ordnance Property.
10. Armouries, Drill Sheds, Military Clothing, and Munitions of War, and Lands set apart for general Public Purposes.

THE FOURTH SCHEDULE

Assets to be the Property of Ontario and Quebec conjointly

Upper Canada Building Fund.
Lunatic Asylums.
Normal School.
Court Houses in |
Aylmer | Lower Canada
Montreal |
Kamouraska. |
Law Society, Upper Canada.
Montreal Turnpike Trust.
University Permanent Fund.
Royal Institution.
Consolidated Municipal Loan Fund, Upper Canada.
Consolidated Municipal Loan Fund, Lower Canada.
Agricultural Society, Upper Canada.
Lower Canada Legislative Grant.
Quebec Fire Loan.
Temiscouata Advance Account.
Quebec Turnpike Trust.
Education — East.
Building and Jury Fund, Lower Canada.
Municipalities Fund.
Lower Canada Superior Education Income Fund.

THE FIFTH SCHEDULE

OATH OF ALLEGIANCE

I A.B. do swear, That I will be faithful and bear true Allegiance to Her Majesty Queen Victoria.

Note. — The Name of the King or Queen of the United Kingdom of Great Britain and Ireland for the Time being is to be substituted from Time to Time, with proper Terms of Reference thereto.

DECLARATION OF QUALIFICATION

I A.B. do declare and testify, That I am by Law duly qualified to be appointed a Member of the Senate of Canada (*or as the Case may be*), and that I am legally or equitably seised as of Freehold for my own Use and Benefit of Lands or Tenements held in Free and Common

Socage (*or* seised or possessed for my own Use and Benefit of Lands or Tenements held in Franc-alleu or in Roture (*as the Case may be*),) in the Province of Nova Scotia (*or as the Case may be*) of the Value of Four thousand Dollars over and above all Rents, Dues, Debts, Mortgages, Charges, and Incumbrances due or payable out of or charged on or affecting the same, and that I have not collusively or colourably obtained a Title to or become possessed of the said Lands and Tenements or any Part thereof for the Purpose of enabling me to become a Member of the Senate of Canada (*or as the Case may Be*), and that my Real and Personal Property are together worth Four thousand Dollars over and above my Debts and Liabilities.

THE SIXTH SCHEDULE

Primary Production from Non-Renewable Natural Resources and Forestry Resources

1. For the purposes of Section 92A of this Act,

    (a) production from a non-renewable natural resource is primary production therefrom if

    (i) it is in the form in which it exists upon its recovery or severance from its natural state, or

    (ii) it is a product resulting from processing or refining the resource, and is not a manufactured product or a product resulting from refining crude oil, refining upgraded heavy crude oil, refining gases or liquids derived from coal or refining a synthetic equivalent of crude oil; and

    (b) production from a forestry resource is primary production therefrom if it consists of sawlogs, poles, lumber, wood chips, sawdust or any other primary wood product, or wood pulp, and is not a product manufactured from wood.

    {Note: Some of the following sections are now spent and others are now covered by other legislation: 40, 41, 47, 50, 63, 70, 71, 80, 83 to 85, 105, 109, 114, 119, 122 to 124, 129, 130, 134, 135, 139 to 143, 146, 147 and The First Schedule}.

RUPERT'S LAND ACT, 1868

31-32 Victoria, c. 105 (U.K.)

An Act for enabling Her Majesty to accept a Surrender upon Terms of the Lands, Privileges, and Rights of "The Governor and Company of Adventurers of England trading into Hudson's Bay,"and for admitting the same into the Dominion of Canada

{31st July, 1868}

Recital of Charter of Hudson's Bay Company, 22 Cap. 2

Whereas by certain Letters Patent granted by His late Majesty King Charles the Second in the Twenty-second Year of His Reign certain Persons therein named were incorporated by the Name of "The Governor and Company of Adventurers of England trading into Hudson's Bay," and certain Lands and Territories, Rights of Government, and other Rights, Privileges, Liberties, Franchises, Posers, and Authorities, were thereby granted or purported to be granted to the said Governor and Company in His Majesty's Dominions in North America:

And whereas by the Constitution Act, 1867, it was (amongst other things) enacted that it should be lawful for Her Majesty, by and with the Advice of Her Majesty's most Honourable Privy Council, on Address from the Houses of the Parliament of Canada, to admit Rupert's Land and the North-Western Territory, or either of them, into the Union on such Terms and Conditions as are in the Address expressed and as Her Majesty thinks fit to approve, subject to the provisions of the said Act:

Recital of Agreement of Surrender

And whereas for the Purpose of carrying into effect the Provisions of the said Constitution Act, 1867, and of admitting Rupert's Land into the said Dominion as aforesaid upon such Terms as Her Majesty thinks fit to approve, it is expedient that the said Lands, Territories, Rights, Privileges, Liberties, Franchises, Powers, and Authorities, so far as the same have been lawfully granted to the said Company, should be surrendered to Her Majesty, Her Heirs and Successors, upon such Terms and Conditions as may be agreed upon by and between Her Majesty and the said Governor and Company as hereinafter mentioned:

Be it therefore enacted by the Queen's most Excellent Majesty, by and with the Advice and Consent of the Lords Spiritual and Temporal, and Commons, in this present Parliament assembled, and by the Authority of the same, as follows:

Short Title

1. This Act may be cited as "Rupert's Land Act, 1868."

Definition of
"Rupert's Land"

2. For the Purposes of this Act the Term " Rupert's Land " shall include the whole of the Lands and Territories held or claimed to be held by the said Governor and Company.

Power to Her Majesty
to accept Surrender
of Lands, etc., of the
Company upon
certain Terms

3. It shall be competent for the said Governor and Company to surrender to Her Majesty, and for Her Majesty by any Instrument under Her Sign Manual and Signet to accept a Surrender of all or any of the Lands, Territories, Rights, Privileges, Liberties, Franchises, Powers, and Authorities whatsoever granted or purported to be granted by the said Letters of Patent to the said Governor and Company within Rupert's Land, upon such Terms and Conditions as shall be agreed upon by and between Her Majesty and the said Governor and Company; provided, however, that such Surrender shall not be accepted by Her Majesty until the Terms and Conditions upon which Rupert's Land shall be admitted into the said Dominion of Canada shall have been approved of by Her Majesty, and embodied in an Address to Her Majesty from both the Houses of the Parliament of Canada in pursuance of the One hundred and forty-sixth Section of the Constitution Act, 1867; and that the said Surrender and Acceptance thereof shall be null and void unless within a Month from the Date of Such Acceptance Her Majesty does by Order in Council under the Provisions of the said last recited Act admit Rupert's Land into the said Dominion; provided further, that no Charge shall be imposed by such Terms upon the Consolidated Fund of the United Kingdom.

Extinguishment of all
Rights of the
Company

4. Upon the Acceptance by Her Majesty of such Surrender all Rights of Government and Proprietary Rights, and all other Privileges, Liberties, Franchises, Powers, and Authorities whatsoever, granted or purported to be granted by the said Letters Patent to the said Governor and Company within Rupert's Land, and which shall have been so surrendered, shall be absolutely extinguished; provided that nothing herein contained shall prevent the said Governor and Company from continuing to carry on in Rupert's Land or elsewhere Trade and Commerce.

Power to Her Majesty
by Order in Council
to admit Rupert's
Land into and form
Part of the Dominion
of Canada

Jurisdiction of
present Courts and
Officers continued

5. It shall be competent to Her Majesty by any such Order or Orders in Council as aforesaid, on Address from the Houses of the Parliament of Canada, to declare that Rupert's Land shall, from a Date to be therein mentioned, be admitted into and become Part of the Dominion of Canada; and thereupon it shall be lawful for the Parliament of Canada from the Date aforesaid to make, ordain, and establish within the Land and Territory so admitted as aforesaid all such Laws, Institutions, and Ordinances, and to constitute such Courts and Officers as may be necessary for the Peace, Order, and good Government of Her Majesty's Subjects and others therein: Provided that, until otherwise enacted by the said Parliament of Canada, all the Powers, Authorities, and Jurisdiction of the several Courts of Justice now established in Rupert's Land, and of the several Officers thereof, and of all Magistrates and Justices now acting within the said Limits, shall continue in full force and effect therein.

MANITOBA ACT, 1870

33 Victoria, c. 3 (Canada)

*(An Act to amend and continue the Act 32 and 33 Victoria, chapter 3;
and to establish and provide for the Government of the Province
of Manitoba)*

{ Note: The long title was repealed and "Manitoba Act, 1870" substituted
by the **Constitution Act, 1982** }

{ Assented to 12th May, 1870 }

Preamble

Whereas it is probable that Her Majesty The Queen may, pursuant to the Constitution Act, 1867, be pleased to admit Rupert's Land and the North-Western Territory into the Union or Dominion of Canada, before the next Session of the Parliament of Canada:

And Whereas it is expedient to prepare for the transfer of the said Territories to the Government of Canada at the time appointed by the Queen for such admission:

And Whereas it is expedient also to provide for the organization of part of the said Territories as a Province, and for the establishment of a Government therefor, and to make provision for the Civil Government of the remaining part of the said Territories, not included within the limits of the Province:

Therefore Her Majesty, by and with the advice and consent of the Senate and House of Commons of Canada, enacts as follows:

Province to be
formed out of N.W.
territory when united
to Canada

Its name and
boundaries

1. On, from and after the day upon which the Queen, by and with the advice and consent of Her Majesty's Most Honorable Privy Council, under the authority of the 146th Section of the Constitution Act, 1867, shall, by Order in Council in that behalf, admit Rupert's Land and the North-Western Territory into the Union or Dominion of Canada, there shall be formed out of the same a Province, which shall be one of the Provinces of the Dominion of Canada, and which shall be called the Province of Manitoba, and be bounded as follows: that is to say, commencing at the point where the meridian of ninety-six degrees west longitude from greenwich intersects the parallel of forty-nine degrees north latitude, — thence due west along the said parallel of forty-nine degrees north latitude (which forms a portion of the boundary line between the United States of America and the said North-Western Territory) to the meridian of ninety-nine degrees west longitude, to the intersection of the same with the parallel of fifty degrees and thirty minutes north latitude, — thence due east along the said parallel of fifty degrees and thirty minutes north latitude to its intersection with the

before-mentioned meridian of ninety-six degrees west longitude, — thence due south along the said meridian of ninety-six degrees west longitude to the place of beginning.

Certain provisions of Constitution Act, 1867, to apply to Manitoba

2. On, from and after the said day on which the Order of the Queen in Council shall take effect as aforesaid, the provisions of the Constitution Act, 1867, shall, except those parts thereof which are in terms made, or, by reasonable intendment, may be held to be specially applicable to, or only to affect one or more, but not the whole of the Provinces now composing the Dominion, and except so far as the same may be varied by this Act, be applicable to the Province of Manitoba, in the same way, and to the like extent as they apply to the several Provinces of Canada, and as if the Province of Manitoba had been one of the Provinces originally united by the said Act.

Representation in the Senate

3. The said Province shall be represented in the Senate of Canada by two Members, until it shall have, according to decennial census, a population of fifty thousand souls, and from thenceforth it shall be represented therein by three Members, until it shall have, according to decennial census, population of seventy-five thousand souls, and from thenceforth it shall be represented therein by four Members.

Representation in the House of Commons

4. The said Province shall be represented, in the first instance, in the House of Commons of Canada, by four Members, and for that purpose shall be divided by proclamation of the Governor General, into four Electoral Districts, each of which shall be represented by one Member: Provided that on the completion of the census in the year 1881, and of each decennial census afterwards, the representation of the said Province shall be re-adjusted according to the provisions of the fifty-first section of the Constitution Act, 1867.

Qualification of voters and members

5. Until the Parliament of Canada otherwise provides, the qualification of voters at Elections of Members of the House of Commons shall be the same as for the Legislative Assembly hereinafter mentioned: And no person shall be qualified to be elected, or to sit and vote as a Member for any Electoral District, unless he is a duly qualified voter within the said Province.

Lieutenant-Governor

6. For the said Province there shall be an officer styled the Lieutenant-Governor, appointed by the Governor General in Council, by instrument under the Great Seal of Canada.

Executive Council

7. The Executive Council of the Province shall be composed of such persons, and under such designations, as the Lieutenant-Governor shall, from time to time, think fit; and, in the first instance, of not more than five persons.

Seat of Government

8. Unless and until the Executive Government of the Province otherwise directs, the seat of Government of the same shall be at Fort Garry, or within one mile thereof.

Legislature

9. There shall be a Legislature for the Province, consisting of the Lieutenant-Governor, and of two Houses, styled respectively, the Legislative Council of Manitoba, and the Legislative Assembly of Manitoba.

Legislative Council

10. The Legislative Council shall, in the first instance, be composed of seven Members, and after the expiration of four years from the time of the first appointment of such seven Members, may be increased to not more than twelve Members. Every Member of the Legislative Council shall be appointed by the Lieutenant-Governor in the Queen's name, by Instrument under the Great Seal of Manitoba, and shall hold office for the term of his life, unless and until the Legislature of Manitoba otherwise provides under the Constitution Act, 1867.

Speaker

11. The Lieutenant-Governor may, from time to time, by Instrument under the Great Seal, appoint a Member of the Legislative Council to be Speaker thereof, and may remove him and appoint another in his stead.

Quorum

12. Until the Legislature of the Province otherwise provides, the presence of a majority of the whole number of the Legislative Council, including the Speaker, shall be necessary to constitute a meeting for the exercise of its powers.

Voting

13. Questions arising in the Legislative Council shall be decided by a majority of voices, and the Speaker shall, in all cases, have a vote, and whenEquality of votesthe voices are equal the decision shall be deemed to be in the negative.

Legislative Assembly

14. The Legislative Assembly shall be composed of twenty-four Members, to be elected to represent the Electoral Divisions into which the said Province may be divided by the Lieutenant-Governor, as hereinafter mentioned.

Quorum

15. The presence of a majority of the Members of the Legislative Assembly shall be necessary to constitute a meeting of the House for the exercise of its powers; and for that purpose the Speaker shall be reckoned as a Member.

Electoral Divisions

16. The Lieutenant-Governor shall (within six months of the date of the Rupert's Land and North-Western Territory Order), by Proclamation under the Great Seal, divide the said Province into twenty-four Electoral Divisions, due regard being had to existing Local Divisions and population.

Qualification of voters

17. Every male person shall be entitled to vote for a Member to serve in the Legislative Assembly for any Electoral Division, who is qualified as follows, that is to say, if he is : —

1. Of the full age of twenty-one years, and not subject to any legal incapacity :

2. A subject of Her Majesty by birth or naturalization :

3. And a *bona fide* householder within the Electoral Division, at the date of the Writ of Election for the same, and has been a *bona fide* householder for one year next before the said date; or,

Special, — for first
election only

4. If, being of the full age of twenty-one years, and not subject to any legal Incapacity, and a subject of Her Majesty by birth or naturalization, he was, at any time within twelve months prior to the passing of this Act, and (though in the interim temporarily absent) is at the time of such election a *bona fide* householder, and was resident within the Electoral Division at the date of the Writ of Election for the same:

Proviso

But this fourth sub-section shall apply only to the first election to be held under this Act for Members to serve in the Legislative Assembly aforesaid.

Proceedings at first
election, etc., — how
regulated

18. For the first election of Members to serve in the Legislative Assembly, and until the Legislature of the Province otherwise provides, the Lieutenant-Governor shall cause writs to be issued, by such person, in such form, and addressed to such Returning Officers as he thinks fit; and for such first election, and until the Legislature of the Province otherwise provides, the Lieutenant-Governor shall, by Proclamation, prescribe and declare the oaths to be taken by voters, the powers and duties of Returning and Deputy Returning Officers, the proceedings to be observed at such elections, and the period during which such election may be continued, and such other provisions in respect to such first election as he may think fit.

Duration of
Legislative Assembly

19. Every Legislative Assembly shall continue for four years from the date of the return of the writs for returning the same (subject nevertheless to being sooner dissolved by the Lieutenant-Governor), and no longer; and the first Session thereof shall be called at such time as the Lieutenant-Governor shall appoint.

*Sessions at least once
a year*

20. There shall be a Session of the Legislature once at least in every year, so that twelve months shall not intervene between the last sitting of the Legislature in one Session and its first sitting in the next Session.

{ Note: Repealed by the **Constitution Act, 1982** }

Certain provisions of
Constitution Act,
1867, to apply

21. The following provisions of the Constitution Act, 1867, respecting the House of Commons of Canada, shall extend and apply to the Legislative Assembly, that is to say: — Provisions relating to the election of a Speaker, originally, and on vacancies, — the duties of the Speaker, — the absence of the Speaker and the mode of voting, as if those provisions were here re-enacted and made applicable in terms to the Legislative Assembly.

Legislation touching
schools subject to
certain provisions

22. In and for the Province, the said Legislature may exclusively make Laws in relation to Education, subject and according to the following provisions: —

(1) Nothing in any such Law shall prejudicially affect any right or privilege with respect to Denominational Schools which any class of persons have by Law or practice in the Province at the Union: —

(2) An appeal shall lie to the Governor General in Council from any Act or decision of the Legislature of the Province, or of any Provincial Authority, affecting any right or privilege of the Protestant or Roman Catholic minority of the Queen's subjects in relation to Education:

Power reserved to Parliament

(3) In case any such Provincial Law, as from time to time seems to the Governor General in Council requisite for the due execution of the provisions of this section, is not made, or in case any decision of the Governor General in Council on any appeal under this section is not duly executed by the proper Provincial Authority in that behalf, then, and in every such case, and as far only as the circumstances of each case require, the Parliament of Canada may make remedial Laws for the due execution of the provisions of this section, and of any decision of the Governor General in Council under this section.

English and French languages to be used

23. Either the English or the French language may be used by any person in the debates of the Houses of the Legislature, and both those languages shall be used in the respective Records and Journals of those Houses; and either of those languages may be used by any person, or in any Pleading or Process, in or issuing from any Court of Canada established under the Constitution Act, 1867, or in or from all or any of the Courts of the Province. The Acts of the Legislature shall be printed and published in both those languages.

Interest allowed to the Province on a certain amount of the debt of Canada

24. Inasmuch as the Province is not in debt, the said Province shall be entitled to be paid, and to receive from the Government of Canada, by Half-yearly payments in advance, interest at the rate of five per centum per annum on the sum of four hundred and seventy-two thousand and ninety dollars.

Subsidy to the Province for support of Government, and in proportion to its population

25. The sum of thirty thousand dollars shall be paid yearly by Canada to the Province, for the support of its Government and Legislature, and an annual grant, in aid of the said Province, shall be made, equal to eighty cents per head of the population, estimated at seventeen thousand souls; and such grant of eighty cents per head shall be augmented in proportion to the increase of population, as may be shown by the census that shall be taken thereof in the year one thousand eight hundred and eighty-one, and by each subsequent decennial census, until its population amounts to four hundred thousand souls, at which amount such grant shall remain thereafter, and such sum shall be in full settlement of all future demands on Canada, and shall be paid half-yearly, in advance, to the said Province.

Canada assumes certain expenses

26. Canada will assume and defray the charges for the following services:—

1. Salary of the Lieutenant-Governor.

2. Salaries and allowances of the Judges of the Superior and District or County Courts.

3. Charges in respect of the Department of the Customs.

4. Postal Department.

5. Protection of Fisheries.

6. Militia.

7. Geological Survey.

8. The Penitentiary.

General provision

9. And such further charges as may be incident to, and connected with the services which, by the Constitution Act, 1867, appertain to the General Government, and as are or may be allowed to the other Provinces.

Customs duties

27. The Customs duties now by Law chargeable in Rupert's Land, shall be continued without increase for the period of three years from and after the passing of this Act, and the proceeds of such duties shall form part of the Consolidated Revenue Fund of Canada.

Customs laws

28. Such provisions of the Customs Laws of Canada (other than such as prescribe the rate of duties payable) as may be from time to time declared by the Governor General in Council to apply to the Province of Manitoba, shall be applicable thereto, and in force therein accordingly.

Inland Revenue laws and duties

29. Such provisions of the Laws of Canada respecting the Inland Revenue, including those fixing the amount of duties, as may be from time to time declared by the Governor General in Council applicable to the said Province, shall apply thereto, and be in force therein accordingly.

Ungranted lands vested in the Crown for Dominion purposes

30. All ungranted or waste lands in the Province shall be, from and after the date of the said transfer, vested in the Crown, and administered by the Government of Canada for the purposes of the Dominion, subject to, and except and so far as the same may be affected by, the conditions and stipulations contained in the agreement for the surrender of Rupert's Land by the Hudson's Bay Company to Her Majesty.

Provisions as to Indian title

Grant for half-breeds

31. And whereas, it is expedient, towards the extinguishment of the Indian Title to the lands in the Province, to appropriate a portion of such ungranted lands, to the extent of one million four hundred thousand acres thereof, for the benefit of the families of the half-breed residents, it is hereby enacted, that, under regulations to be from time to time made by the Governor General in Council, the Lieutenant-Governor shall select such lots or tracts in such parts of the Province as he may deem expedient, to the extent aforesaid, and divide the same among the children of the half-breed heads of families residing in the Province at the time of the said transfer to Canada, and the same shall be granted to the said children respectively, in such mode and on such conditions as to settlement and otherwise, as the Governor General in Council may from time to time determine.

Quieting titles

32. For the quieting of titles, and assuring to the settlers in the Province the peaceable possession of the lands now held by them, it is enacted as follows: —

Grants by H.B. Company

(1) All grants of land in freehold made by the Hudson's Bay Company up to the eighth day of March, in the year 1869, shall, if required by the owner, be confirmed by grant from the Crown.

The same

(2) All grants of estates less than freehold in land made by the Hudson's Bay Company up to the eighth day of March aforesaid, shall, if required by the owner, be converted into an estate in freehold by grant from the Crown.

Titles by occupancy with permission

(3) All titles by occupancy with the sanction and under the license and authority of the Hudson's Bay Company up to the eighth day of March aforesaid, of land in that part of the Province in which the Indian Title has been extinguished, shall, if required by the owner, be converted into an estate in freehold by grant from the Crown.

By peaceable possession

(4) All persons in peaceable possession of tracts of land at the time of the transfer to Canada, in those parts of the Province in which the Indian Title has not been extinguished, shall have the right of pre-emption of the same, on such terms and conditions as may be determined by the Governor in Council.

Lieut.-Governor to make provisions under Order in Council

(5) The Lieutenant-Governor is hereby authorized, under regulations to be made from time to time by the Governor General in Council, to make all such provisions for ascertaining and adjusting, on fair and equitable terms, the rights of Commons, and rights of cutting Hay held and enjoyed by the settlers in the Province, and for the commutation of the same by grants of land from the Crown.

Governor in Council to appoint form, etc., of grants

33. The Governor General in Council shall from time to time settle and appoint the mode and form of Grants of Land from the Crown, and any Order in Council for that purpose when published in the *Canada Gazette*, shall have the same force and effect as if it were a portion of this Act.

Rights of H.B. Company not affected

34. Nothing in this Act shall in any way prejudice or affect the rights or properties of the Hudson's Bay Company, as contained in the conditions under which that Company surrendered Rupert's Land to Her Majesty.

Lieut.-Governor to govern N.W. Territory for Canada

35. And with respect to such portion of Rupert's Land and the North-Western Territory, as is not included in the Province of Manitoba, it is hereby enacted, that the Lieutenant-Governor of the said Province shall be appointed, by Commission under the Great Seal of Canada, to be the Lieutenant-Governor of the same, under the name of the North-West Territories, and subject to the provisions of the Act in the next section mentioned.

Act 32 and 33 V., C. 3, extended and continued

36. Except as hereinbefore is enacted and provided, the Act of the Parliament of Canada, passed in the now last Session thereof, and entitled, "An Act for the Temporary Government of Rupert's Land, and the North-Western Territory when united with Canada," is hereby re-enacted, extended and continued in force until the first day of January, 1871, and until the end of the Session of Parliament then next succeeding.

RUPERT'S LAND AND NORTH-WESTERN TERRITORY ORDER

*(ORDER OF HER MAJESTY IN COUNCIL
ADMITTING RUPERT'S LAND AND THE
NORTH-WESTERN TERRITORY INTO THE UNION)*

{Note: The present title was substituted for the original title in italics by the **Constitution Act, 1982.**}

At the Court at Winds, the 23rd day of June, 1870

PRESENT,

The QUEEN's Most Excellent Majesty

Lord President

Lord Privy Seal

Lord Chamberlain

Mr. Gladstone

Whereas by the "Constitution Act, 1867," it was (amongst other things) enacted that it should be lawful for the Queen, by and with the advice of Her Majesty's Most Honourable Privy Council, on Address from the Houses of the Parliament of Canada, to admit Rupert's Land and the North-Western Territory, or either of them, into the Union on such terms and conditions in each case as should be in the Addresses expressed, and as the Queen should think fit to approve, subject to the provisions of the said Act. And it was further enacted that the provisions of any Order in Council in that behalf should have effect as if they had been enacted by the Parliament of the United Kingdom of Great Britain and Ireland:

And whereas by an Address from the Houses of the Parliament of Canada, of which Address a copy is contained in the Schedule to this Order annexed, marked A, Her Majesty was prayed, by and with the advice of Her Most Honourable Privy Council, to unite Rupert's Land and the North-Western Territory with the Dominion of Canada, and to grant to the Parliament of Canada authority to legislate for their future welfare and good government upon the terms and conditions therein stated:

And whereas by the "Rupert's Land Act, 1868," it was (amongst other things) enacted that it should be competent for the Governor and Company of Adventurers of England trading into Hudson's Bay (hereinafter called the Company) to surrender to Her Majesty, and for Her Majesty by any Instrument under Her Sign Manual and Signet to accept a surrender of all or any of the lands, territories, rights, privileges, liberties, franchises, powers, and authorities whatsoever granted or purported to be granted by certain Letters Patent therein recited to the said Company within Rupert's Land upon such terms and conditions as should be agreed upon by and between Her Majesty and the said Company; provided, however, that such surrender should not be accepted by Her Majesty until the terms and conditions upon which Rupert's Land should be admitted into the said Dominion of Canada should have been approved of by Her Majesty and embodied in an Address to Her Majesty from both the Houses of the Parliament of Canada, in pursuance of the 146th Section of the "Constitution Act, 1867:"

And it was by the same Act further enacted that it should be competent to Her Majesty, by Order or Orders in Council, on Addresses from the Houses of the Parliament of Canada, to declare that Rupert's Land should, from a date to be therein mentioned, be admitted into and become part of the Dominion of Canada:

And whereas a second Address from both the Houses of the Parliament of Canada has been received by Her Majesty praying that Her Majesty will be pleased, under the provisions of the hereinbefore recited Acts, to unite Rupert's Land on the terms and conditions expressed in certain Resolutions therein referred to and approved of by Her Majesty, of which said Resolutions and Address copies are contained in the Schedule to this Order annexed, marked B, and also to unite the North-Western Territory with the Dominion of Canada, as prayed for by and on the terms and conditions contained in the hereinbefore first recited Address, and also approved of by Her Majesty:

And whereas a draft surrender has been submitted to the Governor General of Canada containing stipulations to the following effect, viz: —

1. The sum of 300,000L. (being the sum hereinafter mentioned) shall be paid by the Canadian Government into the Bank of England to the credit of the Company within six calendar months after acceptance of the surrender aforesaid, with interest on the said sum at the rate of 5 per cent. per annum, computed from the date of such acceptance until the time of such payment.

2. The size of the blocks which the Company are to select adjoining each of their posts in the Red River limits, shall be as follows:-

	Acres
Upper Fort Garry and town of Winnipeg, including the inclosed park around shop and ground at the entrance to the town	500
Lower Fort Garry (including the farm the Company now have under cultivation)	500
White Horse Plain	500

3. The deduction to be made as hereinafter-mentioned from the price of the materials of the Electric Telegraph, in respect of deterioration thereof, is to be certified within three calendar months from such acceptance as aforesaid by the agents of the Company in charge of the depots where the materials are stored. And the said price is to be paid by the Canadian Government into the Bank of England to the credit of the Company within six calendar months of such acceptance, with interest at the rate of 5 per cent. per annum on the amount of such price computed from the date of such acceptance until the time of payment.

And whereas the said draft was on the fifth day of July, one thousand eight hundred and sixty-nine, approved by the said Governor General in accordance with a Report from the Committee of the Queen's Privy Council for Canada; but it was not expedient that the said stipulations, not being contained in the aforesaid second Address, should be included in the surrender by the said Company to Her Majesty of their rights aforesaid or in this Order in Council.

And whereas the said Company did by deed under the seal of the said Company, and bearing date the nineteenth day of November, one thousand eight hundred and sixty-nine, of which deed a copy is contained in the Schedule to this Order annexed, marked C, surrender to Her Majesty all the rights of government, and other rights, privileges, liberties, franchises, powers and authorities granted, or purported to be granted, to the said Company by the said Letters Patent therein and hereinbefore referred to, and also all similar rights which may have been exercised or assumed by the said Company in any parts of British North America not forming part of Rupert's Land, or of Canada or of British Columbia, and all the lands and territories (except and subject as in the terms and conditions therein mentioned) granted, or purported to be granted to the said Company by the said Letters Patent:

And whereas such surrender has been duly accepted by Her Majesty, by an instrument under her Sign Manual and Signet, bearing date at Windsor the twenty-second day of June, one thousand eight hundred and seventy.

It is hereby ordered and declared by Her Majesty, by and with the advice of the Privy Council, in pursuance and exercise of the powers vested in Her Majesty by the said Acts of Parliament, that from and after the fifteenth day of July, one thousand eight hundred and seventy, the said North-Western Territory shall be admitted into and become part of the Dominion of Canada upon the terms and conditions set forth in the first hereinbefore recited Address, and that the Parliament of Canada shall from the day aforesaid have full power and authority to legislate for the future welfare and good government of the said Territory. And it is further ordered that, without prejudice to any obligations arising from the aforesaid approved Report, Rupert's Land shall from and after the said date be admitted into and become part of the Dominion of Canada upon the following terms and conditions, being the terms and conditions still remaining to be performed of those embodied in the said second Address of the Parliament of Canada, and approved of by Her Majesty as aforesaid: —

1. Canada is to pay to the Company 300,000L. when Rupert's Land is transferred to the Dominion of Canada.

2. The Company are to retain the posts they actually occupy in the North-Western Territory, and may, within twelve months of the surrender, select a block of land adjoining each of its posts within any part of British North America not comprised in Canada and British Columbia, in conformity, except as regards the Red River Territory, with a list made out by the Company and communicated to the Canadian Ministers, being the list in the Schedule of the aforesaid Deed of Surrender. The actual survey is to be proceeded with, with all convenient speed.

3. The size of each block is not to exceed { 10 } acres round Upper Fort Garry, { 300 } acres round Lower Fort Garry; in the rest of the Red River Territory a number of acres to be settled at once between the Governor in Council and the Company, but so that the aggregate extent of the blocks is not to exceed 50,000 acres.

4. So far as the configuration of the country admits, the blocks shall front the river or road, by which means of access are provided, and shall be approximately in the shape of parallelograms, of which the frontage shall not be more than half the depth.

5. The Company may, for fifty years after the surrender, claim in any township or district within the Fertile Belt, in which land is set out for settlement, grants of land not exceeding one-twentieth part of the land so set out. The blocks so granted to be determined by lot, and the Company to pay a rateable share of the survey expenses, not exceeding 8 cents Canadian an acre. The company may defer the exercise of their right of claiming the proportion of each township for not more than ten years after it is set out; but their claim

must be limited to an allotment from the lands remaining unsold at the time they declare their intention to make it.

6. For the purpose of the last Article, the Fertile Belt is to be bounded as follows: — On the south by the United States' boundary; on the west by the Rocky Mountains; on the north by the northern branch of the Saskatchewan; on the east by Lake Winnipeg, the Lake of the Woods, and the waters connecting them.

7. If any township shall be formed abutting on the north bank of the northern branch of the Saskatchewan River, the Company may take their one-twentieth of any such township, which for the purpose of this Article shall not extend more than five miles inland from the river, giving to the Canadian Dominion an equal quantity of the portion of lands coming to them of townships established on the southern bank.

8. In laying out any public roads, canals, &c., through any block of land reserved to the Company, the Canadian Government may take, without compensation, such land as is necessary for the purpose, not exceeding one twenty-fifth of the total acreage of the block; but if the Canadian Government require any land which is actually under cultivation, or which has been built upon, or which is necessary for giving the Company's servants access to any river or lake, or as a frontage to any river or lake, they shall pay to the Company the fair value of the same, and shall make compensation for any injury done to the Company or their servants.

9. It is understood that the whole of the land to be appropriated within the meaning of the last preceding clause shall be appropriated for public purposes.

10. All titles to land up to the eighth day of March, one thousand eight hundred and sixty-nine, conferred by the Company are to be confirmed.

11. The Company is to be at liberty to carry on its trade without hindrance in its corporate capacity, and no exceptional tax is to be placed on the Company's land, trade, or servants, nor any import duty on goods introduced by them previous to the surrender.

12. Canada is to take over the materials of the electric telegraph at cost price — such price including transport, but not including interest for money, and subject to a deduction for ascertained deterioration.

13. The Company's claim to land under agreements of Messrs. Vankoughnet and Hopkins is to be withdrawn.

14. Any claims of Indians to compensation for lands required for purposes of settlement shall be disposed of by the Canadian Government in communication with the Imperial Government; and the Company shall be relieved of all responsibility in respect of them.

15. The Governor in Council is authorized and empowered to arrange any details that may be necessary to carry out the above terms and conditions.

And the Right Honourable Earl Granville, one of Her Majesty's Principal Secretaries of State, is to give the necessary directions herein accordingly.

(Signed) EDMUND HARRISON.

BRITISH COLUMBIA TERMS OF UNION

(ORDER OF HER MAJESTY IN COUNCIL ADMITTING BRITISH COLUMBIA INTO THE UNION)

{ Note: The present title was substituted for the original title in italics by the **Constitution Act, 1982.** }

At the Court at Windsor, the 16th day of May, 1871

PRESENT

The QUEEN's Most Excellent Majesty

His Royal Highness Prince ARTHUR

Lord Privy Seal

Earl Cowper

Earl of Kimberley

Lord Chamberlain

Mr. Secretary Cardwell

Mr. Ayrton

Whereas by the "Constitution Act, 1867" provision was made for the Union of the Provinces of Canada, Nova Scotia and New Brunswick into the Dominion of Canada, and it was (amongst other things) enacted that it should be lawful for the Queen, by and with the advice of Her Majesty's Most Honourable Privy Council, on Addresses from the House of the Parliament of Canada, and of the Legislature of the Colony of British Columbia, to admit that Colony into the said Union on such terms and conditions as should be in the Addresses expressed, and as the Queen should think fit to approve, subject to the provisions of the said Act. And it was further enacted that the provisions of any Order in Council in that behalf should have effect as if they had been enacted by the Parliament of the United Kingdom of Great Britain and Ireland.

And whereas by Addresses from the Houses of the Parliament of Canada and from the Legislative Council of British Columbia respectively, of which Addresses copies are contained in the Schedule to this Order annexed, Her Majesty was prayed, by and with the advice of Her Most Honourable Privy Council, under the one hundred and forty-sixth section of the hereinbefore recited Act, to admit British Columbia into the Dominion of Canada, on the terms and conditions set forth in the said Addresses.

And whereas Her Majesty has thought fit to approve of the said terms and conditions. It is hereby ordered and declared by Her Majesty, by and with the advice of Her Privy Council, in pursuance and exercise of the powers vested in Her Majesty by the said Act of Parliament, that from and after the twentieth day of July, one thousand eight hundred and seventy-one, the said Colony of British Columbia shall be admitted into and become part of the Dominion of Canada, upon the terms and conditions set forth in the hereinbefore recited Addresses. And, in accordance with the terms of the said Addresses relating to the electoral districts in British Columbia, for which the first election of members to serve in the House of Commons of the said Dominion shall take place, it is hereby further ordered and declared that such electoral districts shall be as follows: —

"New Westminster District" and the "Coast District," as defined in a public notice issued from the Lands and Works Office in the said colony on the fifteenth day of December, one thousand eight hundred and sixty-nine, by the desire of the Governor, and purporting to be in accordance with the provisions of the thirty-ninth clause of the "Mineral Ordinance, 1869," shall constitute one district, to be designated "New Westminster District," and return one member.

"Cariboo District" and "Lillooet District," as specified in the said public notice, shall constitute one district, to be designated "Cariboo District," and return one member.

"Yale District" and "Kootenay District," as specified in the said public notice, shall constitute one district, to be designated "Yale District," and return one member.

Those portions of Vancouver Island, known as "Victoria District," "Esquimalt District," and "Metchosin District," as defined in the official maps of those districts which are in the Land Office, Victoria, and are designated respectively, "Victoria District Official Map, 1858," "Esquimalt District Official Map, 1858," and "Metchosin District Official Map, A.D. 1858," shall constitute one district, to be designated "Victoria District," and return two members.

All the remainder of Vancouver Island, and all such islands adjacent thereto, as were formerly dependencies of the late Colony of Vancouver Island District, shall constitute one district, to be designated "Vancouver Island District," and return one member.

And the Right Honourable Earl of Kimberley, one of Her Majesty's Principal Secretaries of State, is to give the necessary directions therein accordingly.

(Signed) ARTHUR HELPS.

PRINCE EDWARD ISLAND TERMS OF UNION

(ORDER OF HER MAJESTY IN COUNCIL ADMITTING PRINCE EDWARD ISLAND INTO THE UNION)

{Note: The present title was substituted for the original title in italics by the **Constitution Act, 1982.**}

At the Court at Windsor, the 26th day of June, 1873

PRESENT

The QUEEN'S Most Excellent Majesty

Lord President

Earl Granville

Earl of Kimberley

Lord Chamberlain

Mr. Gladstone

Whereas by the "Constitution Act, 1867," provision was made for the Union of the Provinces of Canada, Nova Scotia and New Brunswick into the Dominion of Canada, and it was (amongst other things) enacted that it should be lawful for the Queen, by and with the advice of Her Majesty's Most Honorable Privy Council, on Addresses from the Houses of the Parliament of Canada, and of the Legislature of the Colony of Prince Edward Island, to admit that Colony into the said Union on such terms and conditions as should be in the Addresses expressed, and as the Queen should think fit to approve, subject to the provisions of the said Act; and it was further enacted that the provisions of any Order in Council in that behalf, should have effect as if they had been enacted by the Parliament of the United Kingdom of Great Britain and Ireland.

And whereas by Addresses from the Houses of the Parliament of Canada, and from the Legislative Council and House of Assembly of Prince Edward Island respectively, of which

Addresses, copies are contained in the Schedule to this Order annexed, Her Majesty was prayed, by and with the advice of Her Most Honorable Privy Council, under the one hundred and forty-sixth section of the hereinbefore recited Act, to admit Prince Edward Island into the Dominion of Canada, on the terms and conditions set forth in the said Addresses.

And whereas Her Majesty has thought fit to approve of the said terms and conditions, it is hereby ordered and declared by Her Majesty, by and with the advice of Her Privy Council, in pursuance and exercise of the powers vested in Her Majesty, by the said Act of Parliament, that from and after the first day of July, one thousand eight hundred and seventy-three, the said Colony of Prince Edward Island shall be admitted into and become part of the Dominion of Canada, upon the terms and conditions set forth in the hereinbefore recited Addresses.

And in accordance with the terms of the said Addresses relating to the Electoral Districts for which, the time within which, and the laws and provisions under which the first election of members to serve in the House of Commons of Canada, for such Electoral Districts shall be held, it is hereby further ordered and declared that "Prince County" shall constitute one district, to be designated "Prince County District," and return two members; that "Queen's County" shall constitute one district, to be designated "Queen's County District," and return two members; that "King's County" shall constitute one district, to be designated "King's County District," and return two members; that the election of members to serve in the House of Commons of Canada, for such Electoral Districts shall be held within three calendar months from the day of the admission of the said Island into the Union or Dominion of Canada; that all laws which at the date of this Order in Council relating to the qualification of any person to be elected or sit or vote as a member of the House of Assembly of the said Island, and relating to the qualifications or disqualifications of voters, and to the oaths to be taken by voters, and to Returning Officers and Poll Clerks, and their powers and duties, and relating to Polling Divisions within the said Island, and relating to the proceedings at elections, and to the period during which such elections may be continued, and relating to the trial of controverted elections, and the proceedings incidental thereto, and relating to the vacating of seats of the members, and to the execution of new writs, in case of any seat being vacated otherwise than by a dissolution, and to all other matters connected with or incidental to elections of members to serve in the House of Assembly of the said Island, shall apply to elections of members to serve in the House of Commons for the Electoral Districts situate in the said Island of Prince Edward.

And the Right Honourable Earl of Kimberley, one of Her Majesty's Principal Secretaries of State is to give the necessary directions herein, accordingly.

ARTHUR HELPS

THE YUKON TERRITORY ACT, 1898

61 Victoria, c. 6 (Canada)

An Act to provide for the Government of the Yukon District

{*Assented to 13ᵗʰ June, 1898*}

Her Majesty, by and with the advice and consent of the Senate and House of Commons of Canada, enacts as follows : —

Short title

1. This Act may be cited as **The Yukon Territory Act.**

The Yukon Territory defined and constituted

2. The Yukon Judicial District, as constituted by the proclamation of the Governor in Council bearing date the sixteenth day of August, one thousand eight hundred and ninety-seven, and contained in the schedule to this Act, is hereby constituted and declared to be a separate territory under the name of the Yukon Territory, and the same shall no longer form part of the North-west Territories.

Commissioner

3. The Governor in Council may, by instrument under the Great Seal, appoint for the Yukon Territory a chief executive officer to be styled and known as the Commissioner of the Yukon Territory.

Administration of Government

4. The Commissioner shall administer the government of the territory under instructions from time to time given him by the Governor in Council or the Minister of the Interior.

Council

5. (1) The Governor in Council by warrant under his privy seal may constitute and appoint such and so many persons from time to time not exceeding in the whole six persons, as may be deemed desirable to be a Council to aid the Commissioner in the administration of the territory, and such persons so appointed to the Council shall before entering upon the duties of their offices take and subscribe before the Commissioner such oaths of allegiance and office as the Governor in Council may prescribe.

Quorum

(2) The majority of the Council including the Commissioner shall form a quorum.

(3) Each judge of the court shall be ex officio a member of the Council, but the total number of members of the Council, including the judges, shall not exceed six.

Powers to make
ordinances

6. The Commissioner in Council shall have the same powers to make ordinances for the government of the territory as are at the date of this Act possessed by the Lieutenant Governor of the North-west Territories, acting by and with the advice and consent of the Legislative Assembly thereof to make ordinances for the government of the North-west Territories, except as such powers may be limited by order of the Governor in Council.

Disallowance by
Governor in Council

7. A copy of every such ordinance made by the Commissioner in Council shall be despatched by mail to the Governor in Council within ten days after the passing thereof, and shall be laid before both Houses of Parliament as soon as conveniently may be thereafter, and any such ordinance may be disallowed by the Governor in Council at any time within two years after its passage.

Governor in Council
may make certain
ordinances

8. Subject to the provisions of this Act, the Governor in Council may make ordinances for the peace, order and good government of the territory and of Her Majesty's subjects and others therein, but no ordinance made by the Governor in Council or the Commissioner in Council shall,

Restrictions as to
such ordinances

(a) impose any tax or any duty of customs or any excise or any penalty exceeding one hundred dollars, or

(b) alter or repeal the punishment provided in any Act of the Parliament of Canada in force in the territory for any offence, or

(c) appropriate any public money, lands or property of Canada without authority of Parliament:

Proviso

Provided that this section shall not apply to any law extending or applying or declared applicable to the territory by any Act of the Parliament of Canada.

Existing laws to
remain in force until
altered by the proper
legislative authority

9. Subject to the provisions of this Act, the laws relating to civil and criminal matters and the ordinances as the same exist in the North-west Territories at the time of the passing of this Act, shall be and remain in force in the said Yukon Territory in so far as the same are applicable thereto until amended or repealed by the Parliament of Canada or by any ordinance of the Governor in Council or the Commissioner in Council made under the provisions of this Act.

Territorial Court
constituted

10. (1) There is hereby constituted and appointed a superior court of record in and for the said territory, which shall be called the Territorial Court.

Judges

The said court shall consist of one or more judges, who shall be appointed by the Governor in Council by letters patent under the Great Seal.

Their
qualifications

(2) Any person may be appointed judge of the court who is or has been a judge of a superior or a county court of any province of Canada or of the North-west Territories, or a barrister or advocate of at least ten years' standing at the bar of any such province or of the North-west Territories.

Their
disqualifications

(3) A judge of the court shall not hold any other office or emolument under the Government of Canada, or of any province of Canada or of the said territory, but this provision shall not prevent a judge from being eligible for appointment as a member of the Council of the said territory.

Law as to judges and jurisdiction of the court

11. The law governing the residence, tenure of office, oath of office, rights and privileges of the judge or judges of the court, and the power, authority and jurisdiction of the court shall be the same, *mutatis mutandis*, as the law governing the residence, tenure of office, oath of office, rights and privileges of the judges, and the power, authority and jurisdiction of the Supreme Court of the North-west Territories, except as the same are expressly varied in this Act.

Sittings of the court

12. Sittings of the court presided over by a judge or judges shall be held at such times and places as the Governor in Council or the Commissioner in Council shall appoint.

Officers of the court

13. The Governor in Council may appoint such officers of the court as may be deemed necessary, and may define and specify the duties and emoluments of the officers so appointed.

Provisional appointment of judge and officers

14. The judge of the Supreme Court of the North-west Territories assigned to the Yukon judicial District at the time this Act comes into force, and the officers of that court for the said district, shall be the judge and officers of the Territorial Court until otherwise provided, but the said judge may at his option, at any time within twelve months after this Act comes into force, resume his office as one of the judges of the Supreme Court of the North-west Territories, his transfer to that court being in such case made by Order of the Governor in Council.

Procedure in criminal cases

15. The procedure in criminal cases in the Territorial Court shall, subject to the provisions of any Act of the Parliament of Canada, conform as nearly as possible to the procedure existing in like cases in the North-west Territories at the time of the passing of this Act.

Justices of the peace

16. While in the said Yukon Territory the Commissioner of the territory, each member of the Council thereof, every judge of the court, and every commissioned officer of the North-west Mounted Police, shall ex officio have, possess and exercise all the powers of a justice of the peace, or of two justices of the peace, under any laws or ordinances, civil or criminal, in force in the said territory, and the Governor in Council may, by commission, appoint such other persons justices of the peace or police commissioners, having each the authority of two justices of the peace within the said territory, as may be deemed desirable.

Jurymen to be British subjects

17. No person shall be summoned or sworn as a juryman on any trial in the Territorial Court unless he is a British subject.

Penitentiaries, jails and places of confinement

18. (1) Every lock-up, guard-room, guard-house or place of confinement provided by or for or under the direction of the North-west Mounted Police Force, or the regular military force, or a municipal body, or by the Commissioner or Commissioner in Council of the territory, shall be a penitentiary, jail, and place of confinement for all persons sentenced to imprisonment in the territory, and the Commissioner of the territory shall direct in which such penitentiary, jail or place of confinement any person sentenced to imprisonment shall be imprisoned.

Governor in Council to make rules and regulations as to penitentiaries, etc.

(2) The Governor in Council shall have power to make rules and regulations respecting the management, discipline and policy of every penitentiary, jail or place of confinement used as such in the territory.

Coroners

19. All persons possessing the powers of two justices of the peace in the territory shall also be coroners in and for the said territory.

Appointment of necessary officers, fixing of fees, etc.

20. The Governor in Council may appoint such officers as are necessary for the due administration of justice in the territory, may fix the fees or emoluments of such officers and may fix the fees or emoluments of coroners, justices of the peace, jurors, witnesses and other persons attending or performing duties in relation to the administration of criminal justice, and provide the manner in which such fees and emoluments shall be paid.

Provision for case of commissioner's death

21. In case of the death of the Commissioner the senior member of the Council shall act as Commissioner until a successor is appointed.

ALBERTA ACT

(THE ALBERTA ACT)

{ Note: The present short title was substituted for the original short title in italics by the **Constitution Act, 1982**. }

4-5 Edward VII, c. 3 (Canada)

An Act to establish and provide for the Government of the Province of Alberta

{Assented to 20th July, 1905}

Preamble

Whereas in and by the **Constitution Act, 1871**, being chapter 28 of the Acts of the Parliament of the United Kingdom passed in the session thereof held in the 34th and 35th years of the reign of Her late Majesty Queen Victoria, it is enacted that the Parliament of Canada may from time to time establish new provinces in any territories forming for the time being part of the Dominion of Canada, but not included in any province thereof, and may, at the time of such establishment, make provision for the constitution and administration of any such province, and for the passing of laws for the peace, order and good government of such province, and for its representation in the said Parliament of Canada;

And whereas it is expedient to establish as a province the territory hereinafter described, and to make provision for the government thereof and the representation thereof in the Parliament of Canada: Therefore His Majesty, by and with the advice and consent of the Senate and House of Commons of Canada, enacts as follows: —

Short title

1. This Act may be cited as the **Alberta Act**.

Province of Alberta formed; its boundaries

2. The territory comprised within the following boundaries, that is to say, — commencing at the intersection of the international boundary dividing Canada from the United States of America by the fourth meridian in the system of Dominion lands surveys; thence westerly along the said international boundary to the eastern boundary of the province of British Columbia; thence northerly along the said eastern boundary of the province of British Columbia to the north-east corner of the said province; thence easterly along the parallel of the sixtieth degree of north latitude to the fourth meridian in the system of Dominion lands surveys as the same may be hereafter defined in accordance with the said system; thence southerly along the said fourth meridian to the point of commencement, — is hereby established as a province of the Dominion of Canada, to be called and known as the province of Alberta.

Constitution Acts, 1867 to 1886, to apply

3. The provisions of the **Constitution Acts, 1867 to 1886** shall apply to the province of Alberta in the same way and to the like extent as they apply to the provinces heretofore comprised in the Dominion, as if the said province of Alberta had been one of the provinces originally united, except in so far as varied by this Act and except such provisions as are in terms made, or by reasonable intendment may be held to be, specially applicable to or only to affect one or more and not the whole of the said provinces.

Representation in the Senate

4. The said province shall be represented in the Senate of Canada by four members: Provided that such representation may, after the completion of the next decennial census, be from time to time increased to six by the Parliament of Canada.

Representation in the House of Commons

5. The said province and the province of Saskatchewan shall, until the termination of the Parliament of Canada existing at the time of the first readjustment hereinafter provided for, continue to be represented in the House of Commons as provided by chapter 60 of the statutes of 1903, each of the electoral districts defined in that part of the schedule to the said Act which relates to the North-west Territories, whether such district is wholly in one of the said provinces, or partly in one and partly in the other of them, being represented by one member.

Readjustment after next quinquennial census;

6. (1) Upon the completion of the next quinquennial census for the said province, the representation thereof shall forthwith be readjusted by the Parliament of Canada in such manner that there shall be assigned to the said province such a number of members as will bear the same proportion to the number of this population ascertained at such quinquennial census as the number sixty-five bears to the number of the population of Quebec as ascertained at the then last decennial census; and in the computation of the number of members for the said province a fractional part not exceeding one-half of the whole number requisite for entitling the province to a member shall be disregarded, and a fractional part exceeding one-half of that number shall be deemed equivalent to the whole number, and such readjustment shall take effect upon the termination of the Parliament then existing.

Subsequent readjustments

(2) The representation of the said province shall thereafter be readjusted from time to time according to the provisions of section 51 of the **Constitution Act, 1867**.

Election of members of House of Commons

7. Until the Parliament of Canada otherwise provides the qualifications of voters for the election of members of the House of Commons and the proceedings at and in connection with elections of such members shall, *mutatis mutandis*, be those prescribed by law at the time this Act comes into force with respect to such elections in the North-west Territories.

Executive Council

8. The Executive Council of the said province shall be composed of such persons, under such designations, as the Lieutenant Governor from time to time thinks fit.

Seat of Government

9. Unless and until the Lieutenant Governor in Council of the said province otherwise directs, by proclamation under the Great Seal, the seat of government of the said province shall be at Edmonton.

Powers of Lieutenant
Governor and Council

10. All powers, authorities and functions which under any law were before the coming into force of this Act vested in or exercisable by the Lieutenant Governor of the North-west Territories, with the advice, or with the advice and consent, of the Executive Council thereof, or in conjunction with that Council or with any member or members thereof, or by the said Lieutenant Governor individually, shall, so far as they are capable of being exercised after the coming into force of this Act in relation to the government of the said province, be vested in and shall or may be exercised by the Lieutenant Governor of the said province, with the advice or with the advice and consent of, or in conjunction with, the Executive Council of the said province or any member or members thereof, or by the Lieutenant Governor individually, as the case requires, subject nevertheless to be abolished or altered by the Legislature of the said province.

Great Seal

11. The Lieutenant Governor in Council shall, as soon as may be after this Act comes into force, adopt and provide a Great Seal of the said province, and may, from time to time, change such seal.

Legislature

12. There shall be a Legislature for the said province consisting of the Lieutenant Governor and one House to be styled the Legislative Assembly of Alberta.

Legislative Assembly

13. Until the said Legislature otherwise provides, the Legislative Assembly shall be composed of twenty-five members, to be elected to represent the electoral divisions defined in the schedule to this Act.

Election of members
of Assembly

14. Until the said Legislature otherwise determines, all the provisions of the law with regard to the constitution of the Legislative Assembly of the North-west Territories and the election of members thereof shall apply, *mutatis mutandis*, to the Legislative Assembly of the said province and the elections of members thereof respectively.

Writs for first election

15. The writs for the election of the members of the first Legislative Assembly of the said province shall be issued by the Lieutenant Governor and made returnable within six months after this Act comes into force.

Laws, courts and
officers continued

16. (1) All laws and all orders and regulations made thereunder, so far as they are not inconsistent with anything contained in this Act, or as to which this Act contains no provision intended as a substitute therefor, and all courts of civil and criminal jurisdiction, and all commissions, powers, authorities and functions, and all officers and functionaries, judicial, administrative and ministerial, existing immediately before the coming into force of this Act in the territory hereby established as the province of Alberta, shall continue in the said province as if this Act and the **Saskatchewan Act** had not been passed; subject, nevertheless, except with respect to such as are enacted by or existing under Acts of the Parliament of Great Britain, or of the Parliament of the United Kingdom or Great Britain and Ireland, to be repealed, abolished or altered by the Parliament of Canada, or by the Legislature of the said province, according to the authority of the Parliament, or of the said Legislature;

Proviso

Provided that all powers, authorities and functions which, under any law, order or regulation were, before the coming into force of this Act, vested in or exercisable by any public officer or functionary of the North-west Territories shall be vested in and exercisable in and for the said province by like public officers and functionaries of the said province when appointed by competent authority.

Province may abolish
Supreme Court of
N.W.T.

Proviso

(2) The Legislature of the province may, for all purposes affecting or extending to the said province, abolish the Supreme Court of the North-west Territories, and the offices, both judicial and ministerial, thereof, and the jurisdiction, powers and authority belonging or incident to the said court: Provided that, if, upon such abolition, the Legislature constitutes a superior court of criminal jurisdiction, the procedure in criminal matters then obtaining in respect of the Supreme Court of the North-west Territories shall, until otherwise provided by competent authority, continue to apply to such superior court, and that the Governor in Council may at any time and from time to time declare all or any part of such procedure to be inapplicable to such superior court.

As to certain
corporations in
N.W.T.

(3) All societies or associations incorporated by or under the authority of the Legislature of the North-west Territories existing at the time of the coming into force of this Act which include within their objects the regulation of the practice of or the right to practise any profession or trade in the North-west Territories, such as the legal or the medical profession, dentistry, pharmaceutical chemistry and the like, shall continue, subject, however, to be dissolved and abolished by order of the Governor in Council, and each of such societies shall have power to arrange for and effect the payment of its debts and liabilities, and the division, disposition or transfer of its property.

As to joint-stock
companies

(4) Every joint-stock company lawfully incorporated by or under the authority of any ordinance of the North-west Territories shall be subject to the legislative authority of the province of Alberta if —

(a) the head office or the registered office of such company is at the time of the coming into force of this Act situate in the province of Alberta; and

(b) the powers and objects of such company are such as might be conferred by the Legislature of the said province and not expressly authorized to be executed in any part of the North-west Territories beyond the limits of the said province.

Education

17. Section 93 of the **Constitution Act, 1867** shall apply to the said province, with the substitution for paragraph (1) of the said section 93, of the following paragraph: —

"(1) Noting in any such law shall prejudicially affect any right or privilege with respect to separate schools which any class of persons have at the date of the passing of this Act, under the terms of chapters 29 and 30 of the Ordinances of the North-west Territories, passed in the year 1901, or with respect to religious instruction in any public or separate school as provided for in the said ordinances."

(2) In the appropriation by the Legislature or distribution by the Government of the province of any moneys for the support of schools organized and carried on in accordance with the said chapter 29 or any Act passed in amendment thereof, or in substitution therefor, there shall be no discrimination against schools of any class described in the said chapter 29.

(3) Where the expression "by law" is employed in paragraph 3 of the said section 93, it shall be held to mean the law as set out in the said chapters 29 and 30, and where the expression "at the Union" is employed, in the said paragraph 3, it shall be held to mean the date at which this Act comes into force.

Subsidy to province

18. The following amounts shall be allowed as an annual subsidy to the province of Alberta and shall be paid by the Government of Canada, by half-yearly instalments in advance, to the said province, that is to say: —

For government

(a) for the support of the Government and Legislature, fifty thousand dollars;

In proportion to population

(b) on an estimated population of two hundred and fifty thousand, at eighty cents per head, two hundred thousand dollars, subject to be increased as hereinafter mentioned, that is to say: — a census of the said province shall be taken in every fifth year, reckoning from the general census of one hundred nine hundred and one, and an approximate estimate of the populations shall be made at equal intervals of time between each quinquennial and decennial census; and whenever the population, by any such census or estimate, exceeds two hundred and fifty thousand, which shall be the minimum on which the said allowance shall be calculated, the amount of the said allowance shall be increased accordingly, and so on until the population has reached eight hundred thousand souls.

Annual payment to province

19. Inasmuch as the said province is not in debt, it shall be entitled to be paid and to receive from the Government of Canada, by half-yearly payments in advance, an annual sum of four hundred and five thousand three hundred and seventy-five dollars, being the equivalent of interest at the rate of five per cent per annum on the sum of eight million one hundred and seven thousand five hundred dollars.

Compensation to province for public lands

20 (1) Inasmuch as the said province will not have the public land as a source of revenue, there shall be paid by Canada to the province by half-yearly payments, in advance, an annual sum based upon the population of the province as from time to time ascertained by the quinquennial census thereof, as follows: —

The population of the said province being assumed to be at present two hundred and fifty thousand, the sum payable until such population reaches four hundred thousand, shall be three hundred and seventy-five thousand dollars;

Thereafter, until such population reaches eight hundred thousand, the sum payable shall be five hundred and sixty-two thousand five hundred dollars;

Thereafter, until such population reaches one million two hundred thousand, the sum payable shall be seven hundred and fifty thousand dollars;

And thereafter the sum payable shall be one million one hundred and twenty-five thousand dollars.

Further compensation

(2) As an additional allowance in lieu of public lands, there shall be paid by Canada to the province annually by half-yearly payments, in advance, for five years from the time this Act comes into force, to provide for the construction of necessary public buildings, the sum of ninety-three thousand seven hundred and fifty dollars.

Property in lands, etc.

21. All Crown lands, mines and minerals and royalties incident thereto, and the interest of the Crown in the waters within the province under **The North-west Irrigation Act, 1898**, shall continue to be vested in the Crown and administered by the Government of Canada for the purposes of Canada, subject to the provisions of any Act of the Parliament of Canada with respect to road allowances and roads or trails in force immediately before the coming into force of this Act, which shall apply to the said province with the substitution therein of the said province for the North-west Territories.

Division of assets and liabilities between Saskatchewan and Alberta

Arbitration

22. All properties and assets of the North-west Territories shall be divided equally between the said province and the province of Saskatchewan, and the two provinces shall be jointly and equally responsible for all debts and liabilities of the North-west Territories: Provided that, if any difference arises as to the division and adjustment of such properties, assets, debts and liabilities, such difference shall be referred to the arbitrament of three arbitrators, one of who shall be chosen by the Lieutenant Governor in Council of each province, and the third by the Governor in Council. The selection of such arbitrators shall not be made until the Legislatures of the provinces have met, and the arbitrator chosen by Canada shall not be resident of either province.

Rights of H.B. Co.

23. Nothing in this Act shall in any way prejudice or affect the rights or properties of the Hudson's Bay company as contained in the conditions under which that company surrendered Rupert's Land to the Crown.

Provision as to C.P.R. Co.

24. The powers hereby granted to the said province shall be exercised subject to the provisions of section 16 of the contract set forth in the schedule to chapter 1 of the statutes of 1881, being an Act respecting the Canadian Pacific Railway Company.

Commencement of Act

25. This Act shall come into force on the first day of September, one thousand nine hundred and five.

SASKATCHEWAN ACT

(THE SASKATCHEWAN ACT)

[Note: The present short title was substituted for the original short title in italics by the **Constitution Act, 1982.**]

4-5 Edward VII, c. 42 (Canada)

An Act to establish and provide for the government of the Province of Saskatchewan

[Assented to 20th July, 1905]

Preamble

Whereas in and by the **Constitution Act, 1871**, being chapter 28 of the Acts of the Parliament of the United Kingdom passed in the session thereof held in the 34th and 35th years of the reign of her late Majesty Queen Victoria, it is enacted that the Parliament of Canada may from time to time establish new provinces in any territories forming for the time being part of the Dominion of Canada, but not included in any province thereof, and may, at the time of such establishment, make provision for the constitution and adminstration of any such province, and for the passing of laws for the peace, order and good government of such province and for its representation in the said Parliament of Canada;

And whereas it is expedient to establish as a province the territory hereinafter described, and to make provision for the government thereof and the representation thereof in the Parliament of Canada: Therefore His Majesty, by and with the advice and consent of the Senate and House of Commons of Canada, enacts as follows: —

Short title

1. This Act may be cited as the **Saskatchewan Act.**

Province of Saskatchewan formed; its boundaries

2. The territory comprised within the following boundaries, that is to say, — commencing at the intersection of the international boundary dividing Canada from the United States of America by the west boundary of the province of Manitoba, thence northerly along the said west boundary of the province of Manitoba to the north-west corner of the said province of Manitoba; thence continuing northerly along the centre of the road allowance between the twenty-ninth and thirtieth ranges west of the principal meridian in the system of Dominion lands surveys, as the said road allowance may hereafter be defined in accordance with the said system, to the second meridian in the said system of Dominion lands surveys, as the same may hereafter be defined in accordance with the said system; thence northerly along the said second meridian to the sixtieth degree of north latitude; thence westerly along the parallel of the sixtieth degree of north latitude to the fourth meridian in the said system of Dominion lands surveys, as the same may be hereafter defined in

accordance with the said system; thence southerly along the said fourth meridian to the said international boundary dividing Canada from the United States of America; thence easterly along the said international boundary to the point of commencement, — is hereby established as a province of the Dominion of Canada, to be called and known as the province of Saskatchewan.

Constitution Acts, 1867 to 1886, to apply

3. The provisions of the **Constitution Acts, 1867 to 1886** shall apply to the province of Saskatchewan in the same way and to the like extent as they apply to the provinces heretofore comprised in the Dominion, as if the said province of Saskatchewan had been one of the provinces originally united, except in so far as varied by this Act and except such provisions as are in terms made, or by reasonable intendment may be held to be, specially applicable to or only to affect one or more and not the whole of the said provinces.

Representation in the Senate

4. The said province shall be represented in the Senate of Canada by four members: Provided that such representation may, after the completion of the next decennial census, be from time to time increased to six by the Parliament of Canada.

Representation in the House of Commons

5. The said province and the province of Alberta shall, until the termination of the Parliament of Canada existing at the time of the first readjustment hereinafter provided for, continue to be represented in the House of Commons as provided by chapter 60 of the statutes of 1903, each of the electoral districts defined in that part of the schedule to the said Act which relates to the North-west Territories, whether such district is wholly in one of the said provinces, or partly in one and partly in the other of them, being represented by one member.

Readjustment after next quinquennial census

6 (1) Upon the completion of the next quinquennial census for the said province, the representation thereof shall forthwith be readjusted by the Parliament of Canada in such manner that there shall be assigned to the said province such a number of members as will bear the same proportion to the number of its population ascertained at such quinquennial census as the number sixty-five bears to the number of the population of Quebec as ascertained at the then last decennial census; and in the computation of the number of members for the said province a fractional part not exceeding one-half of that number shall be deemed equivalent to the whole number, and such readjustment shall take effect upon the termination of the Parliament then existing.

Subsequent readjustments

(2) The representation of the said province shall thereafter be readjusted from time to time according to the provisions of section 51 of the **Constitution Act, 1867.**

Election of members of House of Commons

7. Until the Parliament of Canada otherwise provides, the qualifications of voters for the election of members of the House of Commons and the proceedings at and in connection with elections of such members shall, *mutatis mutandis*, be those prescribed by law at the time this Act comes into force with respect to such elections in the North-west Territories.

Executive Council

8. The Executive Council of the said province shall be composed of such persons, under such designations, as the Lieutenant governor from time to time thinks fit.

Seat of Government

9. Unless and until the Lieutenant Governor in Council of the said province otherwise directs, by proclamation under the Great Seal, the seat of government of the said province shall be at Regina.

Powers of Lieutenant Governor and Council

10. All powers, authorities and functions which under any law were before the coming into force of this Act vested in or exercisable by the Lieutenant Governor of the North-west Territories, with the advice, or with the advice and consent, of the Executive Council thereof, or in conjunction with that Council or with any member or members thereof, or by the said Lieutenant governor individually, shall, so far as they are capable of being exercised after the coming into force of this Act in relation to the government of the said province, be vested in and shall or may be exercised by the Lieutenant Governor of the said province, with the advice or with the advice and consent of, or in conjunction with, the Executive Council of the said province or any member or members thereof, or by the Lieutenant Governor individually, as the case requires, subject nevertheless to be abolished or altered by the Legislature of the said province.

Great Seal

11. The Lieutenant Governor in Council shall, as soon as may be after this Act comes into force, adopt and provide a Great Seal of the said province, and may, from time to time, change such seal.

Legislature

12. There shall be a Legislature for the said province consisting of the Lieutenant Governor and One House, to be styled the Legislative Assembly of Saskatchewan.

Legislative Assembly

13. Until the said Legislature otherwise provides, the Legislative Assembly shall be composed of twenty-five members, to be elected to represent the electoral divisions defined in the schedule to this Act.

Election of members of Assembly

14. Until the said Legislature otherwise determines, all the provisions of the law with regard to the constitution of the Legislative Assembly of the North-west Territories and the election of members thereof shall apply, *mutatis mutandis*, to the Legislative Assembly of the said province and the election of members thereof respectively.

Writs for first election

15. The writs for the election of the members of the first Legislative Assembly of the said province shall be issued by the Lieutenant Governor and made returnable within six months after this Act comes into force.

Laws, courts and officers continued

16. (1) All laws and all orders and regulations made thereunder, so far as they are not inconsistent with anything contained in this Act, or as to which this Act contains no provision intended as a substitute therefor, and all courts of civil and criminal jurisdiction, and all commissions, powers, authorities and functions, and all officers and functionaries, judicial, administrative and ministerial, existing immediately before the coming into force of this Act in the territory hereby established as the province of Saskatchewan, shall continue in the said province as if this Act and the **Alberta Act** had not been passed; subject, nevertheless, except with

Proviso

respect to such as are enacted by or existing under Acts of the Parliament of Great Britain, or of the Parliament of the United Kingdom of Great Britain and Ireland, to be repealed, abolished or altered by the Parliament of Canada, or by the Legislature of the said province, according to the authority of the Parliament or of the said Legislature: Provided that all powers, authorities and functions which under any law, order or regulation were, before the coming into force of this Act, vested in or exercisable by any public officer or functionary of the North-west Territories shall be vested in and exercisable in and for the said province by like public officers and functionaries of the said province when appointed by competent authority.

Province may abolish Supreme Court of N.W.T.

(2) The Legislature of the province may, for all purposes affecting or extending to the said province, abolish the Supreme Court of the North-west Territories, and the offices, both judicial and ministerial, thereof, and the jurisdiction, powers and authority belonging or incident to theProvisosaid court: provided that, if upon such abolition, the Legislature constitutes a superior court of criminal jurisdiction, the procedure in criminal matters then obtaining in respect of the Supreme Court of the Northwest Territories shall, until otherwise provided by competent authority, continue to apply to such superior court, and that the Governor in Council may at any time and from time to time declare all or any part of such procedure to be inapplicable to such superior court.

As to certain corporations in N.W.T.

(3) All societies or associations incorporated by or under the authority of the Legislature of the North-west Territories existing at the time of the coming into force of this Act which include within their objects the regulation of the practice of, or the right to practise, any profession or trade in the North-west Territories, such as the legal or the medical profession, dentistry, pharmaceutical chemistry and the like, shall continue, subject, however, to be dissolved and abolished by order of the Governor in Council, and each of such societies shall have power to arrange for and effect the payment of its debts and liabilities, and the division, disposition or transfer of its property.

As to joint-stock companies

(4) Every joint-stock company lawfully incorporated by or under the authority of any ordinance of the North-west Territories shall be subject to the legislative authority of the province of Saskatchewan; —

(a) the head office or the registered office of such company is at the time of the coming into force of this Act situate in the province of Saskatchewan; and

(b) the powers and objects of such company are such as might be conferred by the Legislature of the said province and not expressly authorized to be executed in any part of the North-west Territories beyond the limits of the said province.

Education

17. Section 93 of the **Constitution Act, 1867** shall apply to the said province, with the substitution for paragraph (1) of the said section 93, of the following paragraph: —

"(1) Nothing in any such law shall prejudicially affect any right or privilege with respect to separate schools which any class of persons have at the date of the passing of this Act, under the terms of chapters 29 and 30 of the Ordinances of the North-west Territories, passed in the year 1901, or with respect to religious instruction in any public or separate school as provided for in the said ordinances."

(2) In the appropriation by the Legislature or distribution by the Government of the province of any moneys for the support of schools organized and carried on in accordance with the said chapter 29, or any Act passed in amendment thereof or in substitution therefor, there shall be no discrimination against schools of any class described in the said chapter 29.

(3) Where the expression "by law" is employed in paragraph (3) of the said section 93, it shall be held to mean the law as set out in the said chapters 29 and 30; and where the expression "at the Union" is employed, in the said paragraph (3), it shall be held to mean the date at which this Act comes into force.

Subsidy to province

18. The following amounts shall be allowed as an annual subsidy to the province of Saskatchewan, and shall be paid by the Government of Canada, by half-yearly instalments in advance, to the said province, that is to say: —

For government

(a) for the support of the Government and Legislature, fifty thousand dollars;

In proportion to population

(b) on an estimated population of two hundred and fifty thousand, at eighty cents per head, two hundred thousand dollars, subject to be increased as hereinafter mentioned, that is to say: - a census of the said province shall be taken in every fifth year reckoning from the general census of one thousand nine hundred and one, and an approximate estimate of the population shall be made at equal intervals of time between each quinquennial and decennial census; and whenever the population, by any such census or estimate, exceeds two hundred and fifty thousand, which shall be the minimum on which the said allowance shall be calculated, the amount of the said allowance shall be increased accordingly, and so on until the population has reached eight hundred thousand souls.

Annual payment to province

19. Inasmuch as the said province is not in debt, it shall be entitled to be paid and to receive from the Government of Canada, by half-yearly payments in advance, an annual sum of four hundred and five thousand three hundred and seventy-five dollars, being the equivalent of interest at the rate of five per cent per annum on the sum of eight million one hundred and seven thousand five hundred dollars.

Compensation to province for public lands

20. (1) Inasmuch as the said province will not have the public land as a source of revenue, there shall be paid by Canada to the province by half-yearly payments, in advance, an annual sum based upon the population of the province as from time to time ascertained by the quinquennial census thereof, as follows: —

The population of the said province being assumed to be at present two hundred and fifty thousand, the sum payable until such population reaches four hundred thousand, shall be three hundred and seventy-five thousand dollars;

Thereafter, until such population reaches eight hundred thousand, the sum payable shall be five hundred and sixty-two thousand five hundred dollars;

And thereafter the sum payable shall be one million one hundred and twenty-five thousand dollars.

Further compensation
(2) As an additional allowance in lieu of public lands, there shall be paid by Canada to the province annually by half-yearly payments, in advance, for five years from the time this Act comes into force, to provide for the construction of necessary public buildings, the sum of ninety-three thousand seven hundred and fifty dollars.

Property in lands, etc.
21. All Crown lands, mines and minerals and royalties incident thereto, and the interest of the Crown in the waters within the province under **The North-west Irrigation Act, 1898**, shall continue to be vested in the Crown and administered by the Government of Canada for the purposes of Canada, subject to the provisions of any Act of the Parliament of Canada with respect to road allowances and roads or trails in force immediately before the coming into force of this Act, which shall apply to the said province with the substitution therein of the said province for the North-west Territories.

Division of assets and liabilities between Alberta and Saskatchewan

Arbitration
22. All properties and assets of the North-west Territories shall be divided equally between the said province and the province of Alberta, and the two provinces shall be jointly and equally responsible for all debts and liabilities of the North-west Territories: Provided that, if any difference arises as to the division and adjustment of such properties, assets, debts and liabilities, such difference shall be referred to the arbitrament of three arbitrators, one of whom shall be chosen by the Lieutenant Governor in Council of each province, and the third by the Governor in Council. The selection of such arbitrators shall not be made until the Legislatures of the provinces have met, and the arbitrator chosen by Canada shall not be a resident of either province.

Rights of H.B. Co.
23. Nothing in this Act shall in any way prejudice or affect the rights or properties of the Hudson's Bay Company as contained in the conditions under which that company surrendered Rupert's Land to the Crown.

Provisions as to C.P.R. Co.
24. The powers hereby granted to the said province shall be exercised subject to the provisions of section 16 of the contract set forth in the schedule to chapter 1 of the statutes of 1881, being an Act respecting the Canadian Pacific Railway Company.

Commencement of Act
25. This Act shall come into force on the first day of September, one thousand nine hundred and five.

STATUTE OF WESTMINSTER, 1931

22 George V, c. 4 (U.K.)

An Act to give effect to certain resolutions passed by Imperial Conferences held in the years 1926 and 1930

[11th December, 1931]

Whereas the delegates of His Majesty's Governments in the United Kingdom, the Dominion of Canada, the Commonwealth of Australia, the Dominion of New Zealand, the Union of South Africa, the Irish Free State and Newfoundland, at Imperial Conferences holden at Westminster in the years of our Lord nineteen hundred and twenty-six and nineteen hundred and thirty did concur in making the declarations and resolutions set forth in the Reports of the said Conferences:

And whereas it is meet and proper to set out by way of preamble to this Act that, inasmuch as the Crown is the symbol of the free association of the members of the British Commonwealth of Nations, and as they are united by a common allegiance to the Crown, it would be in accord with the established constitutional position of all the members of the Commonwealth in relation to one another that any alteration in the law touching the Succession to the Throne or the Royal Style and Titles shall hereafter require the assent as well of the Parliaments of all the Dominions as of the Parliament of the United Kingdom:

And whereas it is in accord with the established constitutional position that no law hereafter made by the Parliament of the United Kingdom shall extend to any of the said Dominions as part of the law of that Dominion otherwise than at the request and with the consent of that Dominion:

And whereas it is necessary for the ratifying, confirming and establishing of certain of the said declarations and resolutions of the said Conferences that a law be made and enacted in due form by authority of the Parliament of the United Kingdom:

And whereas the Dominion of Canada, the Commonwealth of Australia, the Dominion of New Zealand, the Union of South Africa, the Irish Free State and Newfoundland have severally requested and consented to the submission of a measure to the Parliament of the United Kingdom for making such provision with regard to the matters aforesaid as is hereafter in this Act contained:

Now, therefore, be it enacted by the King's most Excellent Majesty by and with the advice and consent of the Lords Spiritual and Temporal, and Commons, in this present Parliament assembled, and by the authority of the same, as follows: —

Meaning of "Dominion" in this Act

1. In this Act the expression "Dominion" means any of the following Dominions, that is to say, the Dominion of Canada, the Commonwealth of Australia, the Dominion of New Zealand, the Union of South Africa, the Irish Free State and Newfoundland.

Validity of laws made by Parliament of a Dominion. 28 & 29 Vict. c. 63

2. (1) The Colonial Laws Validity Act, 1865, shall not apply to any law made after the commencement of this Act by the Parliament of a Dominion.

(2) No law and no provision of any law made after the commencement of this Act by the Parliament of a Dominion shall be void or inoperative on the ground that it is repugnant to the law of England, or to the provisions of any existing or future Act of Parliament of the United Kingdom, or to any order, rule or regulation made under any such Act, and the powers of the Parliament of a Dominion shall include the power to repeal or amend any such Act, order, rule or regulation in so far as the same is part of the law of the Dominion.

Power of Parliament of Dominion to legislate extra-territorially

3. It is hereby declared and enacted that the Parliament of a Dominion has full power to make laws having extra-territorial operation.

Parliament of United King- dom not to legislate for Dominion except by consent

4. No Act of Parliament of the United Kingdom passed after the commencement of this Act shall extend, or be deemed to extend, to a Dominion as part of the law of that Dominion, unless it is expressly declared in that Act that that Dominion has requested, and consented to the enactment thereof.

{Note: In so far as it applied to Canada, section 4 was repealed by the *Constitution Act, 1982*}

Powers of Dominion Par- liaments in relation to merchant shipping. 57 & 58 Vict. c. 60

5. Without prejudice to the generality of the foregoing provisions of this Act, sections seven hundred and thirty-five and seven hundred and thirty-six of the Merchant Shipping Act, 1894, shall be construed as though reference therein to the Legislature of a British possession did not include reference to the Parliament of a Dominion.

A.D. 1931.

Powers of Dominion
Parliaments in
relation to Courts of
Admiralty. 53 & 54
Vict. c. 27

6. Without prejudice to the generality of the foregoing provisions of this Act, section our of the Colonial Courts of Admiralty Act, 1890 (which requires certain laws to be reserved for the signification of His Majesty's pleasure or to contain a suspending clause), and so much of section seven of that Act as requires the approval of His Majesty in Council to any rules of Court for regulating the practice and procedure of a Colonial Court of Admiralty, shall cease to have effect in any Dominion as from the commencement of this Act.

Saving for British
North America Acts
and application of the
Act to Canada

7. (1) Nothing in this Act shall be deemed to apply to the repeal, amendment or alteration of the British North America Acts, 1867 to 1930, or any order, rule or regulation made thereunder.

{Note : In so far as it applied to Canada, subsection 7(1) was repealed by the *Constitution Act, 1982* }

(2) The provisions of section two of this Act shall extend to laws made by any of the Provinces of Canada and to the powers of the legislatures of such Provinces.

(3) The powers conferred by this Act upon the Parliament of Canada or upon the legislatures of the Provinces shall be restricted to the enactment of laws in relation to matters within the competence of the Parliament of Canada or of any of the legislatures of the Provinces respectively.

Saving for
Constitution Acts of
Australia and New
Zealand

8. Nothing in this Act shall be deemed to confer any power to repeal or alter the Constitution or the Constitution Act of the Commonwealth of Australia or the Constitution Act of the Dominion of New Zealand otherwise than in accordance with the law existing before the commencement of this Act.

Saving with respect
to States of Australia

9. (1) Nothing in this Act shall be deemed to authorize the Parliament of the Commonwealth of Australia to make laws on any matter within the authority of the States of Australia, not being a matter within the authority of the Parliament or Government of the Commonwealth of Australia.

(2) Nothing in this Act shall be deemed to require the concurrence of the Parliament or Government of the Commonwealth of Australia in any law made by the Parliament of the United Kingdom with respect to any matter within the authority of the States of Australia, not being a matter within the authority of the Parliament or Government of the Commonwealth of Australia, in any case where it would have been in accordance with the constitutional practice existing before the commencement of this Act that the Parliament of the United Kingdom should make that law without such concurrence.

(3) In the application of this Act to the Commonwealth of Australia the request and consent referred to in section four shall mean the request and consent of the Parliament and Government of the Commonwealth.

Certain sections of Act not to apply to Aus- tralia, New Zealand or Newfoundland unless adopted

10. (1) None of the following sections of this Act, that is to say, sections two, three, four, five and six, shall extend to a Dominion to which this section applies as part of the law of that Dominion unless that section is adopted by the Parliament of the Dominion, and any Act of that Parliament adopting any section of this Act may provide that the adoption shall have effect either from the commencement of this Act or from such later date as is specified in the adopting Act.

(2) The Parliament of any such Dominion as aforesaid may at any time revoke the adoption of any section referred to in subsection (1) of this section.

(3) The Dominions to which this section applies are the Commonwealth of Australia, the Dominion of New Zealand and Newfoundland.

Meaning of "Colony" in future Acts. 52 & 53 Vict. c. 63

11. Notwithstanding anything in the Interpretation Act, 1889, the expression "Colony" shall not, in any Act of the Parliament of the United Kingdom passed after the commencement of this Act, include a Dominion or any Province or State forming part of a Dominion.

Short title

12. This Act may be cited as the Statute of Westminster, 1931.

NEWFOUNDLAND ACT

(BRITISH NORTH AMERICA ACT, 1949)

{Note: The present short title was substituted for the original short title in italics by the **Constitution Act, 1982.**}

12-13 George VI, c. 22 (U.K.)

An Act to confirm and give effect to Terms of Union agreed between Canada and Newfoundland

{23rd March 1949}

Whereas by means of a referendum the people of Newfoundland have by a majority signified their wish to enter into confederation with Canada;

And whereas the Agreement containing Terms of Union between Canada and Newfoundland set out in the Schedule to this Act has been duly approved by the Parliament of Canada and by the Government of Newfoundland;

And whereas Canada has requested, and consented to, the enactment of an Act of the Parliament of the United Kingdom to confirm and give effect to the said Agreement, and the Senate and House of Commons of Canada in Parliament assembled have submitted an address to His Majesty praying that His Majesty may graciously be pleased to cause a Bill to be laid before the Parliament of the United Kingdom for that purpose;

Be it therefore enacted by the King's Most Excellent Majesty, by and with the advice and consent of the Lords Spiritual and Temporal, and Commons, in this present Parliament assembled, and by the authority of the same, as follows: —

Confirmation of Terms of Union

1. The Agreement containing Terms of Union between Canada and Newfoundland set out in the Schedule to this Act is hereby confirmed and shall have the force of law notwithstanding anything in the Constitution Acts, 1867 to 1940.

{Note: The original text mentioned the "British North America Acts, 1867 to 1946". The B.N.A. Acts, 1933 and 1946 were repealed by the **Constitution Act, 1982.**}

Repeal of 24 & 25 Geo. 5, c. 2

2. In accordance with the preceding section the provisions of the Newfoundland Act, 1933, other than section three thereof (which relates to guarantee of certain securities of Newfoundland) shall be repealed as from the coming into force of the said Terms of Union.

Short title

3. This Act may be cited as the **Newfoundland Act.**

CANADA ACT 1982

including the

CONSTITUTION ACT, 1982

1982, c. 11 (U.K.)

{29th March 1982}

An Act to give effect to a request by the Senate and House of Commons of Canada

Whereas Canada has requested and consented to the enactment of an Act of the Parliament of the United Kingdom to give effect to the provisions hereinafter set forth and the Senate and the House of Commons of Canada in Parliament assembled have submitted an address to Her Majesty requesting that Her Majesty may graciously be pleased to cause a Bill to be laid before the Parliament of the United Kingdom for that purpose.

Be it therefore enacted by the Queen's Most Excellent Majesty, by and with the advice and consent of the Lords Spiritual and Temporal, and Commons, in this present Parliament assembled, and by the authority of the same, as follows:

Constitution Act, 1982 enacted

1. The **Constitution Act, 1982** set out in Schedule B to this Act is hereby enacted for and shall have the force of law in Canada and shall come into force as provided in that Act.

Termination of power to legislate for Canada

2. No Act of the Parliament of the United Kingdom passed after the **Constitution Act, 1982** comes into force shall extend to Canada as part of its law.

French version

3. So far as it is not contained in Schedule B, the French version of this Act is set out in Schedule A to this Act and has the same authority in Canada as the English version thereof.

Short title

4. This Act may be cited as the **Canada Act 1982.**

SCHEDULE B

CONSTITUTION ACT, 1982

PART I

CANADIAN CHARTER OF RIGHTS AND FREEDOMS

Whereas Canada is founded upon principles that recognize the supremacy of God and the rule of law:

Guarantee of Rights and Freedoms

Rights and freedoms in Canada

1. The **Canadian Charter of Rights and Freedoms** guarantees the rights and freedoms set out in it subject only to such reasonable limits prescribed by law as can be demonstrably justified in a free and democratic society.

Fundamental Freedoms

Fundamental freedoms

2. Everyone has the following fundamental freedoms:

(a) freedom of conscience and religion;

(b) freedom of thought, belief, opinion and expression, including freedom of the press and other media of communication;

(c) freedom of peaceful assembly; and

(d) freedom of association.

Democratic Rights

Democratic rights of citizens

3. Every citizen of Canada has the right to vote in an election of members of the House of Commons or of a legislative assembly and to be qualified for membership therein.

Maximum duration of legislative bodies

4. (1) No House of Commons and no legislative assembly shall continue for longer than five years from the date fixed for the return of the writs at a general election of its members.

Continuation in special circumstances

(2) In time of real or apprehended war, invasion or insurrection, a House of Commons may be continued by Parliament and a legislative assembly may be continued by the legislature beyond five years if such continuation is not opposed by the votes of more than one-third of the members of the House of Commons or the legislative assembly, as the case may be.

Annual sitting of legislative bodies

5. There shall be a sitting of Parliament and of each legislature at least once every twelve months.

Mobility Rights

Mobility of citizens

6. (1) Every citizen of Canada has the right to enter, remain leave Canada.

Rights to move and gain livelihood

(2) Every citizen of Canada and every person who has the status of a permanent resident of Canada has the right

(a) to move to and take up residence in any province; and

(b) to pursue the gaining of a livelihood in any province.

Limitation

(3) The rights specified in subsection (2) are subject to

(a) any laws or practices of general application in force in a province other than those that discriminate among persons primarily on the basis of province of present or previous residence; and

(b) any laws providing for reasonable residency requirements as a qualification for the receipt of publicly provided social services.

Affirmative action programs

(4) Subsections (2) and (3) do not preclude any law, program or activity that has as its object the amelioration in a province of conditions of individuals in that province who are socially or economically disadvantaged if the rate of employment in that province is below the rate of employment in Canada.

Legal Rights

Life, liberty and security of person

7. Everyone has the right to life, liberty and security of the person and the right not to be deprived thereof except in accordance with the principles of fundamental justice.

Search or seizure

8. Everyone has the right to be secure against unreasonable search or seizure.

Detention or imprisonment

9. Everyone has the right not to be arbitrarily detained or imprisoned.

Arrest or detention

10. Everyone has the right on arrest or detention

(a) to be informed promptly of the reasons therefor;

(b) to retain and instruct counsel without delay and to be informed of that right; and

(c) to have the validity of the detention determined by way of *habeas corpus* and to be released if the detention is not lawful.

Proceedings in criminal and penal matters

11. Any person charged with an offence has the right

(a) to be informed without unreasonable delay of the specific offence;

(b) to be tried within a reasonable time;

(c) not to be compelled to be a witness in proceedings against that person in respect of the offence;

(d) to be presumed innocent until proven guilty according to law in a fair and public hearing by an independent and impartial tribunal;

(e) not to be denied reasonable bail without just cause;

(f) except in the case of an offence under military law tried before a military tribunal, to the benefit of trial by jury where the maximum punishment for the offence is imprisonment for five years or a more severe punishment;

(g) not to be found guilty on account of any act or omission unless, at the time of the act or omission, it constituted an offence under Canadian or international law or was criminal according to the general principles of law recognized by the community of nations;

(h) if finally acquitted of the offence, not to be tried for it again and, if finally found guilty and punished for the offence, not to be tried or punished for it again; and

(i) if found guilty of the offence and if the punishment for the offence has been varied between the time of commission and the time of sentencing, to the benefit of the lesser punishment.

Treatment or punishment

12. Everyone has the right not to be subjected to any cruel and unusual treatment or punishment.

Self-crimination

13. A witness who testifies in any proceedings has the right not to have any incriminating evidence so given used to incriminate that witness in any other proceedings, except in a prosecution for perjury or for the giving of contradictory evidence.

Interpreter

14. A party or witness in any proceedings who does not understand or speak the language in which the proceedings are conducted or who is deaf has the right to the assistance of an interpreter.

Equality Rights

Equality before and under law and equal protection and benefit of law

15 (1) Every individual is equal before and under the law and has the right to the equal protection and equal benefit of the law without discrimination and, in particular, without discrimination based on race, national or ethnic origin, colour, religion, sex, age or mental or physical disability.

Affirmative action programs

(2) Subsection (1) does not preclude any law, program or activity that has as its object the amelioration of conditions of disadvantaged individuals or groups including those that are disadvantaged because of race, national or ethnic origin, colour, religion, sex, age or mental or physical disability.

Official Languages of Canada

Official languages of Canada

16. (1) English and French are the official languages of Canada and have equality of status and equal rights and privileges as to their use in all institutions of the Parliament and government of Canada.

Official languages of New Brunswick

(2) English and French are the official languages of New Brunswick and have equality of status and equal rights and privileges as to their use in all institution of the legislature and government of New Brunswick.

Advancement of status and use

(3) Nothing in this Charter limits the authority of Parliament or a legislature to advance the equality of status or use of English and French.

Proceedings of Parliament

17. (1) Everyone has the right to use English or French in any debates and other proceedings of Parliament.

Proceedings of New Brunswick legislature

(2) Everyone has the right to use English or French in any debates and other proceedings of the legislature of New Brunswick.

Parliamentary statutes and records

18. (1) The statutes, records and journals of Parliament shall be printed and published in English and French and both language versions are equally authoritative.

New Brunswick statutes and records

(2) The statutes, records and journals of the legislature of New Brunswick shall be printed and published in English and French and both language versions are equally authoritative.

Proceedings in courts established by Parliament

19. (1) Either English or French may be used by any person in, or in any pleading in or process issuing from, any court established by Parliament.

Proceedings in New Brunswick courts

(2) Either English or French may be used by any person in, or in any pleading in or process issuing from, any court of New Brunswick.

Communications by public with federal institutions

20. (1) Any member of the public in Canada has the right to communicate with, and to receive available services from, any head or central office of an institution of the Parliament or government of Canada in English or French, and has the same right with respect to any other office of any such institution where

(a) there is a significant demand for communications with and services from that office in such language; or

(b) due to the nature of the office, it is reasonable that communications with and services from that office be available in both English and French.

Communications by public with New Brunswick institutions

(2) Any member of the public in New Brunswick has the right to communicate with, and to receive available services from, any office of an institution of the legislature or government of New Brunswick in English or French.

Continuation of
existing
constitutional
provisions

21. Nothing in sections 16 to 20 abrogates or derogates from any right, privilege or obligation with respect to the English and French languages, or either of them, that exists or is continued by virtue of any other provision of the Constitution of Canada.

Rights and privileges
preserved

22. Nothing in sections 16 to 20 abrogates or derogates from any legal or customary right or privilege acquired or enjoyed either before or after the coming into force of this Charter with respect to any language that is not English or French.

Minority Language Educational Rights

Language of
instruction

23. (1) Citizens of Canada

(a) whose first language learned and still understood is that of the English or French linguistic minority population of the province in which they reside, or

(b) who have received their primary school instruction in Canada in English or French and reside in a province where the language in which they received that instruction is the language of the English or French linguistic minority population of the province,

have the right to have their children receive primary and secondary school instruction in that language in that province.

Continuity of
language instruction

(2) Citizens of Canada of whom any child has received or is receiving primary or secondary school instruction in English or French in Canada, have the right to have all their children receive primary and secondary school instruction in the same language.

Application where
numbers warrant

(3) The right of citizens of Canada under subsections (1) and (2) to have their children receive primary and secondary school instruction in the language of the English or French linguistic minority population of a province

(a) applies wherever in the province the number of children of citizens who have such a right is sufficient to warrant the provision to them out of public funds of minority language instruction; and

(b) includes, where the number of those children so warrants, the right to have them receive that instruction in minority language educational facilities provided out of public funds.

Enforcement

Enforcement of
guaranteed rights and
freedoms

24. (1) Anyone whose rights or freedoms, as guaranteed by this Charter, have been infringed or denied may apply to a court of competent jurisdiction to obtain such remedy as the court considers appropriate and just in the circumstances.

Exclusion of evidence bringing administration of justice into disrepute

(2) Where, in proceedings under subsection (1), a court concludes that evidence was obtained in a manner that infringed or denied any rights or freedoms guaranteed by this Charter, the evidence shall be excluded if it is established that, having regard to all the circumstances, the admission of it in the proceedings would bring the administration of justice into disrepute.

General

Aboriginal rights and freedoms not affected by Charter

25. The guarantee in this Charter of certain rights and freedoms shall not be construed so as to abrogate or derogate from any aboriginal, treaty or other rights or freedoms that pertain to the aboriginal peoples of Canada including

(a) any rights or freedoms that have been recognized by the Royal Proclamation of October 7, 1763; and

(b) any rights or freedoms that now exist by way of land claims agreements or may be so acquired.

Other rights and freedoms not affected by Charter

26. The guarantee in this Charter of certain rights and freedoms shall not be construed as denying the existence of any other rights or freedoms that exist in Canada.

Multicultural heritage

27. This Charter shall be interpreted in a manner consistent with the preservation and enhancement of the multicultural heritage of Canadians.

Rights guaranteed equally to both sexes

28. Notwithstanding anything in this Charter, the rights and freedoms referred to in it are guaranteed equally to male and female persons.

Rights respecting certain schools preserved

29. Nothing in this Charter abrogates or derogates from any rights or privileges guaranteed by or under the Constitution of Canada in respect of denominational, separate or dissentient schools.

Application to territories and territorial authorities

30. A reference in this Charter to a province or to the legislative assembly or legislature of a province shall be deemed to include a reference to the Yukon Territory and the Northwest Territories, or to the appropriate legislative authority thereof, as the case may be.

Legislative powers not extended

31. Nothing in this Charter extends the legislative powers of any body or authority.

Application of Charter

Application of Charter

32. (1) This Charter applies

(a) to the Parliament and government of Canada in respect of all matters within the authority of Parliament including all matters relating to the Yukon Territory and Northwest Territories; and

(b) to the legislature and government of each province in respect of all matters within the authority of the legislature of each province.

Exception

(2) Notwithstanding subsection (1), section 15 shall not have effect until three years after this section comes into force.

Exception where express declaration

33. (1) Parliament or the legislature of a province may expressly declare in an Act of Parliament or of the legislature, as the case may be, that the Act or a provision thereof shall operate notwithstanding a provision included in section 2 or sections 7 to 15 of this Charter.

Operation of exception

(2) An Act or a provision of an Act in respect of which a declaration made under this section is in effect shall have such operation as it would have but for the provision of this Charter referred to in the declaration.

Five year limitation

(3) A declaration made under subsection (1) shall cease to have effect five years after it comes into force or on such earlier date as may be specified in the declaration.

Re-enactment

(4) Parliament or the legislature of a province may re-enact a declaration made under subsection (1).

Five year limitation

(5) Subsection (3) applies in respect of a re-enactment made under subsection (4).

Citation

Citation

34. This Part may be cited as the **Canadian Charter of Rights and Freedoms**.

PART II

RIGHTS OF THE ABORIGINAL
PEOPLES OF CANADA

Recognition of existing aboriginal and treaty rights

35. (1) The existing aboriginal and treaty rights of the aboriginal peoples of Canada are hereby recognized and affirmed.

Definition of "aboriginal peoples of Canada"

(2) In this Act, "aboriginal peoples of Canada" includes the Indian, Inuit and Métis peoples of Canada.

Land claims agreements

(3) For greater certainty, in subsection (1) "treaty rights" includes rights that now exist by way of land claims agreements or may be so acquired.

Aboriginal and treaty rights are guaranteed equally to both sexes

(4) Notwithstanding any other provision of this Act, the aboriginal and treaty rights referred to in subsection (1) are guaranteed equally to male and female persons.

Commitment to participation in constitutional conference

35.1 The government of Canada and the provincial governments are committed to the principle that before any amendment is made to Class 24 of section 91 of the "**Constitution Act, 1867**", to section 25 of this Act or to this Part,

(a) a constitutional conference that includes in its agenda an item relating to the proposed amendment, composed of the Prime Minister of Canada and the first ministers of the provinces, will be convened by the Prime Minister of Canada; and

(b) the Prime Minister of Canada will invite representatives of the aboriginal peoples of Canada to participate in the discussion on that item.

PART III

EQUALIZATION AND
REGIONAL DISPARITIES

Commitment to promote equal opportunities

36. (1) Without altering the legislative authority of Parliament or of the provincial legislatures, or the rights of any of them with respect to the exercise of their legislative authority, Parliament and the legislatures, together with the government of Canada and the provincial governments, are committed to

(a) promoting equal opportunities for the well-being of Canadians;

(b) furthering economic development to reduce disparity in opportunities; and

(c) providing essential public services of reasonable quality to all Canadians.

Commitment respecting public services

(2) Parliament and the government of Canada are committed to the principle of making equalization payments to ensure that provincial governments have sufficient revenues to provide reasonably comparable levels of public services at reasonably comparable levels of taxation.

PART IV

CONSTITUTIONAL CONFERENCE

37. Repealed.

PART IV.1

CONSTITUTIONAL CONFERENCES

37.1 Repealed.

PART V

PROCEDURE FOR AMENDING CONSTITUTION OF CANADA

General procedure for amending Constitution of Canada

38. (1) An amendment to the Constitution of Canada may be made by proclamation issued by the Governor General under the Great Seal of Canada where so authorized by

(a) resolutions of the Senate and House of Commons; and

(b) resolutions of the legislative assemblies of at least two-thirds of the provinces that have, in the aggregate, according to the then latest general census, at least fifty per cent of the population of all the provinces.

Majority of members

(2) An amendment made under subsection (1) that derogates from the legislative powers, the proprietary rights or any other rights or privileges of the legislature or government of a province shall require a resolution supported by a majority of the members of each of the Senate, the House of Commons and the legislative assemblies required under subsection (1).

Expression of dissent

(3) An amendment referred to in subsection (2) shall not have effect in a province the legislative assembly of which has expressed its dissent thereto by resolution supported by a majority of its members prior to the issue of the proclamation to which the amendment relates unless that legislative assembly, subsequently, by resolution supported by a majority of its members, revokes its dissent and authorizes the amendment.

Revocation of dissent

(4) A resolution of dissent made for the purposes of subsection (3) may be revoked at any time before or after the issue of the proclamation to which it relates.

Restriction on proclamation

39. (1) A proclamation shall not be issued under subsection 38(1) before the expiration of one year from the adoption of the resolution initiating the amendment procedure thereunder, unless the legislative assembly of each province has previously adopted a resolution of assent or dissent.

Idem

(2) A proclamation shall not be issued under subsection 38(1) after the expiration of three years from the adoption of the resolution initiating the amendment procedure thereunder.

Compensation

40. Where an amendment is made under subsection 38(1) that transfers provincial legislative powers relating to education or other cultural matters from provincial legislatures to Parliament, Canada shall provide reasonable compensation to any province to which the amendment does not apply.

Amendment by unanimous consent

41. An amendment to the Constitution of Canada in relation to the following matters may be made by proclamation issued by the Governor General under the Great Seal of Canada only where authorized by resolutions of the Senate and House of Commons and of the legislative assembly of each province:

(a) the office of the Queen, the Governor General and the Lieutenant Governor of a province;

(b) the right of a province to a number of members in the House of Commons not less than the number of Senators by which the province is entitled to be represented at the time this Part comes into force;

(c) subject to section 43, the use of the English or the French language;

(d) the composition of the Supreme Court of Canada; and

(e) an amendment to this Part.

Amendment by general procedure

42. (1) An amendment to the Constitution of Canada in relation to the following matters may be made only in accordance with subsection 38(1):

(a) the principle of proportionate representation of the provinces in the House of Commons prescribed by the Constitution of Canada;

(b) the powers of the Senate and the method of selecting Senators;

(c) the number of members by which a province is entitled to be represented in the Senate and the residence qualifications of Senators;

(d) subject to paragraph 41(d), the Supreme Court of Canada;

(e) the extension of existing provinces into the territories; and

(f) notwithstanding any other law or practice, the establishment of new provinces.

Exception

(2) Subsections 38(2) to (4) do not apply in respect of amendments in relation to matters referred to in subsection (1).

Amendment of provisions relating to some but not all provinces

43. An amendment to the Constitution of Canada in relation to any provision that applies to one or more, but not all, provinces, including

(a) any alteration to boundaries between provinces, and

(b) any amendment to any provision that relates to the use of the English or the French language within a province,

may be made by proclamation issued by the Governor General under the Great Seal of Canada only where so authorized by resolutions of the Senate and House of Commons and of the legislative assembly of each province to which the amendment applies.

Amendments by Parliament

44. Subject to sections 41 and 42, Parliament may exclusively make laws amending the Constitution of Canada in relation to the executive government of Canada or the Senate and House of Commons.

Amendments by provincial legislatures

45. Subject to section 41, the legislature of each province may exclusively make laws amending the constitution of the province.

Initiation of amendment procedures

46. (1) The procedures for amendment under sections 38, 41, 42 and 43 may be initiated either by the Senate or the House of Commons or by the legislative assembly of a province.

Revocation of authorization

(2) A resolution of assent made for the purposes of this Part may be revoked at any time before the issue of a proclamation authorized by it.

Amendments without Senate resolution

47. (1) An amendment to the Constitution of Canada made by proclamation under section 38, 41, 42 or 43 may be made without a resolution of the Senate authorizing the issue of the proclamation if, within one hundred and eighty days after the adoption by the House of Commons of a resolution authorizing its issue, the Senate has not adopted such a resolution and if, at any time after the expiration of that period, the House of Commons again adopts the resolution.

Computation of period

(2) Any period when Parliament is prorogued or dissolved shall not be counted in computing the one hundred and eighty day period referred to in subsection (1).

Advice to issue proclamation

48. The Queen's Privy Council for Canada shall advise the Governor General to issue a proclamation under this Part forthwith on the adoption of the resolutions required for an amendment made by proclamation under this Part.

Constitutional conference

49. A constitutional conference composed of the Prime Minister of Canada and the first ministers of the provinces shall be convened by the Prime Minister of Canada within fifteen years after this Part comes into force to review the provisions of this Part.

PART VI

AMENDMENT TO THE CONSTITUTION ACT, 1867

50. {Note: The amendment is set out as section 92A of the **Constitution Act, 1867.**}

51. {Note: The amendment is set out as the Sixth Schedule of the **Constitution Act, 1867.**}

PART VII

GENERAL

Primacy of Constitution of Canada

52. (1) The Constitution of Canada is the supreme law of Canada, and any law that is inconsistent with the provisions of the Constitution is, to the extent of the inconsistency, of no force or effect.

Constitution of Canada

(2) The Constitution of Canada includes

(a) the **Canada Act 1982**, including this Act;

(b) the Acts and orders referred to in the schedule; and

(c) any amendment to any Act or order referred to in paragraph (a) or (b).

Amendments to Constitution of Canada

(3) Amendments to the Constitution of Canada shall be made only in accordance with the authority contained in the Constitution of Canada.

Repeals and new names

53. (1) The enactments referred to in Column I of the schedule are hereby repealed or amended to the extent indicated in Column II thereof and, unless repealed, shall continue as law in Canada under the names set out in Column III thereof.

Consequential amendments

(2) Every enactment, except the **Canada Act 1982**, that refers to an enactment referred to in the schedule by the name in Column I thereof is hereby amended by substituting for that name the corresponding name in Column III thereof, and any British North America Act not referred to in the schedule may be cited as the **Constitution Act** followed by the year and number, if any, of its enactment.

Repeal and consequential amendments

54. Part IV is repealed on the day that is one year after this Part comes into force and this section may be repealed and this Act renumbered, consequentially upon the repeal of Part IV and this section, by proclamation issued by the Governor General under the Great Seal of Canada.

54.1 Repealed.

French version of
Constitution of
Canada

55. A French version of the portions of the Constitution of Canada referred to in the schedule shall be prepared by the Minister of Justice of Canada as expeditiously as possible and, when any portion thereof sufficient to warrant action being taken has been so prepared, it shall be put forward for enactment by proclamation issued by the Governor General under the Great Seal of Canada pursuant to the procedure then applicable to an amendment of the same provisions of the Constitution of Canada.

English and French
versions of certain
constitutional texts

56. Where any portion of the Constitution of Canada has been or is enacted in English and French or where a French version of any portion of the Constitution is enacted pursuant to section 55, the English and French versions of that portion of the Constitution are equally authoritative.

English and French
versions of this Act

57. The English and French versions of this Act are equally authoritative.

Commencement

58. Subject to section 59, this Act shall come into force on a day to be fixed by proclamation issued by the Queen or the Governor General under the Great Seal of Canada.

Commencement of
paragraph 23(1)(a)
in respect of Quebec

59. (1) Paragraph 23(1)(a) shall come into force in respect of Quebec on a day to be fixed by proclamation issued by the Queen or the Governor General under the Great Seal of Canada.

Authorization of
Quebec

(2) A proclamation under subsection (1) shall be issued only where authorized by the legislative assembly or government of Quebec.

Repeal of this section

(3) This section may be repealed on the day paragraph 23(1)(a) comes into force in respect of Quebec and this Act amended and renumbered, consequentially upon the repeal of this section, by proclamation issued by the Queen or the Governor General under the Great Seal of Canada.

Short title and
citations

60. This Act may be cited as the **Constitution Act, 1982**, and the Constitution Acts 1867 to 1975 (No. 2) and this Act may be cited together as the **Constitution Acts, 1867 to 1982**.

References

61. A reference to the **"Constitution Acts, 1867 to 1982"** shall be deemed to include a reference to the **"Constitution Amendment Proclamation, 1983"**.

{Note: Added by the **Constitution Amendment Proclamation, 1983.**}

SCHEDULE

to the

CONSTITUTION ACT, 1982
MODERNIZATION OF THE CONSTITUTION

Column I Act affected	Column II Amendment	Column III New Name
1. British North America Act, 1867, 30-31 Vict., c. 3 (U.K.)	(1) Section 1 is repealed and the following substituted therefor: "1. This Act may be cited as the *Constitution Act, 1867.*" (2) Section 20 is repealed. (3) Class i of section 91 is repealed. (4) Class 1 of section 92 is repealed.	Constitution Act, 1867
2. An Act to amend and continue the Act 32-33 Victoria chapter 3; and to establish and provide for the Government of the Province of Manitoba, 1870, 33 Vict., c. 3 (Can.)	(1) The long title is repealed and the following substituted therefor: "*Manitoba Act, 1870.*" (2) Section 20 is repealed.	Manitoba Act, 1870
3. Order of Her Majesty in Council admitting Rupert's Land and the North-Western Territory into the union, dated the 23rd day of June, 1870		Rupert's Land and North-Western Territory Order
4. Order of Her Majesty in Council admitting British Columbia into the Union, dated the 16th day of May, 1871		British Columbia Terms of Union
5. British North America Act, 1871, 34-35 Vict., c. 28 (U.K.)	Section 1 is repealed and the following substituted therefor: "1. This Act may be cited as the *Constitution Act, 1871.*"	Constitution Act, 1871

Column I Act affected	Column II Amendment	Column III New Name
6. Order of Her Majesty in Council admitting Prince Edward Island into the Union, dated the 26th day of June, 1873		Prince Edward Island Terms of Union
7. Parliament of Canada Act, 1875, 38-39 Vict., c. 38 (U.K.)		Parliament of Canada Act, 1875
8. Order of Her Majesty in Council admitting all British possessions and Territories in North America and islands adjacent thereto into the Union, dated the 31st day of July, 1880		Adjacent Territories Order
9. British North America Act, 1886, 49-50 Vict., c. 35 (U.K.)	Section 3 is repealed and the following substituted therefor: "3. This Act may be cited as the *Constitution Act, 1886.*"	Constitution Act, 1886
10. Canada (Ontario Boundary) Act, 1889, 52-53 Vict., c. 28 (U.K.)		Canada (Ontario Boundary) Act, 1889
11. Canadian Speaker (Appointment of Deputy) Act, 1895, 2nd Sess., 59 Vict., c. 3 (U.K.)	The Act is repealed.	
12. The Alberta Act, 1905, 4-5 Edw. VII, c. 3 (Can.)		Alberta Act
13. The Saskatchewan Act, 1905, 4-5 Edw. VII, c. 42 (Can.)		Saskatchewan Act
14. British North America Act, 1907, 7 Edw. VII, c. 11 (U.K.)	Section 2 is repealed and the following substituted therefor: "2. This Act may be cited as the *Constitution Act, 1907.*"	Constitution Act, 1907

Column I Act affected	Column II Amendment	Column III New Name
15. British North America Act, 1915, 5-6 Geo. V, c. 45 (U.K.)	Section 3 is repealed and the following substituted therefor: "3. This Act may be cited as the *Constitution Act, 1915.*"	Constitution Act, 1915
16. British North America Act, 1930, 20-21 Geo. V, c. 26 (U.K.)	Section 3 is repealed and the following substituted therefor: "3. This Act may be cited as the *Constitution Act, 1930.*"	Constitution Act, 1930
17. Statute of Westminster, 1931, 22 Geo. V, c. 4 (U.K.)	In so far as they apply to Canada, (a) section 4 is repealed; and (b) subsection 7(1) is repealed.	Statute of Westminster, 1931
18. British North America Act, 1940, 3-4 Geo. VI, c. 36 (U.K.)	Section 2 is repealed and the following substituted therefor: "2. This Ac t may be cited as the *Constitution Act, 1940.*"	Constitution Act, 1940
19. British North America Act, 1943, 6-7 Geo. VI, c. 30 (U.K.)	The Act is repealed.	
20. British North America Act, 1946, 9-10 Geo. VI, c. 63 (U.K.)	The Act is repealed.	
21. British North America Act, 1949, 12-13 Geo. VI, c. 22 (U.K.)	Section 3 is repealed and the following substituted therefor: "3. This Act may be cited as the *Newfoundland Act.*"	Newfoundland Act
22. British North America (No. 2) Act, 1949, 13 Geo. VI, c. 81 (U.K.)	The Act is repealed.	
23. British North America Act, 1951, 14-15 Geo. VI, c. 32 (U.K.)	The Act is repealed.	

Column I Act affected	Column II Amendment	Column III New Name
24. British North America Act, 1952, 1 Eliz. II, c. 15 (Can.)	The Act is repealed.	
25. British North America Act, 1960, 9 Eliz. II, c. 2 (U.K.)	Section 2 is repealed and the following substituted therefor: "2. This Act may be cited as the *Constitution Act, 1960.*"	Constitution Act, 1960
26. British North America Act, 1964, 12-13 Eliz. II, c. 73 (U.K.)	Section 2 is repealed and the following substituted therefor: "2. This Act may be cited as the *Constitution Act, 1964.*"	Constitution Act, 1964
27. British North America Act, 1965, 14 Eliz. II, c. 4, Part I (Can.)	Section 2 is repealed and the following substituted therefor: "2. This Part may be cited as the *Constitution Act, 1965.*"	Constitution Act, 1965
28. British North America Act, 1974, 23 Eliz. II, c. 13, Part I (Can.)	Section 3, as amended by 25-26 Eliz. II, c. 28, s. 38(1) (Can.), is repealed and the following substituted therefor: "3. This Part may be cited as the *Constitution Act, 1974.*"	Constitution Act, 1974
29. British North America Act, 1975, 23-24 Eliz. II, c. 28, Part I (Can.)	Section 3, as amended by 25-26 Eliz. II, c. 28, s. 31 (Can.), is repealed and the following substituted therefor: "3. This Part may be cited as the *Constitution Act (No. 1), 1975.*"	Constitution Act (No. 1), 1975
30. British North America Act, (No. 2), 1975, 23-24 Eliz. II, c. 53 (Can.)	Section 3 is repealed and the following substituted therefor: "3. This Act may be cited as the *Constitution Act (No. 2), 1975.*"	Constitution Act (No. 2), 1975

CANADA ACT

Authentic copy of the Address to H.M. the Queen adopted by the House of Commons in both official languages and signed by the Speaker Jeanne Sauvé on December 2, 1981.

A similar Address was adopted by the Senate on December 8, 1981 and signed by the Speaker Jean Marchand.

This text was put at our disposal by the Queen's Printer for Canada Mr N. Manchevsky and the reproduction authorized by the Speakers of the Senate and the House of Commons.

To the Queen's Most Excellent Majesty:

Most Gracious Sovereign:

We, Your Majesty's loyal subjects, the House of Commons of Canada in Parliament assembled, respectfully approach Your Majesty, requesting that you may graciously be pleased to cause to be laid before the Parliament of the United Kingdom a measure containing the recitals and clauses hereinafter set forth:

An Act to give effect to a request by the Senate and House of Commons of Canada

Whereas Canada has requested and consented to the enactment of an Act of the Parliament of the United Kingdom to give effect to the provisions hereinafter set forth and the Senate and the House of Commons of Canada in Parliament assembled have submitted an address to Her Majesty requesting that

Her Majesty may graciously be pleased to cause a Bill to be laid before the Parliament of the United Kingdom for that purpose.

Be it therefore enacted by the Queen's Most Excellent Majesty, by and with the advice and consent of the Lords Spiritual and Temporal, and Commons, in this present Parliament assembled, and by the authority of the same, as follows:

Constitution
Act, 1981
enacted

1. The Constitution Act, 1981 set out in Schedule B to this Act is hereby enacted for and shall have the force of law in Canada and shall come into force as provided in that Act.

Termination
of power to
legislate for
Canada

2. No Act of the Parliament of the United Kingdom passed after the Constitution Act, 1981 comes into force shall extend to Canada as part of its law.

French
version

3. So far as it is not contained in Schedule B, the French version of this Act is set out in Schedule A to this Act and has the same authority in Canada as the English version thereof.

Short
Title

4. This Act may be cited as the Canada Act.

Constitution Act, 1981

Part I

Canadian Charter of Rights and Freedoms

Whereas Canada is founded upon principles that recognize the supremacy of God and the rule of law:

Guarantee of Rights and Freedoms

Rights and freedoms in Canada

1. The Canadian Charter of Rights and Freedoms guarantees the rights and freedoms set out in it subject only to such reasonable limits prescribed by law as can be demonstrably justified in a free and democratic society.

Fundamental Freedoms

Fundamental freedoms

2. Everyone has the following fundamental freedoms:

(a) freedom of conscience and religion;

(b) freedom of thought, belief, opinion and expression, including freedom of the press and other media of communication;

(c) freedom of peaceful assembly; and

(d) freedom of association.

Democratic Rights

Democratic rights of citizens

3. Every citizen of Canada has the right to vote in an election of members of the House of Commons or of a legislative assembly and to be qualified for membership therein.

Maximum duration of legislative bodies

4. (1) No House of Commons and no legislative assembly shall continue for longer than five years from the date fixed for the return of the writs at a general election of its members.

Continuation in special circumstances

(2) In time of real or apprehended war, invasion or insurrection, a House of Commons may be continued by Parliament and a legislative assembly may be continued by the legislature beyond five years if such continuation is not opposed by the votes of more than one-third of the members of the House of Commons or the legislative assembly, as the case may be.

Annual sitting of legislative bodies

5. There shall be a sitting of Parliament and of each legislature at least once every twelve months.

Mobility Rights

Mobility of citizens

6. (1) Every citizen of Canada has the right to enter, remain in and leave Canada.

Rights to move and gain livelihood

(2) Every citizen of Canada and every person who has the status of a permanent resident of Canada has the right

(a) to move to and take up residence in any province; and

(b) to pursue the gaining of a livelihood in any province.

Limitation

(3) The rights specified in subsection (2) are subject to

(a) any laws or practices of general application in force in a province other than those that discriminate among persons primarily on the basis of province of present or previous residence; and

(b) any laws providing for reasonable residency requirements as a qualification for the receipt of publicly provided social services.

Affirmative action programs

(4) Subsections (2) and (3) do not preclude any law, program or activity that has as its object the amelioration in a province of conditions of individuals in that province who are socially or economically disadvantaged if the rate of employment in that province is below the rate of employment in Canada.

Legal Rights

Life, liberty and security of person

7. Everyone has the right to life, liberty and security of the person and the right not to be deprived thereof except in accordance with the principles of fundamental justice.

Search or seizure

8. Everyone has the right to be secure against unreasonable search or seizure.

Detention or imprisonment

9. Everyone has the right not to be arbitrarily detained or imprisoned.

Arrest or detention

10. Everyone has the right on arrest or detention

(a) to be informed promptly of the reasons therefor;

(b) to retain and instruct counsel without delay and to be informed of that right; and

(c) to have the validity of the detention determined by way of _habeas corpus_ and to be released if the detention is not lawful.

Proceedings in criminal and penal matters

11. Any person charged with an offence has the right

(a) to be informed without unreasonable delay of the specific offence;

(b) to be tried within a reasonable time;

(c) not to be compelled to be a witness in proceedings against that person in respect of the offence;

(d) to be presumed innocent until proven guilty according to law in a fair and public hearing by an independent and impartial tribunal;

(e) not to be denied reasonable bail without just cause;

(f) except in the case of an offence under military law tried before a military tribunal, to the benefit of trial by jury where the maximum punishment for the offence is imprisonment for five years or a more severe punishment;

(g) not to be found guilty on account of any act or omission unless, at the time of the act or omission, it constituted an offence under Canadian or international law or was criminal according to the general principles of law recognized by the community of nations;

(h) if finally acquitted of the offence, not to be tried for it again and, if finally found guilty and punished for the offence, not to be tried or punished for it again; and

(i) if found guilty of the offence and if the punishment for the offence has been varied between the time of commission and the time of sentencing, to the benefit of the lesser punishment.

Treatment or punishment

12. Everyone has the right not to be subjected to any cruel and unusual treatment or punishment.

Self-crimination

13. A witness who testifies in any proceedings has the right not to have any incriminating evidence so given used to incriminate that witness in any other proceedings, except in a prosecution for perjury or for the giving of contradictory evidence.

Interpreter

14. A party or witness in any proceedings who does not understand or speak the language in which the proceedings are conducted or who is deaf has the right to the assistance of an interpreter.

Equality Rights

Equality before and under law and equal protection and benefit of law

15. (1) Every individual is equal before and under the law and has the right to the equal protection and equal benefit of the law without discrimination and, in particular, without discrimination

based on race, national or ethnic origin, colour, religion, sex, age or mental or physical disability.

Affirmative action programs

(2) Subsection (1) does not preclude any law, program or activity that has as its object the amelioration of conditions of disadvantaged individuals or groups including those that are disadvantaged because of race, national or ethnic origin, colour, religion, sex, age or mental or physical disability.

Official Languages of Canada

Official languages of Canada

16. (1) English and French are the official languages of Canada and have equality of status and equal rights and privileges as to their use in all institutions of the Parliament and government of Canada.

Official languages of New Brunswick

(2) English and French are the official languages of New Brunswick and have equality of status and equal rights and privileges as to their use in all institutions of the legislature and government of New Brunswick.

Advancement of status and use

(3) Nothing in this Charter limits the authority of Parliament or a legislature to advance the equality of status or use of English and French.

Proceedings of Parliament

17. (1) Everyone has the right to use English or French in any debates and other proceedings of Parliament.

Proceedings of New Brunswick legislature

(2) Everyone has the right to use English or French in any debates and other proceedings of the legislature of New Brunswick.

Parliamentary statutes and records

18. (1) The statutes, records and journals of Parliament shall be printed and published in English and French and both language versions are equally authoritative.

New Brunswick statutes and records

(2) The statutes, records and journals of the legislature of New Brunswick shall be printed and published in English and French and both language versions are equally authoritative.

Proceedings in courts established by Parliament

19. (1) Either English or French may be used by any person in, or in any pleading in or process issuing from, any court established by Parliament.

Proceedings in New Brunswick courts

(2) Either English or French may be used by any person in, or in any pleading in or process issuing from, any court of New Brunswick.

Communications by public with federal institutions

20. (1) Any member of the public in Canada has the right to communicate with, and to receive available services from, any head or central office of an institution of the Parliament or government of Canada in English or French, and has the same right with respect to any other office of any such institution where

(a) there is a significant demand for communications with and services from that office in such language; or

(b) due to the nature of the office, it is reasonable that communications with and services from that office be available in both English and French.

Communications by public with New Brunswick institutions

(2) Any member of the public in New Brunswick has the right to communicate with, and to receive available services from, any office of an institution of the legislature or government of New Brunswick in English or French.

Continuation of existing constitutional provisions

21. Nothing in sections 16 to 20 abrogates or derogates from any right, privilege or obligation with respect to the English and French languages, or either of them, that exists or is continued by virtue of any other provision of the Constitution of Canada.

22. Nothing in sections 16 to 20 abrogates or derogates from any legal or customary right or privilege acquired or enjoyed either before or after the coming into force of this Charter with respect to any language that is not English or French.

Minority Language Educational Rights

23. (1) Citizens of Canada

(a) whose first language learned and still understood is that of the English or French linguistic minority population of the province in which they reside, or

(b) who have received their primary school instruction in Canada in English or French and reside in a province where the language in which they received that instruction is the language of the English or French linguistic minority population of the province,

have the right to have their children receive primary and secondary school instruction in that language in that province.

(2) Citizens of Canada of whom any child has received or is receiving primary or secondary school instruction in English or French in Canada, have the right to have all their children receive primary and secondary school instruction in the same language.

(3) The right of citizens of Canada under subsections (1) and (2) to have their children receive primary and secondary school instruction in the language of the English or French linguistic minority population of a province

(a) applies wherever in the province the number of children of citizens who have such a right is sufficient to warrant the provision to them out of public funds of minority language instruction; and

(b) includes, where the number of those children so warrants, the right to have them receive that instruction in minority language educational facilities provided out of public funds.

Enforcement

24. (1) Anyone whose rights or freedoms, as guaranteed by this Charter, have been infringed or denied may apply to a court of competent jurisdiction to obtain such remedy as the court considers appropriate and just in the circumstances.

(2) Where, in proceedings under subsection (1), a court concludes that evidence was obtained in a manner that infringed or denied any rights or freedoms guaranteed by this Charter, the evidence shall be excluded if it is established that, having regard to all the circumstances, the admission of it in the proceedings would bring the administration of justice into disrepute.

General

25. The guarantee in this Charter of certain rights and freedoms shall not be construed so as to abrogate or derogate from any aboriginal, treaty or other rights or freedoms that pertain to the aboriginal peoples of Canada including

(a) any rights or freedoms that have been recognized by the Royal Proclamation of October 7, 1763; and

(b) any rights or freedoms that may be acquired by the aboriginal peoples of Canada by way of land claims settlement.

26. The guarantee in this Charter of certain rights and freedoms shall not be construed as denying the existence of any other rights or freedoms that exist in Canada.

27. This Charter shall be interpreted in a manner consistent with the preservation and enhancement of the multicultural heritage of Canadians.

Rights guaranteed equally to both sexes

28. Notwithstanding anything in this Charter, the rights and freedoms referred to in it are guaranteed equally to male and female persons.

Rights respecting certain schools preserved

29. Nothing in this Charter abrogates or derogates from any rights or privileges guaranteed by or under the Constitution of Canada in respect of denominational, separate or dissentient schools.

Application to territories and territorial authorities

30. A reference in this Charter to a province or to the legislative assembly or legislature of a province shall be deemed to include a reference to the Yukon Territory and the Northwest Territories, or to the appropriate legislative authority thereof, as the case may be.

Legislative powers not extended

31. Nothing in this Charter extends the legislative powers of any body or authority.

Application of Charter

Application of Charter

32. (1) This Charter applies

(a) to the Parliament and government of Canada in respect of all matters within the authority of Parliament including all matters relating to the Yukon Territory and Northwest Territories; and

(b) to the legislature and government of each province in respect of all matters within the authority of the legislature of each province.

Exception

(2) Notwithstanding subsection (1), section 15 shall not have effect until three years after this section comes into force.

Exception where express declaration

33. (1) Parliament or the legislature of a province may expressly declare in an Act of Parliament or of the legislature, as the case may be, that the Act or a provision thereof shall operate notwithstanding a provision included in section 2 or sections 7 to 15 of this Charter.

Operation of exception

(2) An Act or a provision of an Act in respect of which a declaration made under this section is in effect shall have such operation as it would have but for the provision of this Charter referred to in the declaration.

Five year limitation

(3) A declaration made under subsection (1) shall cease to have effect five years after it comes into force or on such earlier date as may be specified in the declaration.

Re-enactment

(4) Parliament or a legislature of a province may re-enact a declaration made under subsection (1).

Five year limitation

(5) Subsection (3) applies in respect of a re-enactment made under subsection (4).

Citation

Citation

34. This Part may be cited as the Canadian Charter of Rights and Freedoms.

Part II
Rights of the aboriginal peoples of Canada

Recognition of existing aboriginal and treaty rights

35. (1) The existing aboriginal and treaty rights of the aboriginal peoples of Canada are hereby recognized and affirmed.

Definition of "aboriginal peoples of Canada"

(2) In this Act, "aboriginal peoples of Canada" includes the Indian, Inuit and Métis peoples of Canada.

Part III
Equalization and regional disparities

36. (1) Without altering the legislative authority of Parliament or of the provincial legislatures, or the rights of any of them with respect to the exercise of their legislative authority, Parliament and the legislatures, together with the government of Canada and the provincial governments, are committed to

(a) promoting equal opportunities for the well-being of Canadians;

(b) furthering economic development to reduce disparity in opportunities; and

(c) providing essential public services of reasonable quality to all Canadians.

(2) Parliament and the government of Canada are committed to the principle of making equalization payments to ensure that provincial governments have sufficient revenues to provide reasonably comparable levels of public services at reasonably comparable levels of taxation.

Part IV

Constitutional Conference

37. (1) A constitutional conference composed of the Prime Minister of Canada and the first ministers of the provinces shall be convened by the Prime Minister of Canada within one year after this Part comes into force.

(2) The conference convened under subsection (1) shall have included in its agenda an item respecting constitutional matters that directly affect the aboriginal peoples of Canada, including the identification and definition of the rights of those peoples to be included in the Constitution of Canada, and the Prime Minister of Canada shall invite representatives of those peoples to participate in the discussions on that item.

(3) The Prime Minister of Canada shall invite elected representatives of the governments of the Yukon Territory and the Northwest Territories to participate in the discussions on any item on the agenda of the conference convened under subsection (1) that, in the opinion of the Prime Minister, directly affects the Yukon Territory and the Northwest Territories.

Part V

Procedure for amending Constitution of Canada

38. (1) An amendment to the Constitution of Canada may be made by proclamation issued by the Governor General under the Great Seal of Canada where so authorized by

(a) resolutions of the Senate and House of Commons; and

(b) resolutions of the legislative assemblies of at least two-thirds of the provinces that have, in the aggregate, according to the then latest general census, at least fifty per cent of the population of all the provinces.

(2) An amendment made under subsection (1) that derogates from the legislative powers, the proprietary rights or any other

rights or privileges of the legislature or government of a province shall require a resolution supported by a majority of the members of each of the Senate, the House of Commons and the legislative assemblies required under subsection (1).

(3) An amendment referred to in subsection (2) shall not have effect in a province the legislative assembly of which has expressed its dissent thereto by resolution supported by a majority of its members prior to the issue of the proclamation to which the amendment relates unless that legislative assembly, subsequently, by resolution supported by a majority of its members, revokes its dissent and authorizes the amendment.

(4) A resolution of dissent made for the purposes of subsection (3) may be revoked at any time before or after the issue of the proclamation to which it relates.

39. (1) A proclamation shall not be issued under subsection 38(1) before the expiration of one year from the adoption of the resolution initiating the amendment procedure thereunder, unless the legislative assembly of each province has previously adopted a resolution of assent or dissent.

(2) A proclamation shall not be issued under subsection 38(1) after the expiration of three years from the adoption of the resolution initiating the amendment procedure thereunder.

40. Where an amendment is made under subsection 38(1) that transfers provincial legislative powers relating to education or other cultural matters from provincial legislatures to Parliament, Canada shall provide reasonable compensation to any province to which the amendment does not apply.

41. An amendment to the Constitution of Canada in relation to the following matters may be made by proclamation issued by the Governor General under the Great Seal of Canada only where authorized by resolutions of the Senate and House of Commons and of the legislative assembly of each province:

(a) the office of the Queen, the Governor General and the Lieutenant Governor of a province;

(b) the right of a province to a number of members in the House of Commons not less than the number of Senators by which the province is entitled to be represented at the time this Part comes into force;

(c) subject to section 43, the use of the English or the French language;

(d) the composition of the Supreme Court of Canada; and

(e) an amendment to this Part.

Amendment by general procedure

42. (1) An amendment to the Constitution of Canada in relation to the following matters may be made only in accordance with subsection 38(1):

(a) the principle of proportionate representation of the provinces in the House of Commons prescribed by the Constitution of Canada;

(b) the powers of the Senate and the method of selecting Senators;

(c) the number of members by which a province is entitled to be represented in the Senate and the residence qualifications of Senators;

(d) subject to paragraph 41(d), the Supreme Court of Canada;

(e) the extension of existing provinces into the territories; and

(f) notwithstanding any other law or practice, the establish= ment of new provinces.

Exception

(2) Subsections 38(2) to (4) do not apply in respect of amendments in relation to matters referred to in subsection (1).

Amendment of provisions relating to some but not all provinces

43. An amendment to the Constitution of Canada in relation to any provision that applies to one or more, but not all, provinces, including

(a) any alteration to boundaries between provinces, and

(b) any amendment to any provision that relates to the use of the English or the French language within a province,

may be made by proclamation issued by the Governor General under the Great Seal of Canada only where so authorized by resolutions of the Senate and House of Commons and of the legislative assembly of each province to which the amendment applies.

Amendments by Parliament

44. Subject to sections 41 and 42, Parliament may exclusively make laws amending the Constitution of Canada in relation to the executive government of Canada or the Senate and House of Commons.

Amendments by provincial legislatures

45. Subject to section 41, the legislature of each province may exclusively make laws amending the constitution of the province.

Initiation of amendment procedures

46. (1) The procedures for amendment under sections 38, 41, 42 and 43 may be initiated either by the Senate or the House of Commons or by the legislative assembly of a province.

Revocation of authorization

(2) A resolution of assent made for the purposes of this Part may be revoked at any time before the issue of a proclamation authorized by it.

Amendments without Senate resolution

47. (1) An amendment to the Constitution of Canada made by proclamation under section 38, 41, 42 or 43 may be made without a resolution of the Senate authorizing the issue of the proclamation if, within one hundred and eighty days after the adoption by the House of Commons of a resolution authorizing its issue, the Senate has not adopted such a resolution and if, at any time after the expiration of that period, the House of Commons again adopts the resolution.

Computation of period

(2) Any period when Parliament is prorogued or dissolved shall not be counted in computing the one hundred and eighty day period referred to in subsection (1).

48. The Queen's Privy Council for Canada shall advise the Governor General to issue a proclamation under this Part forthwith on the adoption of the resolutions required for an amendment made by proclamation under this Part.

49. A constitutional conference composed of the Prime Minister of Canada and the first ministers of the provinces shall be convened by the Prime Minister of Canada within fifteen years after this Part comes into force to review the provisions of this Part.

Part VI

Amendment to the Constitution Act, 1867

50. The Constitution Act, 1867 (formerly named the British North America Act, 1867) is amended by adding thereto, immediately after section 92 thereof, the following heading and section:

"Non-Renewable Natural Resources, Forestry Resources and Electrical Energy

Laws respecting
non-renewable
natural
resources,
forestry
resources and
electrical
energy

92A. (1) In each province, the legislature may exclusively make laws in relation to

(a) exploration for non-renewable natural resources in the province;

(b) development, conservation and management of non-renewable natural resources and forestry resources in the province, including laws in relation to the rate of primary production therefrom; and

(c) development, conservation and management of sites and facilities in the province for the generation and production of electrical energy.

(2) In each province, the legislature may make laws in relation to the export from the province to another part of Canada of the primary production from non-renewable natural resources and forestry resources in the province and the production from facilities in the province for the generation of electrical energy, but such laws may not authorize or provide for discrimination in prices or in supplies exported to another part of Canada.

(3) Nothing in subsection (2) derogates from the authority of Parliament to enact laws in relation to the matters referred to in that subsection and, where such a law of Parliament and a law of a province conflict, the law of Parliament prevails to the extent of the conflict.

(4) In each province, the legislature may make laws in relation to the raising of money by any mode or system of taxation in respect of

(a) non-renewable natural resources and forestry resources in the province and the primary production therefrom, and

(b) sites and facilities in the province for the generation of electrical energy and the production therefrom,

whether or not such production is exported in whole or in part from the province, but such laws may not authorize or provide for taxation that differentiates between production exported to another part of Canada and production not exported from the province.

"Primary
production"

(5) The expression "primary production" has the meaning assigned by the Sixth Schedule.

Existing powers
or rights

(6) Nothing in subsections (1) to (5) derogates from any powers or rights that a legislature or government of a province had immediately before the coming into force of this section."

Idem

51. The said Act is further amended by adding thereto the following Schedule:

"The Sixth Schedule

Primary Production from Non-Renewable Natural Resources and Forestry Resources

1. For the purposes of section 92A of this Act,

(a) production from a non-renewable natural resource is primary production therefrom if

(i) it is in the form in which it exists upon its recovery or severance from its natural state, or

(ii) it is a product resulting from processing or refining the resource, and is not a manufactured product or a product resulting from refining crude oil, refining upgraded heavy crude oil, refining gases or liquids derived from coal or refining a synthetic equivalent of crude oil; and

(b) production from a forestry resource is primary production therefrom if it consists of sawlogs, poles, lumber, wood chips, sawdust or any other primary wood product, or wood pulp, and is not a product manufactured from wood."

Part VII
General

Primacy of Constitution of Canada

    52. (1) The Constitution of Canada is the supreme law of Canada, and any law that is inconsistent with the provisions of the Constitution is, to the extent of the inconsistency, of no force or effect.

Constitution of Canada

    (2) The Constitution of Canada includes

(a) the Canada Act, including this Act;

(b) the Acts and orders referred to in Schedule I; and

(c) any amendment to any Act or order referred to in paragraph (a) or (b).

Amendments to Constitution of Canada

    (3) Amendments to the Constitution of Canada shall be made only in accordance with the authority contained in the Constitution of Canada.

Repeals and new names

    53. (1) The enactments referred to in Column I of Schedule I are hereby repealed or amended to the extent indicated in Column II thereof and, unless repealed, shall continue as law in Canada under the names set out in Column III thereof.

Consequential amendments

    (2) Every enactment, except the Canada Act, that refers to an enactment referred to in Schedule I by the name in Column I thereof is hereby amended by substituting for that name the corresponding name in Column III thereof, and any British North America Act not referred to in Schedule I may be cited as the Constitution Act followed by the year and number, if any, of its enactment.

Repeal and consequential amendments

54. Part IV is repealed on the day that is one year after this Part comes into force and this section may be repealed and this Act renumbered, consequential upon the repeal of Part IV and this section, by proclamation issued by the Governor General under the Great Seal of Canada.

French version of Constitution of Canada

55. A French version of the portions of the Constitution of Canada referred to in Schedule I shall be prepared by the Minister of Justice of Canada as expeditiously as possible and, when any portion thereof sufficient to warrant action being taken has been so prepared, it shall be put forward for enactment by proclamation issued by the Governor General under the Great Seal of Canada pursuant to the procedure then applicable to an amendment of the same provisions of the Constitution of Canada.

English and French versions of certain constitutional texts

56. Where any portion of the Constitution of Canada has been or is enacted in English and French or where a French version of any portion of the Constitution is enacted pursuant to section 55, the English and French versions of that portion of the Constitution are equally authoritative.

English and French versions of this Act

57. The English and French versions of this Act are equally authoritative.

Commencement

58. Subject to section 59, this Act shall come into force on a day to be fixed by proclamation issued by the Queen or the Governor General under the Great Seal of Canada.

Commencement of paragraph 23(1)(a) in respect of Quebec

59. (1) Paragraph 23(1)(a) shall come into force in respect of Quebec on a day to be fixed by proclamation issued by the Queen or the Governor General under the Great Seal of Canada.

Authorization of Quebec

(2) A proclamation under subsection (1) shall be issued only where authorized by the legislative assembly or government of Quebec.

(3) This section may be repealed on the day paragraph 23(1)(a) comes into force in respect of Quebec and this Act amended and renumbered, consequential upon the repeal of this section, by proclamation issued by the Queen or the Governor General under the Great Seal of Canada.

60. This Act may be cited as the Constitution Act, 1981, and the Constitution Acts, 1867 to 1975 (No. 2) and this Act may be cited together as the Constitution Acts, 1867 to 1981.

Schedule I
to the
Constitution Act, 1981
Modernization of the Constitution

Item	Column I Act Affected	Column II Amendment	Column III New Name
1.	British North America Act, 1867, 30-31 Vict., c. 3 (U.K.)	(1) Section 1 is repealed and the following substituted therefor: "1. This Act may be cited as the Constitution Act, 1867." (2) Section 20 is repealed. (3) Class 1 of section 91 is repealed. (4) Class 1 of section 92 is repealed.	Constitution Act, 1867
2.	An Act to amend and continue the Act 32-33 Victoria chapter 3; and to establish and provide for the Government of the Province of Manitoba, 1870, 33 Vict., c. 3 (Can.)	(1) The long title is repealed and the following substituted therefor: "Manitoba Act, 1870." (2) Section 20 is repealed.	Manitoba Act, 1870
3.	Order of Her Majesty in Council admitting Rupert's Land and the North Western Territory into the union, dated the 23rd day of June, 1870		Rupert's Land and North-Western Territory Order
4.	Order of Her Majesty in Council admitting British Columbia into the Union, dated the 16th day of May, 1871		British Columbia Terms of Union
5.	British North America Act, 1871, 34-35 Vict., c. 28 (U.K.)	Section 1 is repealed and the following substituted therefor: "1. This Act may be cited as the Constitution Act, 1871."	Constitution Act, 1871
6.	Order of Her Majesty in Council admitting Prince Edward Island into the Union, dated the 26th day of June, 1873		Prince Edward Island Terms of Union

Item	Column I Act Affected	Column II Amendment	Column III New Name
7.	Parliament of Canada Act, 1875, 38-39 Vict., c. 38 (U.K.)		Parliament of Canada Act, 1875
8.	Order of Her Majesty in Council admitting all British possessions and Territories in North America and islands adjacent thereto into the Union, dated the 31st day of July, 1880		Adjacent Territories Order
9.	British North America Act, 1886, 49-50 Vict., c. 35 (U.K.)	Section 3 is repealed and the following substituted therefor: "3. This Act may be cited as the Constitution Act, 1886."	Constitution Act, 1886
10.	Canada (Ontario Boundary) Act, 1889, 52-53 Vict., c. 28 (U.K.)		Canada (Ontario Boundary) Act, 1889
11.	Canadian Speaker (Appointment of Deputy) Act, 1895, 2nd Sess., 59 Vict., c. 3 (U.K.)	The Act is repealed.	
12.	The Alberta Act, 1905, 4-5 Edw. VII, c. 3 (Can.)		Alberta Act
13.	The Saskatchewan Act, 1905, 4-5 Edw. VII, c. 42 (Can.)		Saskatchewan Act
14.	British North America Act, 1907, 7 Edw. VII, c. 11 (U.K.)	Section 2 is repealed and the following substituted therefor: "2. This Act may be cited as the Constitution Act, 1907."	Constitution Act, 1907

Schedule I

to the

Constitution Act, 1981—Continued

Item	Column I Act Affected	Column II Amendment	Column III New Name
15.	British North America Act, 1915, 5-6 Geo. V, c.45 (U.K.)	Section 3 is repealed and the following substituted therefor: "3. This Act may be cited as the Constitution Act, 1915."	Constitution Act, 1915
16.	British North America Act, 1930, 20-21 Geo. V, c. 26 (U.K.)	Section 3 is repealed and the following substituted therefor: "3. This Act may be cited as the Constitution Act, 1930."	Constitution Act, 1930
17.	Statute of Westminster, 1931, 22 Geo. V, c. 4 (U.K.)	In so far as they apply to Canada, (a) section 4 is repealed; and (b) subsection 7(1) is repealed.	Statute of Westminster, 1931
18.	British North America Act, 1940, 3-4 Geo. VI, c. 36 (U.K.)	Section 2 is repealed and the following substituted therefor: "2. This Act may be cited as the Constitution Act, 1940."	Constitution Act, 1940
19.	British North America Act, 1943, 6-7 Geo. VI, c. 30 (U.K.)	The Act is repealed.	
20.	British North America Act, 1946, 9-10 Geo. VI, c. 63 (U.K.)	The Act is repealed.	
21.	British North America Act, 1949, 12-13 Geo. VI, c. 22 (U.K.)	Section 3 is repealed and the following substituted therefor: "3. This Act may be cited as the Newfoundland Act."	Newfoundland Act

Item	Column I Act Affected	Column II Amendment	Column III New Name
22.	British North America (No. 2) Act, 1949, 13 Geo. VI, c. 81 (U.K.)	The Act is repealed.	
23.	British North America Act, 1951, 14-15 Geo. VI, c. 32 (U.K.)	The Act is repealed.	
24.	British North America Act, 1952, 1 Eliz. II, c. 15 (Can.)	The Act is repealed.	
25.	British North America Act, 1960, 9 Eliz. II, c. 2 (U.K.)	Section 2 is repealed and the following substituted therefor: "2. This Act may be cited as the Constitution Act, 1960."	Constitution Act, 1960
26.	British North America Act, 1964, 12-13 Eliz. II, c. 73 (U.K.)	Section 2 is repealed and the following substituted therefor: "2. This Act may be cited as the Constitution Act, 1964."	Constitution Act, 1964
27.	British North America Act, 1965, 14 Eliz. II, c. 4, Part I (Can.)	Section 2 is repealed and the following substituted therefor: "2. This Part may be cited as the Constitution Act, 1965."	Constitution Act, 1965
28.	British North America Act, 1974, 23 Eliz. II, c. 13, Part I (Can.)	Section 3, as amended by 25-26 Eliz. II, c. 28, s. 38(1) (Can.), is repealed and the following substituted therefor: "3. This Part may be cited as the Constitution Act, 1974."	Constitution Act, 1974

Schedule I

to the

Constitution Act, 1981—Concluded

Item	Column I Act Affected	Column II Amendment	Column III New Name
29.	British North America Act, 1975, 23-24 Eliz. II, c. 28, Part I (Can.)	Section 3, as amended by 25-26 Eliz. II, c. 28, s. 31 (Can.), is repealed and the following substituted therefor: "3. This Part may be cited as the Constitution Act (No. 1), 1975."	Constitution Act (No. 1), 1975
30.	British North America Act (No. 2), 1975, 23-24 Eliz. II, c. 53 (Can.)	Section 3 is repealed and the following substituted therefor: "3. This Act may be cited as the Constitution Act (No. 2), 1975."	Constitution Act (No. 2), 1975

Speaker of the House of Commons

Printed in Canada
Imprimerie Gagné Ltée

CANADA — TERRITORIAL EVOLUTION 1867-1981

On July 1, 1867 the Dominion of Canada was formed by the confederation of three provinces in British North America. This map depicts the evolution of the nation's international, provincial and territorial boundaries from this date to 1981.

BOUNDARIES

PRESENT DAY

- – ·· – ·· – International
- – – – – – Provincial or Territorial
- ·– ·– ·– District
- ············ Unsurveyed
- – ·· – ·· – Dividing Line - Canada and Greenland

BOUNDARIES

HISTORICAL (Many Unsurveyed)

- – – – – International
- ––––– Provincial or Territorial
- ━━━━ Northwest Territories 1870
- ―――― District
- ············ Rupert's Land 1870

CHRONOLOGY

1867 The colonies of CANADA, NOVA SCOTIA and NEW BRUNSWICK unite in a federal state. The provinces of NOVA SCOTIA and NEW BRUNSWICK retain their established boundaries and CANADA is divided into the provinces of ONTARIO and QUEBEC.

1870 RUPERT'S LAND and the NORTH-WESTERN TERRITORY are acquired to form the NORTHWEST TERRITORIES. The province of MANITOBA is created with boundaries 49°N, 50°30'N, 96°W, 99°W.

1871 BRITISH COLUMBIA joins the federation as a province with the boundaries it attained in 1866.

1873 PRINCE EDWARD ISLAND joins Confederation as the seventh province.

1874 New boundaries (provisional) assigned to northern ONTARIO.

1876 District of KEEWATIN is formed from part of the NORTHWEST TERRITORIES.

1877 Boundaries of MANITOBA are adjusted to conform to the Dominion Lands Survey System.

1880 Canada acquires title to the ARCTIC ISLANDS which become part of the NORTHWEST TERRITORIES.

1881 MANITOBA is enlarged by extending its boundaries westward, northward and eastward.

1882 Provisional Districts of ASSINIBOIA, SASKATCHEWAN, ATHABASKA and ALBERTA are created.

1886 Southwestern boundary of KEEWATIN is adjusted to conform with boundaries of the Districts created in 1882.

1889 ONTARIO is enlarged west to Lake of the Woods and north to the Albany River.

1895 UNGAVA, MACKENZIE, YUKON and FRANKLIN are established as additional Districts in the NORTHWEST TERRITORIES. The Districts of ATHABASKA and KEEWATIN are enlarged.

1897 Boundaries are changed for the Districts of FRANKLIN, KEEWATIN, MACKENZIE, UNGAVA and YUKON.

1898 The District of YUKON is separated from the NORTHWEST TERRITORIES to become YUKON TERRITORY with the boundaries as assigned to the District in 1895. The boundaries of QUEBEC are extended northward to the Eastmain River.

1901 The boundaries of YUKON TERRITORY are changed to those of today.

1905 ALBERTA and SASKATCHEWAN are created as provinces with the boundaries as they are today. The District of KEEWATIN is transferred back to the NORTHWEST TERRITORIES.

1912 MANITOBA, ONTARIO and QUEBEC are extended northward to attain their present boundaries.

1920 The boundaries of the Districts within the NORTHWEST TERRITORIES are redescribed as they exist today.

1925 CANADA'S boundaries are extended northward pursuant to provisions of international law.

1927 The boundary between CANADA and NEWFOUNDLAND is defined by the Imperial Privy Council.

1949 NEWFOUNDLAND enters Confederation as the tenth province with the boundaries as delimited in 1927.

Research for this map was carried out under contract by Dr. Norman L. Nicholson, of the Department of Geography, University of Western Ontario for Energy, Mines and Resources Canada.

Cartography by the Cartography and Toponymy Division, Surveys and Mapping Branch, Energy, Mines and Resources Canada.